WALKING WITH GOD
DAY BY DAY

*a year of
meditations*

WALKING WITH GOD
DAY BY DAY

a year of meditations

FORWARD MOVEMENT
Cincinnati, Ohio

Cover Design: Albonetti Design

Published 2011
ISBN 978-0-88028-329-8

Forward Movement, an official, non-profit agency of
The Episcopal Church, is sustained through
sales and tax-free contributions from our readers.

FORWARD MOVEMENT
412 Sycamore Street
Cincinnati, Ohio 45202-4195
USA

1-800-543-1813
513-721-6659
FAX 513-721-0729
Email: orders@forwardmovement.org
www.forwardmovement.org

Foreword

With great pleasure, we present our third annual book of daily meditations. Here you will find the work of twenty authors who present their struggles and victories, their doubts and their faith, as they travel the Christian road. These meditations vary widely in tone and approach, as each author seeks God in particular places and particular times. But isn't this the way we each find God? Every day brings us new opportunities to seek God's presence in our own life.

We encourage you, if you are able, to set aside some time each day. You might like to read the meditation and then spend some time in quiet prayer in response to what you've read. Or maybe you will wish to combine these meditations with our quarterly devotional publication, *Forward Day by Day*. Mostly, we hope this volume will be helpful in your spiritual life, as you seek God in the changes and chances that each day brings.

May God's blessings be known to you, day by day.

Scott Gunn
Executive Director
Forward Movement

New year, new promise

It is a new day; a new year. "If anyone is in Christ, there is a new creation: everything old has passed away; see, everything has become new!" (2 Corinthians 5:17).

On the first day of a new calendar year an impulse arises to turn over a new leaf. We make resolutions for greater self-care—to increase exercise and recreation or reduce consumption and stress. There is promise in a new year; there is resolve to shed old and destructive ways and adopt a new attitude. If only we can remain disciplined in our resolve, we can achieve physical perfection.

The apostle Paul writes about how people use their bodies. Some folks thought that the spirit and the body were two distinct and disconnected arenas—as if you could be spiritual with no connection to the ways you are physical. Some people still think that. For Saint Paul those arenas are not separate, but one. All those warnings against debauchery and lust arise because he believes the body is the temple for the Holy Spirit. It matters how we care for and use the gift that is the body. But that temple is not perfect for a reason. "We have this treasure [freedom and glory] in clay jars, so that it may be made clear that this extraordinary power belongs to God and does not come from us" (2 Corinthians 4:7).

On this first day of this new year, before you make any resolutions for physical perfection, consider how God can use your imperfections to make known the great power that is grace and glory. In prayer and devotion, let the Spirit of God make its dwelling in your flesh, imperfect though it may be. Let Christ make of you his new creation in body, mind, and spirit. —*Ruth Lawson Kirk*

Resolve to remember

We're just coming off the lull between the two major end-of-year holidays, Christmas and New Year's Eve. It feels good.

The gifts are opened; the thank-you notes are done. The entertaining and travel are completed, or nearly so. It's not yet time to take down the decorations. (That's for the day after Epiphany in our household.) Many people have been off work; for those who had to go to an office, it was easy parking and light duty.

After the frantic days and weeks leading up to this period, it's good to have some down time, some relaxation time, some thinking time, some time to play. It's a little bit of sabbath in our own ordinary time, a time to relax and relate to family and friends.

If we're looking for resolutions to shape us in the new year, this might be a good one: To remember the feeling of these easier days and find ways to keep that feeling in our everyday life. Take a few minutes for yourself each day; talk to family members; communicate with friends.

I'm planning to keep my stress levels down and my contact with God up, and never let a day go by without reminding the most important people in my life that I love them very much. It's the best resolution that comes to mind just now. —*Sarah Bryan Miller*

The tenth day of Christmas

On the tenth day of Christmas,
my true love gave to me, ten lords-a-leaping...

—TRADITIONAL CAROL

It's *still Christmas!* Not that the secular world pays any attention to the liturgical calendar or gives credence to the fact that Christmas is a *season* that *follows* the Incarnation, the glorious moment of God breaking into our world in a new and incredible way. The secular world follows its own schedule, a schedule focusing on the build-up to Christmas and urging us to spend, spend, spend, and party, party, party.

I'm one of those Christians who embraces following the liturgical calendar. I love saying to people, in the days before Christmas, "Happy Advent!" I love singing the Advent hymns. By the time I get to Christmas Eve and to the big services in church with all the organ stops pulled out, I am so ready, so *hungry* for that Incarnation, that I can feel it in my bones.

And then, on December 26, I'm more than ready to say to people, "Merry Christmas!" Of course, by that time in the secular world, everyone's already moved on. "Happy New Year!" they reply.

The Incarnation—God with us—is worthy of celebration every day of our lives, but especially so in the season of Christmas.

The world puts Christmas away for another year. Me? I just keep celebrating on this, the tenth day of Christmas. —*Lauren Stanley*

Letting go

I am not ready for the year to begin—not ready for the resolutions and lists of things to do, not ready to put away the ribbons and crèche that are Christmas. I want to stay in the world of family, friends, and joy. Only two more days and one last Epiphany party and the house will need to be delivered back to its normal austerity. But, oh, my heart! It does not want this yet.

Some years ago my son Evan attended a Montessori school where the children could choose whether to participate in the many lessons they had been taught. One day Evan stopped participating. The teacher, thinking he would get back to his work by the end of the day, said nothing to him. But he did not get back to his work by day's end. Instead, he went on a participation strike for six weeks. At the time, I thought he was just being stubborn. But now I wonder: what was it that he didn't want to let go of?

Letting go and going on—Richard Rohr says that this is one of the central tasks of the Christian life: "In order to come to fuller life and spirit we must constantly let go of present life and spirit." I often think of this as having to do with the big issues of my life, but rarely apply it to the simple rhythms of my day, my week, or my year. But it does apply.

As the Christmas season draws to a close, think about this: What do you need to give yourself to that is right in front of you, even if means letting go of something? And what is the "fuller life" you will come to in doing this? —*Melissa Skelton*

Valuable in God's sight

One of the television programs my husband and I enjoy is *Antique Road Show*. It is fun to see people bring in possessions to be appraised and watch their delight when told each item's worth.

I have noticed that objects seem to be worth more if they have never been taken out of the box, played with, or used. They must be pristine—the less used the better. Alterations lower the value. Use rubs off the finish.

God has other values. God delights to see gnarled hands shaped by hard work in the service of others. As we age, most of us rub off the shiny finish God gave us at birth. On the outside we may be less than pristine. But God looks inside and rejoices when we use our special talents.

Do you have a talent for loving people? Or a listening ear for someone in trouble? Can you make a supportive phone call or visit when someone is sick? How many cans of food can you spare for those who have none? Do you invite friends to church? Do you speak to newcomers and get to know them? Do you give the best hugs around? A simple smile can make someone's day. A silent prayer may lead to great changes.

All those are talents in God's sight. Some of us have been given spectacular gifts that benefit the world—in music, literature, leadership, teaching, medicine, and other fields. We all value those skills. But even if those are not our gifts, we too have gifts that are meant to be used.

God knows your talents because God gave them to you. God is waiting for you to use them—use them all. Place them before the Lord. Watch God's delight reflected in those around you. —*Nancy R. Duvall*

What's your sign?

"Where is the child who has been born king of the Jews?
For we observed his star at its rising, and have come to pay him homage."
When King Herod heard this, he was frightened, and all Jerusalem with him.

—MATTHEW 2:2-3

Astronomer Parke Kunkle didn't intend to upset the world. But his observations turned the world upside down for millions. Citing the long-known fact of Earth's precession—its natural wobble on its axis—Kunkle, shortly after Epiphany in 2011, was quoted (aptly enough in the Minneapolis *Star Tribune*) describing how this has changed the way constellations now appear. Because of cyclical divergence widening, the star signs delineated in the zodiac in Babylon 3,000 years ago do not conform to their star configurations as aligned today. Thus, declared Kunkle, the zodiac is now off by about a month. As this news went viral, life-defining certainties were suddenly upended: Geminis became Taureans. Identities and destinies seemed transformed. Bloggers wanted their signs back.

Thankfully, today we remember that there is other earth-shattering news in the stars, news that changes us for good. A shining star still points to an unchanging truth: the Way, Truth, and Life of Jesus Christ.

By grace, our identity in him never changes. Our sign is forever secure. In Christ, the sign of the cross stands over the whole of our lives, freeing us to live wholly/holy for him. The cruciform love of God is the shining star under which our days and destinies are forever blessed and by which the best life of all can be lived.

Christ's dawning star and saving life continue to turn the world upside down. It can turn your life right-side up. Trust that sign and follow that star. —*John Van Nuys*

Arrows

One summer at my parish we hosted Reading Camp, a week-long program for children from the local area. It met in the parish hall, which is behind the church, so Victoria, my wife as well as the camp director, chalked large blue arrows on each of the sidewalk squares leading to the parish hall. The arrows helped the kids find their way. Later that week there was a torrential rain, and it washed away all the arrows, without a trace.

But the camp went on. By then, everyone knew the way to the parish hall. The arrows were gone, but their direction was still with us. No one wandered off or got lost.

It was a busy and great camp, and I was tired after we finished on the last day. That night I went to bed early, and in my own twilight between sleeping and waking I could almost hear the sounds of all the kids' voices one more time. Then I woke up completely and found myself in a darkened room that was absolutely quiet. But the life of the camp and those kids' voices were inside me. The outward sign was gone, but its energy remained. In me.

The magi were pointed by a star to the presence of Jesus. They observed his star at its rising and followed it for many miles to pay homage to the Messiah. They were willing to look up, to see the pointers in their lives, and to find a new direction (Matthew 2).

Everything we do in the church is a pointer. The fellowship, the organization, the budget, the liturgy, and the building are all arrows that point beyond themselves. They point to love that will be with us when all the arrows are gone. —*Rob Slocum*

Refinishing wood

Few tasks give me more satisfaction than refinishing wood. To take a beaten-up old chair or chest and strip it, repair it, sand it, and rub a new finish into it coat by coat is deeply gratifying.

My most recent project was a set of dining room chairs. Though well-built of oak and maple, they had been covered with truly ugly paint at least twice, once in red and black and later in green. Naugahyde—*naugahyde!*—covered the cane seats.

Somehow I knew there were handsome chairs under all that mess. I peeled away the naugahyde, removed the broken canes, and delivered the chairs for stripping and recaning. Then began the long process of cleaning and sanding—and *sanding*—and refinishing. Coat by coat, I rubbed in the oil, buffed it with cloth, rubbed it again with fine steel wool, and then applied more oil. Coat by coat, the beautiful grain of the oak and maple emerged, and the clarity of the wood deepened. It seemed I could look right down into it.

Scars remain, but six handsome chairs now testify to the beauty that had lain hidden all those years.

As with these chairs, the accretions of the years often obscure the beauty God creates in us. We bear wounds. We are disfigured by sin. We paint ourselves with various guises. But God never accepts this false self. Day by day, year by year, he sands down our rough spots, repairs our brokenness, and rubs healing balm into us. God never stops working on us.

This is sanctification: God knows that precious children lie beneath our battered surfaces, and he will bring us forth.

—*Betsy Rogers*

What the heavens declare

The heavens declare the glory of God,
and the firmament shows his handiwork.

—PSALM 19:1

It is amazing to watch the beauty of the Earth and the sky—all that God has made.

A couple of years ago, when the moon and Jupiter were two-stepping across the sky, it was fun to look for them each night, notice their brightness, their different positions, their relationship to each other as the moon waxed and waned through the month.

"Although they have no words or language, and their voices are not heard, their sound has gone out to all lands," writes the psalmist (Psalm 19:3, 4). A website called earthsky.org showed some great pictures of that sound going out—diagrams, charts, all kinds of information on the travels of the moon and Jupiter.

Each clear, early evening that January, we could see a bright star in the south. We learned that Jupiter is the biggest planet in our solar system, and it is always bright in Earth's sky. The moon and Jupiter were near each other then, and nearer to Earth than they usually are, and it was a joy to see them. Jupiter, the moon, and Earth travel at different speeds in different orbits, and are not always so close nor so bright, so we felt lucky to witness it.

Sometimes we are so busy with what we have to do each day that we don't think to look up, to notice the sky and what is happening there. We take for granted the Lord's care over us. I wonder if Moses, Isaiah, the psalmists, Galileo, Michelangelo, Van Gogh and others like them took the time to watch the night sky. I'm sure some of them did. We all should. —*Lois Sibley*

The sunrise of our souls

One winter morning I was standing at the end of a wooden pier extending into Weeks Bay, a small estuary near where I lived in Alabama. It was 5:00 a.m. I heard waves rippling, birds squawking, and an occasional mullet plopping into the water. But I saw virtually nothing—no moon, no lights on the shore across the bay, few stars. This was one of the longest nights of the year. The darkness seemed almost epidemic.

The light arrived hesitantly at first. The water of the bay turned from black, to black laced with gray, to gray laced with silver, and finally to brown, the color of tea. The western sky gradually turned from black to gray while the eastern sky moved more quickly through several colors, from black, to gray, to pink, to bright rose, and finally to many hues at once as different clouds captured the sunbeams from beyond the horizon. Finally, the first ray of sunlight broke through, bold and brazen, and the nebulous sounds and shapes of the darkness grew clear and distinct in the sunlight.

That first brilliant ray of light suggests Christmas, when Christ first appeared in the Bethlehem manger. Most of Christian life, however, is lived in a season more like Epiphany, with daily encounters and skirmishes in which Christ searches out and subdues the enemy in the hidden places of our souls, and establishes his rule. In Epiphany, the waiting is over, the light has arrived, and the celebration of its arrival is concluded; we live in the light. The light invades every corner and crevice, sweeping away the night; the darkness is in retreat. Pockets of darkness remain, some of them horrible and painful, but more and more, the world begins to glisten. See it shine!
—*Richard H. Schmidt*

Nourished by God's gifts

Reading through the Bible you will notice God's people share a lot of meals. A piece of garden fruit is shared between a man and a woman. Roasted meat is eaten by everyone in the house before making a quick exodus. People sit in groups to eat manna in the wilderness, then in the same way to eat bread that has been blessed and broken, shared by the multitudes who gather around Jesus. In his stories Jesus talks about table etiquette and wedding feasts.

When people speak of loved ones in heaven they often imagine them feasting. One friend tells me he imagines heaven's feast to be dark chocolate and red wine. Isaiah imagined a feast of fine foods and great wines spread before the peoples. We call the bread and wine of Holy Communion a foretaste of the heavenly banquet.

Eating is a daily need—a function of our biology. It's a common bond among the creatures of God, who all need sustenance for survival. Eating can become disordered and diseased. Gluttony and anorexia, food riots and hoarding—our relationship with food can become twisted, but it can also be a source of grace and healing. Some foods are full of comfort. Some meals increase the sense of belonging. What makes eating a holy time is more in the attitude of the heart as we recognize God's gifts for us and God's presence with us. Prayer strengthens gratitude and reminds us of the relationship we have with God and with our neighbor.

Whether you eat alone or with companions today, remember God is present, and provides for you the fruit of the earth and the bread of life. —*Ruth Lawson Kirk*

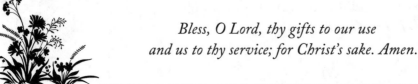

Bless, O Lord, thy gifts to our use
and us to thy service; for Christ's sake. Amen.

Preaching without words

*No one after lighting a lamp puts it under the bushel basket,
but on the lampstand, and it gives light to all in the house.*

—MATTHEW 5:15

Some people are reluctant to admit that they are Christians. Maybe they're afraid others will judge them, based on preconceptions about what being a Christian means. Or maybe their belief is so intensely personal that it feels wrong to bring it up in casual conversation.

Other folks are much bolder. They figure that if Jesus was willing to die for us, we should at least be willing to admit that we follow him. I've always wondered, though, what it says about us if we have to tell others that we're Christians. Shouldn't they be able to see that in our lives, without our having to come right out and say it? If we are really living out the gospel of Jesus Christ, shouldn't people tell *us* that we're Christians, rather than the other way around?

Francis of Assisi once said, "Preach the gospel at all times. If necessary, use words." That's a helpful reminder to all of us that no matter how boldly we proclaim our faith, without godly actions those words are empty. But if our words and actions line up to reveal the love of Christ, we won't need to worry about whether to tell others that we're Christians—they will have already discovered that on their own. —*Robert Macauley*

Offering our selves

And here we offer and present unto thee, O Lord, our selves, our souls and bodies, to be a reasonable, holy, and living sacrifice unto thee ..."
—HOLY EUCHARIST: RITE ONE, *THE BOOK OF COMMON PRAYER*

I always stop when I hear these formal words. We are presenting *our selves*? What a powerful concept for me—that I offer my whole self to God *as a sacrifice*. Not just my mind, which can wander at times, even during a eucharist. Not just my soul, which some days seems to be some ethereal thing to which I do not pay sufficient attention. Not just my body, which I don't always offer to God, especially when I am eating chocolate. But my *whole self.*

What would the world be like, I wonder, if all of us were to actually do this? To sacrifice ourselves to God completely?

Famine and war and man-made destruction would cease, and peace—God's peace—would reign, because by sacrificing our selves, we wouldn't allow others to go hungry, we wouldn't attack each other, we wouldn't hurt each other.

If I am sacrificing myself, and you are sacrificing yourself, and every other person is doing the same thing, wouldn't we then—finally—bring about the kingdom of God? Wouldn't then the wolf live with the lamb, the leopard lie down with the kid, the calf and the lion and the fatling be together?

Isaiah says a little child shall lead them (Isaiah 11:6), and these words, in the portion of the service in which we remember what Jesus, that little child-all-grown-up, did for us, call us to transform ourselves into sacrifices. Our lives are not about our *selves.* Rather, our lives are about serving God and all of God's beloved children. —*Lauren Stanley*

Following the instructions

What does the LORD require of you but to do justice, and to love kindness, and to walk humbly with your God?

—MICAH 6:8

When all else fails, the saying goes, follow the instructions. Micah 6:8 gives the instructions for faithful living as clearly as anything I know.

Imagine the world if we all were to do justice and love kindness and walk humbly with God. No more competitiveness and clawing for the top, no more cruelty and oppression, no more idolatry in all its insidious forms. Striving would give way to service, hard-heartedness to gentleness, indifference and cynicism to faithfulness.

How tragically unrealistic it all sounds...until I look much closer to home, until I imagine my own life if I were truly to do justice and love kindness and walk humbly with my God. Would I be content with volunteering in our food pantry and committee work and check-writing, or would I find more ways to make a difference for the poor? Would I continue to complain about politics or would I truly engage in civic life? Would I indulge in the caustic humor that amuses me or let those moments pass by? Would I bumble along with "coldness of heart and wanderings of mind" ("Before Worship," *The Book of Common Prayer*, p. 833), or learn to worship and pray with more attentiveness and joy?

"Renew your church, Lord, beginning with me," Saint Augustine prayed. May I be renewed, and come to follow the instructions more fully—to do justice, and love kindness, and walk humbly with my God.
—*Betsy Rogers*

Follow the drum major

If you pursue justice, you will attain it and wear it like a glorious robe.

—ECCLESIASTICUS 27:8

Born on January 15, 1929, Martin Luther King Jr. was assassinated on April 4, 1968. He was thirty-nine years old.

As a seminarian, I visited Atlanta's King Center. Looking at King's pulpit robe, I caught my reflection superimposed on it in the glass— and winced. I felt unworthy to be a pastor. Awed by King's legacy and discouraged by how his dream has languished, I thought, "I'll never be good enough to do what God is asking of me—let alone presume to further King's dream in any way."

Twenty-three years have passed. By grace, I am a pastor. God's insistence prevailed over my reticence. King's words still challenge me. As I revisit my reflection before King's example, I realize that God wasn't asking me to put on King's robe, but rather my own.

King often referred to himself as a "drum major for righteousness." He knew the work was God's and countless others—not his alone. I often preach: Do what you can—where you are—as you are able—as the Lord leads you.

Saving the world? Only God can do that. God already has. But it is up to us to stand up when someone is being beaten down; to make sure that all who are loved by God are loved by us as well.

You don't have to write the symphony. You just have to play your part. You don't have to lead the march. Just follow the drum major. When we all take small steps together, big things happen. King and others did what they could. Surely we can, too. Take up that mantle. Robe yourself in Christ. Follow where God leads. As you do, King's dream lives. —*John Van Nuys*

"While you're up…"

What human position do you think pleases God the most? I bet your first thought was when we are on our knees in prayer. Well, God does like that a lot. Maybe you thought of God's pleasure in seeing us hug one another, comforting the sorrowful, or expressing our love to others. God is happy when God sees us do those things, too.

I think God is most pleased when God sees us respond to the request "While you are up would you…?" That is a standard joke in our family. We even say it while we are all still sitting down, and someone always gets up and brings what is needed.

As Christians do we remember to put ourselves out "while we are up" and bring others what is needed? Because we are Christ's hands and feet in this world, it is our job to "be up" for others, to serve as Christ served and continues to serve us and others.

In my opinion, love is a Christian's world view. Our job and pleasure is serving where God puts us—in our homes as we raise our children or honor our marriages, in our schools as we teach and help build character, in our work places where we give our best to the job we have been given, in our churches where we praise our God and reach out to those who need our love, our help, and our trust in God.

Next time you are asked to do something "while you are up," remember that Jesus was up for us—up on a cross, because he loved us. He still loves us, and we can show him we love him in countless ways "while we are up" for others. —*Nancy R. Duvall*

Rituals and rhythms

Each morning when I walk my little Westie, as we round the corner by the local grocery store and begin the final stretch toward home, I begin to say to him: "Do you want to go home? Let's go home."

At these words his ears flatten to his head and he begins to pick up speed. And as I repeat the word "home" he goes faster and faster until he turns into my walkway and dashes up the three stairs to the front door, ready to enter, find his toy, and cavort across the living room with it. This ritual says: "I am elated to have been on my walk in the outside world and now I am home for celebration, for food, and for rest."

Rituals are at the center of what it means to be a human being. For me, a person often too much in her head, rituals provide a concrete lifeline to the real stuff of my life. Meal rituals, bedtime rituals, rituals related to birthdays, anniversaries, and to the lives of other people important to me—all of these give a kind of holy rhythm to my life.

Likewise, the rhythms of Holy Eucharist, some form of the Daily Office, and some form of prayer that is uniquely my own provide the same kind of concrete connection to God that my other rituals provide to the stuff of my life. Without these rhythms of prayer, I feel adrift in a world of spiritual and religious generalities, a person walking around with an idea of home but no real home to occupy.

What are the rituals that hold your life together? What rituals of prayer help to support your relationship to God, to yourself, and to others? —*Melissa Skelton*

Christmas is over

I have finally put most of our decorations away, except that the wreath is still on the front door and the two funny snowmen are still sitting on the bookcase (well, it *is* still winter). And the "Joy to the World" plaque is still on the wall. I think I'll wait a bit. I'll just have another cup of coffee and sit down and sift through my memories of the season:

We did our Advent letter a bit early and had fun choosing a photo for it. We settled on the photo of the four angel-carolers making music around the small tree on a shelf. Our letter was mostly news of what our children are doing, with a bit about my husband and me.

There was a light sprinkling of snow here just before Christmas. That morning, when I looked out and saw our beautiful blue spruce with a dusting of snow on it, I had to get my camera and take a photo. It's a graceful tree and always makes me appreciate again the beauty of so many of the trees in our area.

Our two grandsons were shepherds in the Christmas pageant this year. They looked very cute and AJ got to say that famous line, "Let us go to Bethlehem and see what has happened."

Then we went to the Christmas Eve service, enjoyed the choir's special music and the whole service following. It is a joy to hear the Christmas story again and to know the comfort of God's love for all people wherever they are around the world. The day ends with prayers for them, for their safety, and for provision for all of their needs, with many thanksgivings for God's grace and care. —*Lois Sibley*

"I'll pray for you"

Does prayer do any good? You'll never prove it does. When something good happens (or something bad, for that matter), one can attribute it to any number of causes. It's hard to argue against those who believe in luck or good fortune, and chance is a part of life as God has set it up.

Often an event will have multiple causes. I believe prayer is one of those causes, but this is a matter of faith, not of conclusive demonstration or experiment. I trust that my praying helps those I pray for, but prayer—like everything else in our relationship to God—is a mystery, and ultimately, we must leave it so.

But I know for sure that prayer helps *me*. It quiets my sometimes troubled heart and reminds me that I, together with those I pray for, depend on God. We are not in control of our destinies, and the mere fact that we pray acknowledges that we are not.

Prayer also helps me feel part of a community, for although I am usually alone when I pray, no one actually prays alone. The prayers of many millions of others, from all over the world and from throughout history, are joined to ours as they ascend like incense to the throne of God (Psalm 141:2). I envision people who are praying as a choir singing songs that are heard in heaven.

We can pray for people even when they don't believe in God or prayer. Prayer is a gift we can always give to others. Richard Hooker said it best: "Prayer is that which we always have in our power to bestow and they never in theirs to refuse." —*Richard H. Schmidt*

Glimpse of glory

Staying at a wonderful little retreat center in the bluffs above the Mississippi River, I stumbled one afternoon on the remains of what once had clearly been a very handsome building, now in an advanced state of decay. Neoclassical in design, it had a kind of Jeffersonian look to it. Handsome bricks and stonework made curving walls and steps and pathways around it. I went inside, irresistibly drawn. The rooms had been elegant, trimmed in expensive woodwork and lit by tall, beautifully proportioned windows. Every room had a bath; most had fireplaces. A large central atrium rose a story and a half to a glass roof.

But the ruin was advanced. Windows stood shattered, doors hung crooked and ajar, pillars lay like corpses, collapsing plaster left gaping holes in the walls. Leaves and debris blew around the floors.

Out by the road, I discovered a battered old sign, barely visible in the undergrowth, bearing the letters "…Abbey…Glimpse o…y." Local lore supplied the phrase: "Glimpse of glory." Once long before there had been an abbey here; was this old building a part of it? Its remains surely provided a glimpse of its former glory.

As I walked and prayed, the thought grew in my mind: does God look at us, broken and self-neglected and, yes, decayed, and see a glimpse of glory? Does God find a glimpse of glory *in me*? Through the days of my retreat this understanding unfolded in my heart, and I left with the certain conviction that every bush is burning, every moment is holy, and that in every last person on earth God sees a glimpse of glory.
—*Betsy Rogers*

The whiffle-poose

One day when my dad, Jimmy Slocum, was in a playful mood, he told the story of the "whiffle-poose," an imaginary bird that flies backwards—because, he said with a twinkle in his eyes, it's more interested in where it has been than where it's going. The story was funny, but the problem is real. It's easy to see that the "whiffle-poose" is flying blind and sure to crash, but it's harder to recognize when we're the ones stuck in the past.

The past can be tempting and comforting because we know the traps and pitfalls. Even the bad news is familiar and well-worn. We know how things worked and didn't work, and we know our part of the story, where we fit in, and where we'll end up. But there are no guarantees for the future. Every opportunity has its unknown dangers, and we don't know what happens next. We can feel vulnerable when our usual barriers are ineffective or gone. Whichever way we go, we step into the unknown, and that's scary. We may be tempted to say, "The old wine is good" and turn away from the new wine of Christ's surprising love (Luke 5:39).

I have greyhounds. These dogs are sight hounds, which means that seeing is their primary sense for perceiving. Sometimes they just look away when they're spooked by what they see. They don't want to face it. When something like a scary-looking cat confronts them, they look at something else. We too are sometimes reluctant to face the future and look at where we're going. It can help to know that God will be present, even in an unknown future, and will show us our way. When we open our eyes, we discover that God travels with us. —*Rob Slocum*

Journeying

"Journey" is an important theme in religious life. The followers of Jesus called themselves followers of the Way. Jesus called *himself* the Way. We have a vast tradition of pilgrimage in fact and literature—from fourth-century Egeria's diary from Jerusalem, to Chaucer's fourteenth-century *Canterbury Tales* from imagined English pilgrims, to modern day pilgrims young and old in Iona or Assisi or walking the Camino Real through Spain.

In that other great religious tradition, sports, there is also the theme of journey, on-the-road-to, which is ubiquitous in the sporting world. In the spring, NCAA basketball teams will be on the road to the finals in New Orleans. During the Olympics, feature stories traces various athletes' journeys to the Gold (medal). Every year there is a "Road to the Superbowl."

Many of us characterize our spiritual life as a journey and our-selves as pilgrims, seeking God, seeking the Holy, seeking, seeking. We call ourselves seekers. We place ourselves, or sometimes simply find ourselves, on the Way. We know that life is a journey; life in God is a journey; life together is a journey.

What do we hope to find? Is the destination the thing, or is it about the journey? Was Jesus "On the Road to the Cross?" Is Advent the "Journey to Christmas" and Lent the "Journey to Easter?" Are we willing and able to hold them both, journey and destination, in tension—developing the eyes to see and the ears to hear the wonders and the mysteries as we move among them—so that in the end, wherever and whatever that end is, we know we have come near the heart of God? —*Penny Nash*

The diagnosis

I shall not die, but live, and declare the works of the LORD.
—PSALM 118:17

I'm not dead yet.
—*MONTY PYTHON AND THE HOLY GRAIL*

My life turned upside down one afternoon in November: I went to see a specialist for what my doctors and I thought was just a breast abscess and learned that we were seriously mistaken.

Soon after, it was confirmed that I have inflammatory carcinoma, a rare and aggressive breast cancer. That week brought consultations, procedures, and an impressive set of puncture wounds; I met new doctors and learned a new vocabulary. The next week brought the start of a brutal regimen of chemotherapy.

The diagnosis of cancer has been a very difficult thing to grasp (understatement alert!), and I find myself dissolving into tears over small realizations of a wholly changed world. I go to bed feeling at peace with it, and awaken sobbing at 2 a.m.

The hardest part has been telling people about my diagnosis, particularly those I care about the most: my children and father, my dear friends and colleagues. The wonderful part has been the reaction, both from friends and from people I hardly know: unexpected kindness from medical professionals; an overwhelming response from friends and acquaintances; offers of rides, of food, of reading matter (these are people who know me well), of a sympathetic ear, of prayer.

I trust that Jesus is walking with me down this road; I have invited my friends to walk along, too, and asked for their prayers: for healing, for grace, for acceptance, for peace.
—*Sarah Bryan Miller*

Blindfolds, blinders, and glasses

So much of the spiritual journey is about perception.

I have been thinking about blindfolds and blinders. Watching *Bonanza* as a child taught this city dweller that blindfolding horses makes them manageable because they can't perceive the threat that surrounds them. I remember a trust exercise where one person is blindfolded and led only by the vocal direction of a guide. At first one steps very timidly, hands outstretched, building confidence that the voice is trustworthy. Blindfolds rob you of perception. But blinders only narrow the view, limiting the eye from distractions that are peripheral. Again with the horses, blinders allow a rider to move along busy lanes because the horse can focus only on the road ahead.

Have there been times when you felt blindfolded in your approach to God? Did you have someone to lead you along the way until it was time to receive your sight again? What has served as your blinders, narrowing your attention so that you can focus on God's presence in the path before you?

What about those times when our eyes need the support of glasses or contacts in order to clearly see what is in the distance and what is close at hand? I imagine faith as that pair of glasses. With them on, we can more clearly see the work of God in the world around us. The glasses are not rose-colored. We still see the suffering caused by the turbulence of the earth and her people. But with the glasses of faith we are also able to see the effects of love's out-pouring as victims are comforted, charity is offered, and new life begins again.

With the vision of faith, perhaps we can see beyond what we fear and walk in safety, trusting the guidance of the Holy Spirit.
—*Ruth Lawson Kirk*

Sunrise

Awake, my soul, stretch every nerve.
—*THE HYMNAL 1982*, #546

The new day begins with glory when sunlight fills the clouds and the eastern horizon. Golden light breaks the darkness like a crack in the dome of the sky. Jacob Boehme, a seventeenth-century mystic, describes the sunrise in terms of "the morning-redness." It's the color of new life and hope, the promise of a new day that's visible in majestic skies. The color of dawn may be orange or red. Perhaps you can see the sunrise in the reddish-orange ink William Blake used in his illuminated printing, with dawn's light breaking into every word.

The sunrise says to wake up. Roosters crow. The world is stirring. People get out of bed and stand up. We "come into the daylight's splendor" (*The Hymnal 1982*, #339). Look up!

The Buddha was once asked, "What are you?" He answered, "I am awake!" To be awake is to be available to the present moment, without distractions or buffers. Being awake is living in a new day. Its possibilities come alive in our words and steps.

I once visited a cemetery in Spartanburg, South Carolina, where the graves were positioned to face east. They face the horizon of each new morning, waiting to rise in glory in the first light of that final day. At the opening of Morning Prayer we say, "Lord, open our lips. And our mouth shall proclaim your praise." We can see God's bright glory in the morning, and praise the giver of light. We are awake!

—*Rob Slocum*

Crockpot and microwave Christians

You could call me a crockpot Christian. Food in a crockpot simmers and marinates and stews over a long time at a fairly low temperature. The juices and flavors seep gradually into the ingredients. At some point—no one can say exactly when—the food is cooked. My life as a Christian has been like that. I can't remember when I wasn't a Christian. My devotion hasn't always glowed intensely, but I've spent my life marinating in Christian beliefs and conversation, and over the years I've slowly grown into a deeper discipleship. I'm not done yet.

Some people become Christians in a very different way. I call them microwave Christians. Food is placed into the microwave raw or frozen, then zapped and—presto!—it's done and ready to serve. God has zapped some of my Christian friends, in some cases while they were still frozen. They can tell you the day and the hour when they became Christians; they'll never forget the moment God changed their lives. Their discipleship has been deep and intense from the beginning.

When crockpot Christians and microwave Christians get together, the dynamics are fascinating. They don't always trust or appreciate each other. One prefers sedate traditional worship and the other upbeat contemporary worship. If crockpot Christians seem to take their faith too casually, microwave Christians can seem fanatical about theirs.

Each group has its distinctive strengths. Crockpot Christians offer experience and a balanced perspective. They've seen lean years and fat years in the church and have staying power. Look to them for loyalty and wisdom. Microwave Christians offer enthusiasm, energy, and joy. They're eager to share their faith, try new things, and tackle the opposition. Each group needs what the other offers—and I thank God we're not all alike. —*Richard H. Schmidt*

A bird in the hand

A cold winter brought a wren to live in a mop hanging on our garage wall. I saw his little uplifted tail when I passed on the way to our garage refrigerator. He was nestled where the soft dust mop parted. Every afternoon we made sure he had gotten in again before we closed the garage doors for the night.

One morning I went out to the refrigerator, leaving the house door open. When I returned I stepped into our bedroom and saw our wren at the windows, frantically trying to get out. I went over to him, alarming him so much that he flew into the kitchen. I closed hall doors and called my husband for help.

When he came we looked around for the wren and found him under a kitchen chair. He was looking out at us, not daring to move. Getting down on the bird's level, my husband began to talk to him in a soft, soothing tone. He got closer and closer and suddenly grabbed the little bird. Our wren jumped up with a chirp, escaping capture, and landed this time with his back to us.

Once again soft tones, an extended hand, and this time—success! The bird was quiet in my husband's hand. He took the wren to the back door and let him go. Where did he head? To his mop he went.

God knows our needs and God treats us tenderly when we need help. He might not grab us, but God did give us Jesus, who shows us how to act with love and trust. Christ walks with us to the door and says, "You can make it, for you are my beloved. I am watching over you. Take care of yourself." —*Nancy R. Duvall*

One thing at a time

We live in a fast-paced society where we're often multitasking. We answer emails while we talk on the phone; we listen to music while we exercise; we help our kids with their homework while we cook dinner. There is so much to do and so little time to do it.

Hans Küng once said "Hurry is not of the devil; it is the devil." Those words apply to our modern world because we can get so caught up in accomplishing so many things that we never really pay attention to any single one of them.

To combat the busy-ness of our world, we need to slow down. One way to do that is with "walking meditation," where we pay total attention to the simple act of walking. We feel the pressure of our feet upon the earth, and the transition from heel to toe with each step. Nothing is lost; nothing is taken for granted.

As the father of four, I'm able to enlist some aid in simplifying my life. I challenge my kids to catch me doing more than one thing at a time, no matter how important it is. They love the game, and I love the reminder: if I'm going to help them with their homework, I should just help them with their homework. If I ask how their day was, I should be still enough to listen to what they say.

I may not get as much accomplished that way, but what I lose in quantity I make up for—and then some—in quality. —*Robert Macauley*

Winter fun

I used to go ice skating every winter. There were two choices in our neighborhood. We could walk almost two miles to Cranberry Pond, a small lake among the trees. Or we could go out on the ice floes in Mill Cove just beyond our backyard, where twice a day a brackish river drained into the ocean with the tide, then started back in. As the water receded, the ice floes fell and rested on the mud flats. But the ice there was never even and flat like the ice at Cranberry Pond. In Mill Cove, we had to climb and jump from one hard, crunchy ice floe to another. I liked doing that. Not many tried it, so I often had the whole space to myself.

Sometimes I did go with my brothers and sisters on the long walk to Cranberry Pond. It was a lovely place to sit on the logs at the edges, put on my skates, and talk with friends. I could skate around that circular pond until I was so cold and tired I just had to quit and hurry home to get warm.

There was lots of time to think, too, on the walk to and from Cranberry Pond, as well as while skating. Even on the ice-covered mudflats close to home, there was time to think, maybe especially there in the silence. Who made these beautiful places and why are they there? Just for us to enjoy?

And there was time to dream about spring and summer, to remember rowing the boat again and swimming down at the beach or off our own dock. And maybe there would be fish to catch. Once I caught four tinker mackerel right off our dock. —*Lois Sibley*

What peace looks like

When I was growing up, "Peace" was a common greeting. It was the late 1960s and the nation was engulfed in the antiwar movement. We said "Peace" to everyone, flashed the two-fingered peace sign, wore peace shirts and peace jewelry, and drew the peace symbol on everything. Our goal was to end the Vietnam War. Now, even in the midst of wars overseas, when we say "Peace" we tend not to be calling for the end of those wars, but instead bidding God's peace to each other. God's peace is not just the end of war. It is an overflowing blessing, a wish that we all have more than enough of all that we truly seek in this life: love, joy, security, health.

This is what God's peace looks like: Take a water glass and slowly begin filling it. When it is one-sixteenth full, you have the average situation of people in this world, so many of whom live on less than one dollar per day. At the one-quarter mark, you have what most people in the developed world have. At the halfway mark, you are where the upper 20 percent of the world lives. At the three-quarters mark, you have what the upper 5 percent has. When the glass is absolutely filled to the brim, you are where the upper one-tenth of 1 percent lives.

But only when the water is flowing over the rim and running abundantly down the sides, flooding the area where the glass sits, have you reached the point that God desires for all of us. Because God does not desire that we lack anything that we truly need.

When we bid "Peace" to each other, this is what we are bidding: An overflowing, overabundance of God's absolute love for us.
—*Lauren Stanley*

Answered by mystery

Then the LORD answered Job out of the whirlwind...:
"Where were you when I laid the foundation of the earth?"

—JOB 38:1-7, 34-41

Brian Williams, General George Patton, Garrison Keillor, Maya Angelou: Imagine they were reading aloud these words from Job. We have this scripture's text, but not its tone—which is the key to its understanding.

Did God answer Job in a matter-of-fact tone like a nightly news anchor? Like a Brian Williams, was God just laying out facts in an evidentiary case to logically convince and thereby answer Job?

Did a General Patton-like God thunder angrily, assaulting Job with a series of impossible questions to forcefully, unilaterally put Job back in his place?

Did God spill out of that whirlwind like a disheveled Garrison Keillor out of a Midwest snowstorm to put his arm around Job and say, "Kid, you've got some good questions. How about adding these to your list?" Was God adding questions not to humiliate Job, but to point out wistfully that the answer Job seeks is beyond comprehension?

Or did God, like the wise poet Maya Angelou, gracefully step out of chaos, asking questions in a compassionate tone that conveyed both deep understanding and even deeper love? Was God in those questions gently, lovingly saying, "Child, the questions are limitless—as is my love for you"?

If Jesus were sitting now beside you, reading this scripture, would his tone be factual, furious, wistful, or loving? It wouldn't matter. Because Jesus would be with you. That is all the answer we need—and it's the answer we already have.

—*John Van Nuys*

Feed your soul

The story goes that a Cherokee grandfather is teaching his grandchild about life and tells his grandchild this story:

"A fight is going on inside me," he says to the child. "It is a terrible fight, and it is between two wolves. One wolf is evil: he is anger, envy, sorrow, regret, greed, arrogance, self-pity, guilt, resentment, inferiority, lies, false pride, superiority, and ego." He continues, "The other is good: he is joy, peace, love, hope, serenity, humility, kindness, benevolence, empathy, generosity, truth, compassion, and faith. The same fight is going on inside you and inside every other person, too."

The child thinks about it for a minute and then asks solemnly, "Grandfather, which wolf will win?"

His grandfather replies, "The one you feed."

For centuries, coming out of the monastic tradition, Christians have adopted something called a "rule of life"—a pattern by which a person feeds the holy and human parts of themselves. A rule is a consciously adopted pattern of prayer, study, rest, and work that feeds "the good wolf" while at the same time withdraws energy from all that the "bad wolf" represents.

What we feed in our life matters. What we spend our time and energy on shapes who we are and the choices we make.

Who is the "good wolf" you want to nurture? Describe what he or she is like.

What is the pattern of prayer, study, rest, and work that would feed the holy and human part of you? —*Melissa Skelton*

Snow days

Can any of you by worrying add a single hour to your span of life?
—LUKE 12:25

The first storm was something like an out-of-control Hollywood production: hyped to the hilt. Every element examined, it benefited from the poor non-news judgment of some in the broadcast media *(Snowpocalypse! The storm of the century! Don't dare drive!)*, who chose to dwell endlessly on the threat of bad weather rather than report on, say, the genuinely serious situation in the Middle East.

The real thing failed to stand up to critical scrutiny. The actuality fell short of the forecast. It was a serious storm, but when you've been promised Snowmageddon, some ice, sleet, and a half-foot of snow are bound to disappoint. Give it two stars, for the budget if nothing else.

The second storm slipped quietly into town, unheralded by meteorologists and excitable TV and radio personalities alike. There were no runs on supermarkets. We just awoke on Saturday morning and there it was, hiding the newspapers in the driveway and adding a little too much zest to driving conditions. It was like the little independent film that comes out of nowhere to win a "Best Picture" Oscar nomination. Give it three stars, for style.

We have a tendency to build up our fears—to exaggerate how bad things might be, to worry about things we can't control—when the sensible thing is to prepare as best we can and then move on. Keep things in perspective. Jesus was right, we can't add a single hour to our life spans by worrying. But if you're in the Midwest in February, it's a good idea to carry a scraper in the trunk of your car. You never know when it might snow. —*Sarah Bryan Miller*

Apostle of the North

The church calendar today commemorates Anskar, ninth-century missionary to the Scandinavians and Germans and an exemplar of humility and steadfastness in Christian service.

Anskar was a French monk, born in 801. In 826, in response to Danish King Harald's plea, he led a missionary group first to Denmark and then to Sweden. Eventually he settled in Germany, where in 831 he became the first Archbishop of Hamburg. He worked there, in Bremen and in Scandinavia until his death in 865, preaching the gospel and bringing many to Christ, ending the slave trade, building hospitals, redeeming captives, and serving humbly among his flock.

In 845 heathens attacked and burned Hamburg, destroying Anskar's church, monastery, and library. Undaunted, he continued his work—and befriended the heathen chieftain who had led the attack.

It's hard for twenty-first-century Americans to imagine those medieval times—the wild and primitive lands, the warring tribes, the plundering hordes, the ravaging diseases. What a beacon of light and hope Anskar's hospitals, library, and churches must have been in those dark places!

But we have our own darkness to contend with today. Perhaps it's not so different. We have our own "warring tribes," in our bitterly divisive public discourse and in our own hearts. We have our plundering hordes, though they might occupy executive suites or reveal themselves in our own acquisitiveness. We face sickness of body and spirit.

"If I were worthy in my Lord's sight," Anskar said, "I would ask of him to grant me one miracle—that he would make me a good man." Anskar's humility and faith, strength and servanthood, are a beacon of light and hope for us today as surely as when he walked this earth. —*Betsy Rogers*

Redemption in your hand

There was once a convent in Nashville, Tennessee where part of their building was known as the "tobacco juice floor."

One day the sisters went to the Nashville railway yards to seek contributions. A sister approached an engineer in a locomotive and held up her hand asking alms for the poor. Unimpressed by her appeal, the engineer filled her open hand with tobacco juice. She calmly wiped off her palm on her habit, and said, "That was for me. Now what do you have for God's poor?"

He offered nothing at that moment, but some time later there was a knock on the door of the convent. The engineer brought a gift. Actually, it was a lot of money, enough money to build a new floor of the convent. The tobacco juice floor.

Rejection feels bad. That's what happened when the sister held up her hand for an offering. The engineer rejected her request in a way that was personal, demeaning, and repulsive. But the sister didn't take it personally. She distinguished herself from what happened, and that opened the door for something better. Instead of responding with an insult, or storming away, she held her ground. She stayed true to her mission. She calmly repeated her request, and gave the engineer another chance. And though it took him a while to act on it, he finally gave what she asked, and much more. It was his redemption.

If we're lost and needing to be found, we may discover that God's forgiveness can appear in the hands of another person. The charitable and patient sister gave the engineer a chance for redemption and generosity. Instead of turning away from him, she held out her hand. Again. —*Rob Slocum*

Prodigal forgiveness

The parables of Jesus perpetually offer new discoveries, no matter how familiar they are. Take the parable of the prodigal son, for instance (Luke 15:11-32). I've always viewed that parable through the lens of the older son, because I've always been a rather upstanding sort. Having worked hard and tried to do things the right way, I have been known to resent other people getting something they don't deserve. When I read that parable, I usually try to see ways that I can rejoice for folks like that.

Then, a few years ago, I was overcome with a sense of my own deficiencies. I saw how I struggled to love other people, and how much I wanted to do things on my own, for my own benefit. For the first time I could see myself in the younger son. Instead of being filled with exhortation and challenge, that story became for me a tale of welcome and celebration. It allowed me to enter more deeply into my sin, trusting that no matter what I might have done—or what I might ever do—God was waiting for me to return, just like the father in that story.

Viewed in that light, the end of the story wasn't bitter, but joyous. As I imagined sitting down to the feast laid out for the prodigal—me— who had returned, I was overcome with pity and respect for the older sons among us, who work so hard and focus so much on deservedness that they cannot rejoice over the return of a lost soul. In that moment I understood that I was both of the sons at various points in my life, and I stood in awe of Jesus' parables, which show us things about ourselves that we've never seen before. —*Robert Macauley*

Riding the rope

The belfry of a church I once served housed a giant bell, and the rope which rang the bell hung through the ceiling into the balcony at the rear of the church. To ring the bell, one stood in the balcony and pulled down on the rope. As the bell turned on its axle, it pulled the rope back up through the ceiling. So heavy was the bell that if you held tightly to the rope, you were lifted into the air, then dropped to the floor again as the bell turned back and released the rope. Once the tolling began, even a fully grown man could ride through the air by holding onto the rope.

One Sunday morning, a mother and her seven-year-old son David were in the balcony before worship. I pulled down on the rope. I noticed David watching in fascination. "You can take a ride through the air on this if you wish," I said. "Hold on tight. You don't want to let go until you're back on the floor again, but I'll stand here to catch you if you do!"

David's eyes lit up. He leapt from the pew and reached for the rope. Up he soared into the air. He laughed and giggled as he rode up and down.

A moment later, I noticed David's mother glaring in our direction. "David! We are in church!" she said.

I felt reprimanded. Had I done something wrong? Had I encouraged irreverent, ungodly behavior? Was church a place where having fun was not permitted? Did church have to be serious business? Should it be? What would Jesus have done?

I think Jesus would have taken a ride on the rope.

—*Richard H. Schmidt*

42

All one family

Now that we have two adopted grandsons who are African American, we are more interested than ever in Black History Month.

We look for children's storybooks that include pictures of children of different races. We want our grandsons to know and be proud of the stories of Absalom Jones, Harriet Tubman, Booker T. Washington, Rosa Parks, Lucretia Mott, Marian Anderson, Martin Luther King Jr., and other noble African Americans.

We are collecting books for them to enjoy as they grow, including books by Sidney Poitier, Barack Obama, and Desmond Tutu. Our boys will know where they came from. They will read *The Door of No Return* and perhaps one day visit their ancestors' villages in Africa.

Adopted into our family, these children already know they too are descended from folks who crossed the ocean on the Mayflower. I smile to think of their great-grandparents and the looks on all the great-greats' faces if they knew they had these African American great-grandchildren.

All of us who believe in Jesus Christ the Redeemer know we are adopted into the family of God, based on the biblical promises we have been taught and believe.

When parents decide to adopt, after all the meetings, interviews, home visits, forms, and decisions, it comes down to choices. They choose the child they want to adopt. In Ephesians 1, we read that God chose us in Christ, before the foundation of the world. He destined us for adoption as his children. In Christ, we have redemption through his blood and the forgiveness of our sins, according to the riches of God's grace.

It's a plan, Paul tells us, a plan for the fullness of time. Thanks be to God. —*Lois Sibley*

A comfortable yoke

As a child of the church I knew "the Comfortable Words." After the confession of sin and the absolution, the priest would say, "Hear what comfortable words our Savior Jesus Christ saith unto all who truly turn to him. Come unto me, all ye that travail and are heavy-laden, and I will refresh you." The verse continues, "Take my yoke upon you and learn from me."

Jesus is speaking to those who seek God's wisdom for their life. The truth is God doesn't put the yoke on us like the farmer does for a pair of oxen. We have to choose the yoke. I am free to travel alone, yoke myself to another partner, or join myself to God.

When I hear these comfortable words I remember that the living Christ is willing to shoulder my burdens with me. I regret that "comfortable" has lost its connection to fortitude and become more anemic, like some feathery blanket. Yoked with Jesus, I am comforted but not cosseted. Christ gives me strength for the journey and shares my burden, but I still have to walk. I do occasionally stumble and fall, but joined to Jesus, I regain my footing more quickly.

Walking the Camino de Santiago across northern Spain taught me the great power of those comfortable words. In weariness my fellow pilgrims manifested the presence of the One who will always strengthen weak knees and help find the next resting place. Now I gladly take the yoke, meeting my Companion in prayer, in the words of scripture, and in the company of others who have also chosen the way of comfort. The heavy burden of my brokenness is lifted with the assurance of forgiveness and the strength for a new beginning on the road with my constant Companion and never-failing Friend.

—*Ruth Lawson Kirk*

I love to tell the story

When I die, I want people to sing "I Love to Tell the Story" at my funeral because that's what I love to do: tell the story.

Now, while I revel in telling many kinds of stories, I'm not talking about just any story here. I'm talking about *the* story, the gospel, the good news of God in Christ Jesus, the Incarnate Chosen One of the Lord, who came down to earth to be one of us, to live as one of us, to teach us, to lead us, to suffer as one of us, to die for all of us.

It's a great story, and believe you me, I can start telling it at the drop of a hat. Give me an opening, any opening, and boom! I'm off to the races.

Of course, I know this drives some people nuts. The ones who love me simply roll their eyes and sometimes joke: "There she goes again!"

The ones who don't love me so much wish I'd stop. The ones who don't know me wonder who I am. "What are you, a minister or something?"

It's so fun to tell them, "Why, yes, I am an Episcopal priest," which takes the discussion down new paths...but that's another story for another time.

It's not that I run around saying, "Hey! Did you hear about the time Jesus wept?" It's just that I love to find a way to bring a discussion around to what God wants. "God is calling us," I say. "This is our mission in life," I add. It doesn't matter what the topic is, I can find a way to make it relate to the gospel.

Did I mention that I love, absolutely love, to tell the story?
—*Lauren Stanley*

I'm a lousy driver

Purge me from my sin, and I shall be pure;
wash me, and I shall be clean indeed.

—PSALM 51:8

I'm a lousy driver. My skills aren't the problem. How I exercise them by speeding is. I first attended defensive driving school in my twenties. The second time I was thirty-something. The third time I was in my forties. As I then said to my spouse with full anger—and irony: "I don't know why they keep making me go. I never learn anything!"

It's been four years since my last ticket. I have a ritual now when I get in my car. As I turn the ignition key, I say aloud, "I'm a lousy driver." Hearing those words reminds me of who I am as defined by past choices and still-present inclinations to speed, and helps me to be mindful to drive differently.

A parishioner once asked why worship included a prayer of confession. "I don't recite that," he said. "All those things in those prayers, I'm not guilty of all that!" I was tempted to give him a lecture on original sin. Instead, I told him about my driving record and "ignition liturgy."

Hearing that, he nodded, saying, "I'm always going too fast, too."

Confessing our sins is not a self-improvement program. It is acknowledging our need for grace and recognizing our unworthiness apart from that grace. The more we know we need grace, the more we rely on it—and not on ourselves. And given all of our track records, that is definitely good news.

So, however you acknowledge, name, or confess it, you are a sinner. Join the club. Give your past to God and live differently, knowing that as you do, you are forgiven. —*John Van Nuys*

Growing

Like most spiritual things, spiritual growth is best done in community. We wrestle with others, not so much to sharpen our blades against one another as to engage spiritual questions and allow ourselves to be transformed in community.

It never ceases to amaze me how much I learn from people whom I would not necessarily think to go to with a burning spiritual question. Sometimes an offhand comment by someone I hardly know goes to the very heart of something I've been fretting about for weeks. I have an "aha moment" and the door to a new understanding is unlocked. Sometimes a deliberate discussion with a teacher or mentor leads me to formulate my own—different—take on one of the mysteries, which I could not have done if I were simply in my room, puzzling alone.

Our spiritual growth is not linear or progressive or predictable. We don't need a percentile calculator to see how we stack up against others in our spiritual growth. We are simply individuals with free will who strive to be in community as the Body of Christ to love God and love our neighbors as ourselves.

The beauty is that our own growth strengthens the community just as it strengthens us. Others support us in our spiritual growth, whether or not we are aware of that support. And we support others, even when we are not necessarily trying.

It just happens naturally when we are intentional about being in community—when we are present to God and to one another—just as it happens that green shoots come out of bulbs in February.
—*Penny Nash*

Seeing through a child's eyes

I'm driving in a car with my four-year-old son, the child of two Episcopal priests. He is belted into the back seat, can barely see out the window, and is sucking his thumb. Ahead of me by the side of the road stands a hapless hitchhiker, holding up a sign with a destination scrawled on it. I do not stop. As we drive by the man, a child's voice pipes up from the back seat: "Sorry, Jesus!" it says.

Oh, my son. How is it that you see and say things that I am either afraid to see or say, or am so profoundly perplexed about that I have forced them down to a level that silences them?

The artist Fritz Eichenberg made a wood engraving once of a line of poor men waiting to be given food. And there in the line is Jesus, a blanket around his shoulders, waiting for the same meal that the poor of our world daily await.

I fear that by seeing the world this way I will feel overwhelmed by the need of those who are Christ among us: the poor, the hungry, the disadvantaged, the homeless. How can I allow the eyes of my son to be my own without feeling overwhelmed, paralyzed, and guilty?

Could it be that the answer lies in the sensibility of my child? He is simply open to the outrageous idea that Christ is the man by the side of the road thumbing a ride: Christ is the stranger to be greeted, Christ the hungry one to be fed. My son is open, not weighed down by guilt and an overwhelming sense of responsibility. He is open and ready. Are we? —*Melissa Skelton*

"Lady, this is Jesus"

A friend of mine told me a story about a church where she used to work. She was in charge of children's programs, and one of her goals was to get the kids more involved in the liturgy. She suggested a "Children's Eucharist," and while the kids and their parents thought that was a great idea, some people in the parish didn't. Some wondered if the children had sufficient grasp of eucharistic theology to do justice to the sacrament, while others felt the service would lack the necessary reverence and piety.

After much preparation, the Sunday of the first Children's Eucharist arrived. The priest read a prayer that the children of the parish had written—with a little help from him—and the children took turns giving bread and wine to the parishioners. Then it was time for one of the more skeptical members of the parish to go forward to the altar rail. She was worried that the child dispensing the bread wouldn't know the right words. Maybe the kid would think it was a joke, or just wouldn't be taking it seriously.

The parishioner did her best to keep a good attitude, but as she knelt on the cushion at the rail, she was expecting the worst. Then a child about nine years old came over to her, the plate in one hand and a thin wafer in the other. But instead of saying "The Body of Christ, the bread of heaven," as the priest normally would, the child said, "Lady, this is Jesus."

That parishioner learned a valuable lesson that day, and she never doubted the children's programs again. —*Robert Macauley*

Saint Valentine's Day

Three different Saint Valentines are mentioned in early church records, all commemorated on February 14 and all of them martyrs. But nothing can be verified about any of them, and none is linked to romantic love. That association may have originated with Chaucer, who noted that it was on Saint Valentine's Day that the birds began seeking mates. And so now we send heart-shaped greeting cards, boxes of chocolates, and bouquets of flowers to our sweethearts.

Valentine's Day is largely about sentimentality. There's nothing bad in that, but there's nothing particularly good in it, either. It's important not to confuse sentimentality with love. Love can be sentimental but it can also be challenging, confusing, and demanding. The essential thing about love is commitment. Sentiment comes and goes; commitment remains and you can count on it. Commitment says: "I am there for you whether I feel like it or not, whether it's fun or not, whether you deserve it or not. Come what may, you can bank on me."

The marriage vows are about commitment—"for better for worse, for richer for poorer, in sickness and in health." God says the same thing, to everyone. To show that he means it, God sent his Son Jesus. Commitment is what we see in the face of Jesus Christ (some think of Jesus in more sentimental terms, like a Valentine card, but that is to diminish him). God's commitment to us is why the opening lines of the wedding service say that marriage "signifies to us the mystical union between Christ and his Church."

Commitment starts with God. That is the great original. Our commitments to one another are reflections of it and point to it.
—*Richard H. Schmidt*

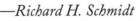

Freedom lies in an open hand

I'm told that there are trappers in South America who want to capture monkeys without harming them, to take them to zoos and such. The trappers take a large gourd and empty it on the inside, just as we make a jack-o-lantern at Halloween. Then they carve a small hole in the side of the gourd just big enough for the monkey's paw to squeeze through. Inside the gourd they place some tasty nuts that the monkey will love to eat and then secure the trap so it won't go anywhere.

When the monkey arrives, he slips his paw into the gourd, and it just fits. But then he closes his paw on the nuts, and he's trapped! Of course, the monkey can leave at any time. He's free to go if he lets go of the nuts. But he doesn't want to do that! He wants the nuts. So he will stay there with his paw in the gourd until the trappers arrive to take him away.

Sometimes we trap ourselves by our unwillingness to let go. We get stuck. We hold on to something that's really gone, unavailable, or inappropriate—maybe a time of life, a way of thinking, or an ended relationship. We tie ourselves down in ways that prevent us from living the life that's available to us.

If your hand isn't open, you can't receive a gift. There's no room if your hands are full. If your hand is closed, you may turn away a friend, or someone who could be a friend.

If you look at your hand, what do you see? Is it closed, like a fist? Are you holding on, clutching at something? Are you full? Are you stuck? Or is your hand open for all you can receive? —*Rob Slocum*

Risky business

Let the same mind be in you that was in Christ Jesus,
who, though he was in the form of God, did not regard equality with God
as something to be exploited, but emptied himself...

—PHILIPPIANS 2:5-7

Cormac McCarthy's typewriter recently sold for $254,500. McCarthy is the Pulitzer-prize winning author whose novels include *All the Pretty Horses, The Road,* and *No Country for Old Men.* He's been compared to William Faulkner, and many critics believe McCarthy will eventually receive the Nobel Prize in Literature.

McCarthy's novels were all written using his Olivetti Lettera 32 typewriter, bought at a pawnshop in 1963. In the typewriter's letter of authentication, McCarthy estimated that he had typed approximately five million words over fifty years on it. No doubt McCarthy would still be pecking away on that machine if it hadn't given up the ghost. If what you've got works, stay with it.

Then there's a grandmother I know named Kathy. When offered early retirement, Kathy thought of her daughter and dreamed of being closer to her grandchildren. So this lifelong Hoosier is now headed to the Pacific Northwest. Boxing up her house, saying goodbye to friends, changing everything in her life—all because of love.

What do you need to hold onto for dear life? What do you need to let go? What risks is God inviting you to take? What part of your life needs to pass away so a better, more Christlike life can arise?

Each day is an opportunity to become who we are: a new creation in Jesus Christ. Get involved in that risky business. Take a leap of faith. Let God's resurrecting life reorder you for good. —*John Van Nuys*

In the cold

For some years we had a capriciously malfunctioning garage door. It would frequently rise up unbidden, baring our over-full and under-organized garage to the passing world. On one notable February day, though, it bared the passing world to us.

The weather was bitter, with near-zero temperatures overnight. Early that morning I approached my car. Inside I found a young man awakening in the back seat, where he had sought refuge from the cold the night before, lured in by the unintentionally open garage door.

Dumbstruck and frightened, I rushed back into the house and I called the police. They picked the man up quickly. Though I regretted unleashing the law on him, I took some comfort in knowing that at least for the time being he would have food and shelter in the county jail.

I have since wrestled with my reaction. Of course I've read news accounts of homeless people committing serious crimes. But I've also read Genesis 18 and Hebrews 13 about entertaining angels unaware. I'm reasonably sure this young man was not an angel, but who knows? And he was (and still is) a beloved child of God. He was suffering, cold, and hungry. Surely I could have found a kinder way to respond. Our fear of the other so often stands in the way of discipleship.

This experience saddened me deeply; no one should be homeless in such cold. Quickly, of course, it became a story that I shared with friends. But it is most emphatically not a "good story." It's a terrible story of society's failure, *our* failure to care for our own.

Every day, in ways that are sometimes obvious and sometimes more hidden, we confront the choice between fear and discipleship. May God strengthen us to choose well.

—*Betsy Rogers*

Where are you, God?

When I was a child, I often stood at my bedroom window after I was supposed to be in bed and looked out into the night. On a cold, crisp night the sky might be filled with light from all the stars, and perhaps the moon was looking down at me.

Sometimes I opened the window and listened to the waves lapping at our dock on their way out to sea with the tide. In the silence, the action of the waves against the dock was a comforting sound that started me thinking and asking, "Where are you, God? Are you up there? Do you see me? Are you really the one who made this land, this river, the moon and stars? I want to know. How can I know? Tell me, God."

I waited for answers, but none came to me. So I closed the window, crawled under my blankets, and fell asleep wondering.

It was years before I heard the answers to those questions. When my two younger sisters convinced me to go with them to Bible Club, I began to hear about God, the Lord Jesus, and the Holy Spirit, about creation and redemption, about prayer and worship and God's love for us. And I began to read God's Word as a guide for life.

I was in college before I found books that answered more of my questions. That happened through small group Bible study, worship, friendship, and encouragement. I found God's will for my life. I thank you, Jesus for answering my many questions.

Now I wonder if some of the children I see are asking similar questions. Do they have someone to help them find the answers? I hope so, and I send up a prayer that God will hear and answer them, as he did for me. —*Lois Sibley*

"How can I say no?"

One of my friends told this story about her mother and a young man she met in Europe just before World War II.

During college her mother went with a chaperone and a group of other young women to Europe. As they sat having lunch in a German beer garden, a young man asked if one of the girls would dance with him. My friend's mother volunteered.

As they whirled to the music she practiced the little German she knew, and he offered the little English he knew. He asked if he could come the next day to her hotel to walk in the gardens. She agreed.

A pleasant time was had the next morning as they strolled, and in parting they exchanged addresses. Her group departed the following day.

Several years later, as the Nazis rose to power, the young man's family gathered to discuss their situation. They were Jewish and were alarmed at what was beginning to happen. The family wanted to go to America, but they needed to be sponsored by an American, and to have jobs for those who came. None of them knew any Americans—until the son remembered the girl he had known for two days. He wrote, asking if she could find a job for him and a place for him and his sister to stay.

She wrote back that she would sponsor them. She went to a Jewish merchant and asked if he would give the young man a job.

He said, "How can I, as a Jew, say no, when you, as a Christian, say yes?"

The young man, now old, became mayor of his town, known for his integrity and compassion.

What we say as Christians makes a difference— sometimes between life and death. —*Nancy R. Duvall*

Mardi Gras

It will soon be Mardi Gras time in Mobile and New Orleans. Mardi Gras is the last big blow-out before the self-denial and penitence of Lent. For some, Mardi Gras has become an extended blow-out, even a series of blow-outs, encouraging precisely the sort of behaviors requiring penitence during Lent. Some may even do the Mardi Gras blow-out and then skip the self-denial and penitence, but that's not how it's supposed to be. Lent is the main thing, Mardi Gras its preamble.

Self-denial and penitence are not fashionable nowadays. Encouraged by television and Madison Avenue, many people want more, bigger, fancier, and sexier everything, and see no reason why they should not have it. Why deny myself a pleasure to which I have ready access? Why deny myself anything, ever, for any reason? Here's why: the persistent pursuit of pleasure, even if it does no damage to another, can cause the soul to rot from within. Lent is a call back to a more honest, realistic, healthy—and happy—outlook, reminding us that we depend on God and are responsible to God for our stewardship of creation, including our lives themselves. Penitence and self-denial are not merely saying no to something—they are saying yes to something else. In declining to spend time, money, and energy on one thing, we are choosing to spend them on another.

When I lived on the Gulf Coast, I enjoyed Mardi Gras with its parades, silly costumes, plastic beads, and Moon Pies. Silly things can delight the soul—the "holy fool" is a classic spiritual figure. But we need a balance between the silly and the serious, and when the drive for pleasure becomes mindless and blocks out everything else, we have entered a very dangerous place. —*Richard H. Schmidt*

"You always have the poor with you"

Jesus told us that we would always have the poor with us (Matthew 26:11; Mark 14:7), and now that sometime seems to be an excuse for letting the poor be poor, for not doing enough to end the poverty that threatens to overwhelm this world.

Poor people have always been blamed for their circumstances. They have sinned, people assume, or their parents have. Poverty often is seen as a deserved punishment for something done or left undone.

But the sin of poverty isn't being poor.

The sin of poverty is that we who have more than enough allow others to live without enough. Without enough food, clean water, homes, medicine, jobs.

The sin of poverty is that we who have enough too often go through our lives ignoring the poor at best, blaming them for their circumstances at worst.

Having lived overseas as a missionary, among some truly poor people, it's all I can do some days not to yell and scream, "We are the sinners! Not them! Us!" I have to restrain myself whenever someone in this country tries to tell me that the poverty we have here is just as bad as it is overseas. I have to restrain myself when I hear people say, "If they would just get their act together." And I have to restrain myself whenever I think to myself, "I know better than these other people. I'm a better person, not only because I get it, but because I've lived among the poor." That's my sinful hubris speaking.

Poverty is a sin, yes. Being poor is not. But it is a bad circumstance that can overwhelm people and kill them.

What are we doing to end poverty, to make sure that those who do not have enough finally get their fair share?
—*Lauren Stanley*

Solemn and whole

The fruit of the Spirit is love, joy, peace, patience, kindness, generosity, faithfulness, gentleness, and self-control.

—GALATIANS 5:22

Lent seems like a solemn season. The word solemn can mean "stately or formal" and describes moments in worship and ritual. When my cousin retired from the U.S. Navy I was struck by the solemn rituals, like the slow salute with each sailor moving in perfect unison as the American flag was presented. We have those moments in worship as well, but Lent is not a stately, formal time.

The word solemn also means "deeply earnest, serious, grave, and sober." Here is Lent's solemnity. We take seriously the destructive consequences of our lives apart from God's grace and are deeply earnest about our desire for God's transforming power. We take a self-inventory and sober up to acknowledge the sense of distance from God, between others, and even from our own truest self—a distance that comes from our prodigal choices. Like the story of that son and father, Lent is the time to come to our right mind and return to the embrace of a loving Father.

It is interesting that the root of the word solemn comes from the Latin word for "whole." Our solemn work in Lent is to devote time for our wholeness, which can only be complete when we are at one with God and with others in the power of God's transforming love. This does not mean forty days of doom and gloom, but forty days for us to contemplate and act in ways that bring us alive to God so that all the fruit of the Spirit is borne in our lives—love, joy, peace, patience, kindness, generosity, faithfulness, gentleness, and self-control. This is solemn work. —*Ruth Lawson Kirk*

Engaging God

One of the joys of the Christian life is the assurance that God is in control. Taken too far, though, this can lead to a dangerous passivity. We might be tempted to believe that just because something happened, God wanted it to happen. Yet it is clear from scripture that God wants us to grapple with the world and strive to change it for the better.

A good example of this is Abraham's bargaining with God in Genesis 18:23-33. When God told Abraham he would destroy Sodom and Gomorrah, the passive response would have been silent obedience. Instead, though, Abraham beseeched God to spare Sodom and Gomorrah if he could find just fifty righteous people there, and God agreed. Then Abraham started bargaining with God: how about forty righteous people? he asked. Pretty soon he'd haggled God down to ten, and then it was up to Abraham to find them.

In the end, there weren't even ten, and Sodom was destroyed. Sometimes, though, there is a happy ending. Recently my wife and I found a house that seemed perfect for us and our family, but the sellers chose another bidder. I struggled for weeks to come to peace with that, but I couldn't. Finally, one afternoon on the way home from work, I said out loud as I drove, "God, I think you made a mistake. I think that house was meant to be ours."

Blasphemy? No, I think it was faithful engagement. I needed to let God know what was in my heart, even as I was ready to accept that the answer was not what I wanted it to be. In the end, though, the other bid fell through, and we were able to buy our dream house. Not because I helped God see the light, of course; rather, because it was God's will all along, and it gave me the chance to engage God, as Abraham had. —*Robert Macauley*

The women's group

My parish has two women's groups. One is a traditional daytime group, specializing in lunch, speakers, and good works. The other is for women who work outside the home. Most are baby boomers, with a few fellow travelers leavening the mix. We meet one Friday night per month.

Some meetings have set programs. Some are loose, and I—often unable to drive places lately—recently volunteered my house as a meeting place for one program.

It seemed like a good idea at the time, despite my current physical weakness due to treatment for cancer; the house was clean, and all I really had to do was a little setup—with a lot of help from my best friends—and fix some mulled wine.

Then I realized that I hadn't considered the work involved in cleanup. Oh, well: It would get done when it got done.

These were thoughtful guests. Early on, Ann asked, "What time do you need us to leave?" I usually tire out a little before 9:00 p.m., I replied. She nodded crisply.

It was a lovely evening, with a good group filling the family room, eating and drinking and making comfortable conversation. Then, just before 9:00 p.m., Ann announced, "Okay, now we're going to clean up."

They moved into the kitchen, dealt with leftovers, pitched the trash, tossed the recyclables into the bin, and moved onto the dirty dishes, making light work of it all. Then, with cheery goodbyes, they headed out.

When you're sick, the little things mean a lot. All those who help are a blessing—and, on this night, that included those who gave me a much-needed social evening and even cleaned up the mess. —*Sarah Bryan Miller*

Sirens

My first home parish, St. Paul's in Macon, Georgia, was a few blocks from the city's main hospital and emergency room. The church was located near the street, and it was not unusual for the sermon or eucharistic prayer to be interrupted by the sounds of an ambulance rushing by with its wailing siren. This may have been the occasion for some people to say a silent prayer for the patient going to the hospital, while others just wanted the noise to end. Either way, the problem was outside and passing. It involved someone else. It was their problem, which might or might not be viewed with compassion.

Benedict's Rule (Chapter 36) encourages his monks to find Christ in the community member who is sick. As Jesus says, help given to the most needy of his brothers and sisters is help given to him (Matthew 25:40). This service is not a reluctant duty endured for the sake of a principle. We find Christ as we extend radical hospitality to help the sick, disoriented, or impoverished. Their need is not just someone else's problem. It's not even just a problem. It's life and salvation for all of us. As we help others, we discover Christ's love present, and our true selves. We're connected with others in love, and their problems are ours.

During a time of plague in England, John Donne warned not to ask for whom the death bell tolls, because it tolls "for thee"—for each one of us. And today the sirens ring for us, as we hear the sounds of suffering and distress in our own communities, calling us to serve.
—*Rob Slocum*

Counsel for the defense

No one has greater love than this, to lay down one's life for one's friends.
—JOHN 15:13

In college "Mike" was known for his smarts and his partying. Few shone brighter or sunk lower. I saw Mike at homecoming after twenty-seven years. He had become a lawyer, working as a federal public defender.

Mike was assigned to defend an accused arsonist, who had terrorized multiple states, inadvertently incinerating two victims. When the media identified Mike as defense counsel, death threats began. Mike took an apartment to protect his family. As the case absorbed months of Mike's attention, his marriage came apart. His spouse left, taking the children.

Undeterred, Mike continued his defense. When prosecutors announced they would seek the death penalty, thus creating a new precedent, Mike, a staunch opponent of the death penalty on religious grounds, threw down the gauntlet.

Staring down the U.S. Attorney General, Mike said, "If you seek the death penalty, I will try this case in every state. Instead of months, this case will take years. If you win a conviction in any state, I will appeal, which will take years. I will not quit until all my client's legal remedies are exhausted." Attorney General Janet Reno blinked. Mike ultimately prevailed and, while his client was found guilty, his life was spared.

It takes great love to give one's life for friends—more so for the condemned. Jesus calls us to give our lives for others—the good and the guilty. The cost is steep; outcomes are often mixed; we are often scorned. Nonetheless, we follow Jesus whose cruciform love pardons us all. —*John Van Nuys*

Sew long, old friend

A long era is ending in my life. On my sixteenth birthday I was given a cabinet sewing machine. Today it is out of date. All this machine does is sew forward and backward and make buttonholes. Now they do everything but sing and dance, and I might have missed one that does that, too.

For many years I made many of my daughter's and my clothes, bathrobes for my sons and husband, table skirts, bed skirts, pillows, curtains, ballet costumes, prom gowns. Clothes were taken up or let out. I ran the sewing machine needle through my finger twice making tutus with yards of netting. Sewing was not always fun, but it was challenging.

With failing sight and less need to save money, I no longer sew. In fact, I can no longer thread the needle. A cosmic shift is taking place. I need to give my machine to someone who can use it. The trouble is finding who that might be. I have a feeling that far fewer people sew than when I was a young mother.

As with our talents, I think God wants us to use our things generously. Nothing pleases me (and, I hope, God) more than to see something I no longer use help someone else. We are only the temporary keeper of things—none of them as important as we think. Even our talents, mental capacity, memory, physical strength, and health are not promised to us forever.

Change is a certainty in our lives. The love of God, the example of how to live given us by Jesus, and the help of the Holy Spirit are the only constants. What else could we want? What more could we need? Look up, not around. Think eternal. —*Nancy R. Duvall*

New wineskins

No one sews a piece of unshrunk cloth on an old cloak...
And no one puts new wine into old wineskins.

—MARK 2:21-22

The Pharisees are already outraged by Jesus. He consorts with harlots and tax collectors. He violates the sabbath. When the Pharisees challenge him, supremely confident of their orthodoxy, he turns their words and actions back on them, leaving them feeling dull-witted and furious. And now, for those alert enough to catch his meaning, he is calling their cherished Law a threadbare garment, an old wineskin.

They had asked him why he and his disciples do not fast. Using the oblique language that he sometimes favors, Jesus explains that the old vessels of the past are worn out, altogether insufficient for the new heaven and the new earth that he ushers in. The old covenant of the Law cannot contain the excitement, the exhilarating, explosive power of God's new covenant of love.

Fasting bespeaks mourning and gloom; even John's disciples fast, mourning their guilt in preparation for God's judgment day. But sackcloth and ashes have no place at the wedding feast of God's kingdom. Its hallmarks are not gloom and mourning, but blessing and joy!

Sometimes we cling to our worn garments, our old wineskins. Offered the new wine of celebration and love, we seem to prefer the bitter vinegar of long faces and old legalisms. But God invites us to dress up in new clothes and party—to rejoice, to dance and sing!

What feasting does God spread before us today? —*Betsy Rogers*

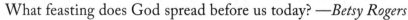

Becoming heaven

I'm a big fan of James Lipton's program *The Actor's Studio*. In it, actors and actresses come before a mostly student audience and answer rapid-fire questions about their careers, their personal histories, and their approaches to acting.

When Martin Sheen, actor, Roman Catholic, and political activist, was Lipton's guest, I tuned in to see just how explicit Sheen would be about his faith in front of an audience of New York City acting and directing students. Sheen did not disappoint. He spoke of what his Catholicism meant to him and the connection between his faith and his choices to get involved in the acts of civil disobedience that had landed him in jail some fifteen times.

My favorite part of each interview is right at the end when Lipton asks each guest an identical series of questions, a series that always ends with this same question: "If heaven exists, what would you like to hear God say to you once you reach the Pearly Gates?" Sheen looked down, laughed, shook his head and said, "Well, I don't believe we go to heaven, I believe we become heaven."

Becoming heaven—what an idea. What would it look like for me to begin to create in myself and in the world around me something of the peace, justice, dignity, connectedness to other, and beauty that heaven is supposed to be? What would heaven be if it were a realized state of being rather than a future destination?

What would your "becoming heaven" look like?

In what way can you take one step toward becoming the heaven you envision? —*Melissa Skelton*

Fasting

Fasting, once a staple of the faithful Christian life, is a practice often misunderstood and unappreciated today: "If it's available and I want it, why shouldn't I have it?"

Fasting's bad name today may derive from the excesses of a few overly rigorous zealots who turned it into a pinched, life-denying trap. It's not meant to be that way. Too much of a good thing becomes a bad thing. If our fasting weakens us rather than strengthens us, it isn't a true fast and we should stop it.

To fast is to decline something good for the sake of something better. Gratitude and joy characterize true fasting; it isn't intended to be painful. Jesus fasted and assumed his followers would fast. He spoke to them in the Sermon on the Mount about *when* you fast, not *if* you fast (Matthew 6:16-17). Food, for example, is a good thing, necessary for life. But many of us, in our obsession about eating (or not eating), act as if our diet were more necessary than God, even as if it were God. Willingly to say no to certain foods at certain times, even though they are available to us and we are entitled to them, acknowledges our dependence and gratitude to God and has led many to a deeper faithfulness and joy. Those of us living in prosperous times and places also learn when we fast that our "needs" are not what we thought they were.

But be careful: when you fast, do it *for God*. "It's Lent, so I'll swear off sweets and be a size slimmer when I buy my new Easter outfit"— that may be a good thing for you to do, but it isn't an appropriate Lenten discipline and it certainly isn't fasting. It's dieting, and that's something else. —*Richard H. Schmidt*

Praying the labyrinth

I built a labyrinth recently, on a cold morning with hoarfrost on the ground and a chill breeze coming off the river. The sun was just rising, and as its rays reached the meadow where I worked, those rays danced on the frost, making me think of angels dancing on glistening diamonds.

It took an hour to lay out the labyrinth for the people who would be using it later in the day as part of a retreat in which they would be asked to contemplate what it means to be a beloved child of God and to live in God's beloved community. At the end of the retreat, they would walk this labyrinth.

As they entered, I planned to give each person a bag of stones to lay down on the labyrinth lines. The stones, I would tell the people, were their prayers. Each stone represented someone for whom they wanted to pray. Pray for your family, I would say, for your friends, for people you know and people you don't know, for those in need and those who are blessed. Pray for the world, for the earth, the river, the sky. Pray for spring to come. It doesn't matter, I would tell them, for *what* you pray, only *that* you pray as you walk and put down your stones and walk some more.

I didn't wait for the stones to begin my prayers. My prayers poured out with the flour I was using to outline the labyrinth.

It was a prayerful hour that cold morning with the sun just rising, and a chill breeze coming off the river, and angels keeping me company as they danced on glistening diamonds and carried my prayers to heaven.

—*Lauren Stanley*

Love creates a space

And so the yearning strong, with which the soul will long,
shall far outpass the power of human telling;
for none can guess its grace, till Love create a place
wherein the Holy Spirit makes a dwelling.
—THE HYMNAL 1982, #516

These words are the third stanza of one of my favorite hymns, "Come down, O love divine." It is easy to sing and asks the Spirit to come into our hearts and lead us to God. The third verse is my favorite because it helped me learn how to forgive.

For years I have tried to love and forgive an acquaintance who often puts me or my ideas down. I had honestly tried to forgive this person for several years, but was not having much luck until one Sunday when we sang this hymn.

I noticed the last few lines: "for none can guess its grace, till Love create a place wherein the Holy Spirit makes a dwelling."

It came to me that I must make a place in my heart where I could love this person, whether or not she loved me, so that the Holy Spirit could enter both our hearts.

It has since been easier to ignore the times when my feelings are hurt and think, *I must give the Holy Spirit a place to enter my heart with love for others.* This is a decision I have to consciously make. It is not always easy. I often go around thinking of retorts I could have made, wondering what I am doing that provokes this behavior, thinking about it way too much. God has shown me a new way with this hymn.
—*Nancy R. Duvall*

Let God find you

There is no place where God is not.
God is there in a thousand wonders,
upholding rocky barriers,
filling the buttercups with their perfume
and refreshing the lonely pines with the breath of his mouth.
—CHARLES HADDON SPURGEON

There are times when we feel that we're wandering in the wilderness. Maybe something tragic has befallen us, or our spiritual life has simply run dry. We're besieged by doubt, and we don't know where to turn. We look for God everywhere, but it seems that God is nowhere to be found.

At times like that, it's good to stand still. When we continue to look for God, we're like a lost hiker who is trying so hard to find his way home that he ends up going deeper into the forest. People are searching for the person who is lost, but he's not where they expect him to be, because his desperation is driving him away from salvation.

God's love shines through scripture: God created the world because he delights in his creation; he sent the prophets to call us to repentance; and he loves us so much that his Son died for us. That means that God loves us far more than we could ever love him, and he's searching for us with even greater fervency than we're yearning to be found.

So the next time you can't find God, consider staying right where you are, and letting God find *you*. That's an act of faith.
—*Robert Macauley*

Fields in winter

March: not the Midwest's finest hour. In much of the nation's midsection the snowstorms are mostly over, but the trees remain bare, the grass stubble is still dead, the flower beds show no signs of life. Typical March weather is cold and wet. The ambient colors are dull shades of gray and brown. Whether from melting snow piles or March rains, there's mud everywhere, and those of us who have dogs just throw up our hands and abandon any hope of clean kitchen floors.

On such a March day I drove through the countryside near our home. The farm fields appeared empty and lifeless. But as I drove the clouds lifted a bit, and thin sunlight filtered down, with a hint of warming. Suddenly I recognized something new in those fields: I saw the life latent in the soil. Illinois farmland is rich and fertile, and in that instant I saw not bare earth but the summer bounty it would produce. The ground seemed to lift and move, ready to burst with the life that lay just beneath the surface.

So often we are like those winter fields. We feel empty, drab, and lifeless. Summer bounty seems either a dim memory or an unreachable dream.

God sees the life latent in us, having breathed it into us. God calls it forth, so that season by season we receive power to bear fruit. God's grace warms us like the sun, brings things hidden in us to life, and puts us to work as co-creators of this abundance.

What fruit does God call forth from us today? —*Betsy Rogers*

Identity crisis

Who do you say that I am?
—MARK 8:29

A recent Baylor University study surprisingly revealed that Americans believe in not one, but four different gods.

A third of Americans believe in an "Authoritarian God" who is involved intimately with his creation, actively punishing transgressors. A fourth believe in a "Benevolent God" who has moral laws and is grieved by sin, but is ultimately motivated by love to forgive. Sixteen percent believe in a "Critical God" who sees and judges humanity's actions, but is not involved in the affairs of people or nations. Belief for this group is constituted by an ethical life lived toward God, not an interactive relationship with God. Finally, 26 percent believe in a "Distant God" that is not a personal deity or a being at all, but rather an impersonal, cosmic force that created life, which we can discover—or not.

According to Jesus, whatever your image of God is, it must involve the cross. As the Incarnation of God, Jesus made plain on Calvary that ours is undeniably the Crucified God who is both the God of love, compassionately blessing the meek, and the God of justice, angrily driving out the moneychangers. Can we hold those two competing truths together simultaneously? A God whose love is fulfilled on the cross *and* a God whose power the cross could not destroy? According to Jesus, the cross is the only place where the answer is to be found, where the true nature of God is disclosed, and where our fullest, best lives are discovered.

Dare to live that answer as you daily follow Christ. Take up your cross to incarnate God's costly, cruciform love in self-sacrificing acts of your love. —*John Van Nuys*

Was that a crocus?

TGIF. It's Friday, and after a wearying commute at the end of the business week, I am glad to be home. I'm wondering about our plans for the weekend as I get out of the car and head for the stairs and the quiet of home.

I look down. Is that a crocus? It's purple, and there is a yellow one, too. Oh, joy. Spring is coming, finally. It's been a long, hard winter and I am glad to see these tiny promises of warmth and beauty in the soil beside the front steps.

I think of the seed catalogs that have been coming in the mail for weeks. Maybe this will be the time for me to sit down with pen and paper and plan for my gardens. I like to have a spot of color here, a bit of beauty there, wherever my eye will be drawn when I step out of the house. Ah, let's make a list this weekend. What do I need? Seeds for parsley and chives, first of all—my winter supply in the freezer is almost gone. And lettuce and peas, and...hmmmm...better slow down.

Check the calendar. Weren't you going to babysit the little boys tomorrow (grandsons, so their mom could go to a craft fair)? Yes. And my sister Jean is coming over for tea in the afternoon, around 3:00 p.m., as we did at Grandma's house.

What was that verse I read this morning? "I can do all things through him who strengthens me" (Philippians 4:13). Yes, but I don't think Paul meant we should cram our days and nights with busyness; that's not what he had in mind when he wrote that. I guess I better study that chapter a little more carefully and not jump to conclusions. Good idea. Do that now, and make the garden list later.

—*Lois Sibley*

The broom

Teach me, my God and King, in all things thee to see.
—GEORGE HERBERT,
THE HYMNAL 1982, #592

We can sweep a floor to the glory of God, said George Herbert, a seventeenth-century Anglican priest. God can be seen in all things when they are done for God. The task then becomes an expression of faith, not a burden. The devotion transforms both the sweeping and the one who sweeps. It "makes the action fine."

God finds us, and we find God, through the things of this world. God is present in creation, and works through it. We find God in the details and everyday contexts of our lives. Benedict states in his Rule (Chapter 31) that the vessels of the kitchen are as holy as the vessels of the altar. The infinite God is not beyond our world or our most basic needs.

God's love is available, particular, tangible, and knowable in the midst of the situations we face. We can place our hands in God's hands so that divine generosity, love, and forgiveness are known through us. Our actions can then reflect both God's invitation and our choice. We may be amazed to discover that we are most ourselves when our choices most fully reflect God's will. Austin Farrer calls this "double agency," and it's visible in the cooperation of the divine and human agents in a single expression of love. We can know God present and active in our lives in all kinds of ways—as we work with a computer, a paintbrush, or a broom. *—Rob Slocum*

Throw it up the stairs

Last year I had surgery on my foot. For three months afterwards I was hobbling around on crutches or scooting around on a little metallic blue contraption called a knee scooter. During that time I learned much about the mobility I had taken for granted for most of my life, but more importantly, I learned the value of throwing things ahead of myself in order to muster the strength to go forward.

Picture this: a woman on crutches at the bottom of a short flight of stairs with a backpack on her back. She cannot ascend the stairs using her crutches with the weight of the backpack. So she throws the backpack to the landing three steps above her. This then allows her to hop up the stairs with the crutches, motivated by the vision of seeing some part of herself already at her destination.

As I did this over and over again, it occurred to me that there was more than the physical business of getting up stairs going on here. It was something about where I put my energy, my heart—and what can happen if I put some of it out in front of myself.

The vision of the New Jerusalem in chapter 21 of the Book of the Revelation is, for me, about the need we all have for some magnetic future that we can recognize as our own to stand before us as we muster our strength to overcome what can feel like inertia or difficult barriers.

Where in your life do you need to throw your backpack ahead of you? What might you do to give even a small amount of energy to the magnetic future before you? —*Melissa Skelton*

Walking in the light

As long as I am in the world, I am the light of the world.
—JOHN 9:5

All four gospels have a version of the story of Jesus healing the blind man. John uses it as a vehicle to demonstrate there are different kinds of blindness—but that Jesus is the light of the world.

Jesus healed many people, but in most of the cases they—or their families and friends—had to ask him first. Not this time; Jesus responds to a question from his disciples: is the blindness a result of the man's sin, or that of his parents? He uses the blind beggar to make his point. At that time, many people believed that physical handicaps were a result of somebody's sinning, and that parents' sins could be visited on their children. By healing the blind man, Jesus is dispelling more than one kind of darkness.

As the account goes on, we also see that there are some who resist the light and what it shows. Jesus violates the law concerning working on the sabbath when he cures the blind man. The Pharisees and other Jewish authorities are so focused on that, and on looking for reasons to discount Jesus and his ministry, that they lose sight of the miracle that's right in front of them: "Though I was blind, now I see."

Sometimes we can lose sight of what's right for us as surely as the Pharisees did.

Jesus healed the blind man, and he saw the light—literally as well as figuratively—for the first time. The Pharisees, though their eyes were perfectly functional, chose to keep them closed. We need to keep our eyes open to God's possibilities for us and for the world. —*Sarah Bryan Miller*

Blooming in the desert

Deep in the southern California desert, not far from the Mexican border, we're on a hunt—for wildflowers.

We are not disappointed. Here, in the seemingly forbidding landscape of the Anza-Borrego Desert State Park, the blooming season is just under way in early March. So off we go in my brother's aging Jeep, careening along washes, bouncing through crater-sized chuckholes, and plunging down drop-offs that have me saying my prayers.

This country looks thoroughly forbidding: gravel, rock, and sand as far as the eye can see. But when we pull to the side of a wash and get out, what wonders await us! Desert lilies, asters, primroses, lupines, penstemon, ghost flowers, poppies, heliotrope, sand verbena, and many more exquisite flowers find what they need in this desolate place and bloom. A week or two later, we might find them in profusion, but now they are more apt to appear as single blossoms surrounded by barren earth.

These surprising flowers are gifts, striking reminders that God is at work here, too, in this unlikely place.

Like the desert, we might feel barren and dry, but God bestows good gifts on us even in our most desolate places. The gifts of the Spirit bloom not just in the lush tropical microclimates of profound devotion but also in the seemingly inhospitable ecology of the everyday. When we stop to look and open our hands to receive, we find peace, joy, love, patience, and kindness ready to blossom in us, to enrich our own lives and to be shared with others. God's beauty waits to bloom in us as surely as in the desert. —*Betsy Rogers*

Feeding my people

Those who refresh others will themselves be refreshed.
—Proverbs 11:25 (New Living Translation)

Every year during the season of Lent, my congregation gathers on Wednesday evening for a meal of soup and bread. Volunteers make the soup, everyone brings some bread, and we conclude with Evening Prayer. One year, an elderly woman volunteered to make the soup every Wednesday. We all thought that would be great, until we tasted the soup. Someone described it as "boiled weeds," and I think that was probably a pretty accurate description. No one really knew what to do, so we all dove in and choked down the concoction, hoping that things would improve the next week. Unfortunately, our hope was in vain.

I have to say, in hindsight, it was one of the finest hours for our congregation. People offered compliments and were gracious. They always said thank you, and though there were lots of leftovers, everyone came back, week after week. They understood that providing the weekly pot of "boiled weeds" for her parish brought obvious joy to our cook. She worked really hard to make the soup, and she was so proud.

On the last Wednesday in Lent, our group gathered for our final meal of boiled weeds. When the soup was served, it was chicken soup. Much to everyone's surprise, it was delicious. People kept saying again and again, "This is really good."

Finally our cook yelled, "You all seem so surprised." So we shut up and kept eating. And all our hearts were filled with joy.

Jesus said, "Feed my people," but he never gave us any recipes. And thank God for that, because we would all certainly obsess over the measurements and ingredients and miss out on the immeasurable joy of sharing. —*Jason Leo*

God's way of arranging things

The goodness of God is in the eye of the beholder. You either see the hand of God in things or you don't. No one can prove to another's satisfaction that God exists, much less that God is good, loves people, or acts in people's lives. That's why the best evangelism isn't trying to convince nonbelievers to see what they do not see, but bringing them to a point where they see it themselves.

My son Andy once came up with a good illustration of this. "There may be an order to things that we cannot perceive," he said. "It's as if there were lots of books in a bookcase and someone had arranged them alphabetically by author. Someone else walks into the room and looks at the bookcase—but this person does not know the alphabet. He would see order in the books only if they were arranged by color or size or binding. The universe may be like that bookcase. It's possible that God does things and arranges things, but we don't see it because we don't know God's alphabet."

Sometimes I find myself in a sticky bind and then things unexpectedly work themselves out—or someone works them out—despite my bumbling and misdirected efforts to set them right. God does not bail us out of every jam. Sometimes he lets us tough it out. But sometimes, for reasons known only to himself, God drops into our lives a bit of—what shall we call it? Good fortune? Divine providence? I call it grace.

Grace is the unearned, undeserved, unexpected goodness of God. You can explain it any way you want. I see God's hand moving the books around on the bookshelf. —*Richard H. Schmidt*

Crocus—the harbinger of renewal

More than half my life ago, I lived in North Dakota, where the winters can be harsh and where your first winter can be brutal beyond belief. Mine was.

An uncle of mine who lived in Virginia took pity on me that winter, when I was shivering constantly and craving sunlight and warmth. He began writing to me about spring in Virginia, about green grass and budding trees, about cherry blossoms and daffodils and tulips, and especially about crocuses, those beautiful little flowers that are the first to blossom.

I didn't know what a crocus (or "croci," as my uncle and I jokingly called them) looked like in those days; I had to find a photo in a book. They are pretty flowers, but my love affair with them has nothing to do with their beauty. My love affair with them is deeply intertwined with resurrection.

I see these flowers poking their heads out through the snow, valiantly bursting open with brilliant colors, and I think, "Soon, very soon, this cold winter will be gone. Soon, very soon, the sun shall return. Soon."

These little flowers are my harbingers of the earth's renewal and, in some ways, of my own renewal. In them I find assurance: yes, the winter will end, the snow will go away, the green grass will return, the trees will bud, and spring will run riot again.

In the darkness of winter, all of life can seem dark and dreary: the body yearns for sunlight and warmth, the spirit yearns for resurrection and renewal.

Every year, I search diligently for the "croci." When I find them, I rejoice: resurrection is on its way!

—*Lauren Stanley*

Confession and forgiveness

*Confess your sins to one another, and pray for one another, so that you may
be healed. The prayer of the righteous is powerful and effective.*

—JAMES 5:16

Those who engage in confession regularly need only mention the
sins they have committed recently. For those who come from religious
traditions where confession—now often called "reconciliation"—isn't
emphasized, there's more ground to cover. I made my first confession
when I was in my twenties. It took weeks to prepare and quite a long
time to share with my spiritual director.

There are two things I'll always remember about the two hours
it took me to go over everything I could remember doing wrong. The
first was how unsurprised the wise old priest who was listening to me
catalog my sins was. He didn't minimize the severity of what I had
done, because it was important enough to me, at least, to mention. But
he also wasn't shocked or aghast at anything I said. Even when he gave
me some mild penance (in the form of prayers and scripture readings), it
wasn't to punish me, but to refocus my mind on what God was calling
me to do. His response helped me to see the truth of the scripture that
reads, "There is no one who is righteous, not even one" (Romans 3:10).

My most vivid memory, though, was of something that happened
when it was all over. My confessor had proclaimed me forgiven by
God and anointed me with oil. I got up to leave, the sheaf of papers
listing all my transgressions still in my hand. The priest stopped me.
"You can put those in the wastebasket," he said. "They don't belong
to you anymore." In that moment, perhaps more than at
any other moment in my life, I felt completely forgiven.
—*Robert Macauley*

Let love flow

Fresh, clean water is a gift. When I was a child we vacationed in Vermont, and my father would visit a spring and fill jerry cans with sweet, clear water. Now I visit the water aisle in a Vermont grocery store and buy the spring water in jugs. Water from around the world is available for purchase in vending machines and convenience stores.

Think about the impact of bottled water. When I buy a single bottle, I'm paying about $9.00 a gallon for water. When I throw the bottle in the trash, I'm adding to the stream of plastic waste that does not deteriorate for thousands of years. What does that have to do with the spiritual life?

A relationship with God is meant to shape a relationship with the rest of God's creation. My spiritual life is only a little about me and my God; it is mostly about me and my neighbors near and far, now and in the future. As Saint John wrote, "No one has ever seen God; if we love one another, God lives in us, and his love is perfected in us" (1 John 4:12). The work of Lent is meant to strengthen my identity as one made in God's image so that I live in solidarity with all whom God loves. So I think again about drinking that bottled water.

By filtering tap water and using glasses or refilling clean bottles, we can express our love for future generations by reducing our impact on the environment. Or when we buy a bottle of water we can donate the cost of another bottle to an organization that helps people in developing countries improve access to safe drinking water. Then our water consumption expresses solidarity and service.

Lord, when did I see you thirsty and give you water to drink?
—*Ruth Lawson Kirk*

Let us pray

Every Sunday night, Dr. Harold Ockenga walked into his pulpit at Park Street Church and said with a firm and dramatic voice: "If my people who are called by my name humble themselves, pray, seek my face, and turn from their wicked ways, then I will hear from heaven, and will forgive their sin and heal their land." Then came a long pause followed by "Let us pray."

The verse is 2 Chronicles 7:14, and I can still hear Dr. Ockenga say it. It gave me chills. Who knew what he would say after that? I loved listening to Dr. Ockenga, and it was worth every minute of it for me.

Some preachers are like that, so impressive and wise-sounding that you hang on their every word. After reading Charles Haddon Spurgeon's *Morning and Evening* for years, I think he was probably like that, too. He put words together so beautifully.

Some preachers pray better than they preach. Their prayers are full of caring and concern for people they know and love, as well as people they don't know but have been asked to pray for. Often their prayers are timely, as they pray about things we are all concerned about, and we appreciate their praying about it for us.

Our Lord Jesus certainly knew how to pray. Read through the middle of the Gospel of John, say chapters 13–17, where Jesus is teaching the disciples what he wants them to know and remember, and then read his prayers for them just before they go out to the garden where Jesus will be betrayed. If you are caught up in the story, you won't be able to stop reading, but will go on into chapter 18 and following.

That's okay. It's a story we need to read often. —*Lois Sibley*

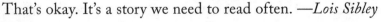

Pour it on

*Mary took a pound of costly perfume....anointed Jesus' feet,
and wiped them with her hair. The house was filled with the fragrance.*

—JOHN 12:3

In 1996 an arsonist torched Ebenezer Presbyterian Church, a white-frame country church in Rush County, Indiana.

The fellowship hall was a total loss. The sanctuary remained standing, but with heavy smoke damage. Carpeting, walls, pews—everything was blackened. The sight was dispiriting. Yet the morning after, grieving church members were there, cleaning and salvaging.

They removed the center aisle carpeting. An elderly farmer in soot-covered overalls knelt with pliers and chisel, carefully pulling up every remaining carpet tack and nail. Friends told him just to pound the hundreds of nails into the floor, that new carpet would cover them.

"No, that would just leave them in the wood. Go ahead with your work. I'll follow, but I'm going to do this right." His friends shook their heads in frustration. I shook mine in wonder as I watched the old man remove another nail. He just kept at it, steadily working away, inching his way forward on his knees down the center aisle to the chancel and the smoke-stained cross hanging high above it.

The potent stench filling the sanctuary was inescapable. But the fragrant outpouring of that man's love for his church and Savior was stronger. Pouring out ourselves in love is how we are to live. When we give generously and selflessly, God is anointed by our actions—and our world reeking of violence and fear is filled with the beautiful, potent fragrance of compassion and love. When it comes to love, our world needs all we can give. Pour it on.

—*John Van Nuys*

Let yourself out of jail

I grew up in the South, where encountering someone preaching repentance on a street corner with Bible in hand was a weekly occurrence and where back roads were punctuated with signs warning us to repent before it was too late. My skeptical family and I regarded these ideas as nonsense, just another example of how odd and useless the church and its teachings were.

Fast forward. After many years in the church, I am in a session with my spiritual director. I am working on a situation in which I have simply messed up, having made a mistake in the way I handled something. In the midst of my increasingly fainthearted justifications of what I have done, my spiritual director turns to me and says: "Why don't you just let yourself out of jail on this one? Just go back, apologize, and tell the person you've had a change of mind and heart about this."

I know it sounds simple-minded, but the little phrase "letting yourself out of jail" along with the permission given me to own up to my mistakes actually taught me more about repentance than all those signs and street corner preachers put together.

Repentance is about a change of mind, a way in which we're given a second chance. It is a way out of a blind alley or a way back from a road to nowhere. Repentance is the way our lives are renewed and our relationships restored.

What kind of repentance is calling to you at this time in your life? What jail might you let yourself out of? —*Melissa Skelton*

This brother of yours

*This brother of yours was dead and has come to life;
he was lost and has been found.*

—LUKE 15:32

The party is in progress. The merciful father has welcomed his prodigal son back with joy and slain the fatted calf. But the obedient son is filled with resentment. Addressing his father, he speaks of his brother as "this *son of yours*," his voice ringing with condemnation.

The father turns it around. He assures the eldest son of his love, and then speaks of the prodigal. "This *brother of yours*," he says, "was lost and has been found."

The difficult people in our lives don't belong to someone else: they belong to us. We might in frustration seek to put distance between ourselves and someone who vexes us. "*Your* husband," we might say, or "*that* woman," as we voice our judgment about their behavior. But God's truth is that these people in fact belong to us, and we to them. We can try to separate ourselves from them, to place them outside our sphere of relationships and caring, but they will persist in slipping back in, because that's where they belong. That's where we all belong, together.

Thank heavens! Because at one time or another we all find ourselves in the shoes of the prodigal son. We get lost. We become estranged from those we love. We fail in our responsibilities. We sink into self-indulgence, carelessness, and wickedness, which presents so many different and alluring temptations to us.

But God's amazing grace finds us, draws us home, and folds us together into an embrace where, by a miracle of God's unsearchable love, we all belong. —*Betsy Rogers*

Impressionism

It's a small thing on which to build a touring art exhibit: three large canvasses of water lilies, painted as a triptych by the aged Claude Monet. They were sold to three different museums; now, with a new frame to tie them together, they're temporarily reunited.

It's a small thing, but on this day it's just the right size: large enough to be worth the trip to the museum, but not so large as to overwhelm the viewer. The three paintings really belong together; they are more than the sum of their parts.

People leaned right into the paintings (their noses perilously close to the canvas), much to the distress of the guards stationed on either side. What did they hope to see? Impressionist paintings don't look like much up close. The wonder of the technique is in the way unshaded blobs of paint turn, with a little distance, into evocative, arresting landscapes or portraits. You must stand back to appreciate them.

That can be true in life, too. We naturally focus on what's directly in front of us—making this deadline, getting to that appointment, worrying about setbacks and surprises—to the exclusion of the larger picture. Much of the time, it doesn't seem to make a lot of sense.

But God, the master painter, does not intend for us to view this creation with our noses to the canvas. Step back; take it all in, and see how miraculously the forms of God's world take shape before us.
—*Sarah Bryan Miller*

A breath of spring

In early spring, my dog and I go for our morning run. It's a jog actually, and requires stopping several times for Milo to…examine his world. It is a cold morning. I am bundled up, including a scarf over my mouth and nose. Even then, I can see my breath.

Upon our return, I am sweating heavily and need to cool down. I turn Milo loose in the courtyard; he immediately begins to explore "his" territory. I walk up and down and notice that the daffodils have died. This latest cold snap has done them in. They came in way too early this year, due to a delightfully beautiful two weeks. Now, however, their time has passed.

I squat down to pull out the stems…and see a *puff* of air rise from the earth.

"Milo! Back off, you silly mutt!"

But Milo isn't next to me. He is across the yard and promptly runs over, snuffling and pushing his nose into the dirt. He sits next to me, looking from the ground to my face, as though to ask, "So…whatchya doing?"

I pull out the remains of another daffodil. Again! There's that *puff* of air! I must be leaning too close, I think. I'm seeing my own breath.

I pull another…*puff!*

Finally, I realize: What I am seeing is the earth itself, breathing, exhaling, letting go.

"Milo!" I say. "Watch this!"

Pull…*puff!* Pull…and pull and…*puff! Puff!*

I am witnessing a small miracle: I am watching the earth *breathe!*

As never before, I now understand that God's creation is fully alive, just as I am. —*Lauren Stanley*

Justified while yet a sinner

We can become so overwhelmed by our undeservedness—Lent being one of those times—that it's hard to imagine ever being accepted by God. Day in and day out, we hear about human sinfulness, which is compounded by deprivation (for those who give something up for this penitential season) and winter weather.

The parable of the Pharisee and the tax collector (Luke 18) is a tonic at times like that. It's a very brief story: a Pharisee (or religious leader) goes to the temple and ticks off all the wonderful things he does in the name of God (and there are a lot of them). Then a tax collector (a profession looked down upon in those days) slips in through a side door and begs God to have mercy on him, without even raising his eyes to the heavens. And guess who Jesus said went away justified? Not the religious leader.

It's a wonderful story of repentance and redemption, a glimmer of hope in the midst of Lent. But the power of the parable only comes out when we imagine what might have happened next. That's the thing about parables: they're short and sweet, and leave a lot to the imagination. Most of us want the tax collector to turn away from his old life and start doing wonderful things in the name of God, so that he can return to the temple the next weekend all cleaned up and justified.

But, as Robert Farrar Capon asks, "Why are you so bent on destroying the story by sending the [tax collector] back for his second visit with the Pharisee's speech in his pocket?" The miracle of the story isn't that the tax collector will be justified if he amends his life; the miracle lies in his justification in that moment when he trusts entirely in God's mercy. —*Robert Macauley*

Homeward bound

Homecomings aren't always easy. When Jesus returns to his hometown and teaches in the synagogue on the sabbath, he encounters hostility. The people think they know just who he is (and isn't) because they know his family. In Mark's narrative (6:1-6), the people ask, "Is not this the carpenter, the son of Mary and brother of James and Joses and Judas and Simon, and are not his sisters here with us?" They take offense at Jesus, and he is amazed by their unbelief. It's not an easy homecoming.

Thomas Wolfe, author of the novel *Look Homeward, Angel*, is well known for saying "you can't go home again." Of course, he's right. The buildings and even the people of a former home may be there, but "home" may be gone. The actual place can be very different from the remembered home. I'm told that people returning from time overseas may experience reverse culture shock when the place they return to isn't the home they remember. Life has gone on without them. People and relationships have changed. The place is different.

Mother Debra Trakel once mentioned at St. James Church in Milwaukee that the expression "hobo" is a contraction of the phrase "homeward bound." We can hope that the homeless people we meet, and all "hobos," will reach their destination and find a good home.

In a way we are all hobos—homeward bound. The completion of our home is ahead of us, in the completion of our lives in God's hands. God is our sanctuary, our oasis, our refuge, our greatest adventure, our place of security, our home. As in John Newton's hymn text, "Amazing grace" (*The Hymnal 1982*, #671), "'tis grace that brought me safe thus far, and grace will lead me home." In God we find our homecoming.
—*Rob Slocum*

Favored by God

Today is the Feast of the Annunciation, the day the archangel Gabriel appeared to Mary and proclaimed to her, "Greetings, favored one!"

I love this day, because on this day, a young woman minding her own business heard from God's messenger that she was favored. When she woke up that morning, did she believe it? Did she believe, with all her heart and soul and mind and strength that God favored *her*?

Mary wasn't favored because she said "Yes" to God. Gabriel didn't bring her contingent blessings; Gabriel simply announced to her, in no uncertain terms, who she was in God's creation: one of God's beloved children.

This is our core identity. We are God's beloved. Not because of anything we have done or might do. But because God says so. Each of us is one of God's favored.

How often do we hear that message from God? Have we ever heard it? In the deepest parts of our being, we all want to know that we are loved. We want to know that someone loves us as much as we love in return.

When we know that we are loved, we can endure anything because, as Paul teaches, love "bears all things, believes all things, hopes all things, endures all things" (1 Corinthians 13:7). When we know that we are loved, we know that we are not alone, even in our deepest sorrows, even in our greatest joys.

To be favored is to be blessed. To be blessed is to be loved. To be loved is to have our lives fulfilled, our purpose defined, our hopes met.

That's why I love this day. Because on this day, a young girl was told that she was favored by God. And because she was, I believe that I am as well. —*Lauren Stanley*

The role of a lifetime

Immediately they left their nets and followed him.
—MARK 1:18

Leave everything? Immediately? Impossible!

Not so fast. We see it all the time. Many of us have experienced it.

When my cousin accepted the blind date, the doorbell rang, she opened the door, locked eyes with a total stranger, and immediately knew: "This is the man I am going to marry." Love at first sight.

Romantic love is wonderfully irresistible. But ongoing love often requires the sublimation of self, for the child who is sick or the cause that is worthy. What is the secret to being loving?

During a recent Oscar Awards chat, actor nominees discussed the risky process of giving a performance, of opening one's essence at the bidding of a director. Anne Hathaway said, "If I have a director I know I can trust, I completely put myself in his hands. I don't always know where I am going—and I don't have to." Commenting on his vocation, Brad Pitt said, "When I am doing this, I know that I am at my purpose." Mickey Rourke said this of the director who put him through eleven months of physical training: "When I sat down, I knew he wanted my blood. I thought, 'I'm going to give it to you because I respect you and I know that you will take me with you to a place that is good.'"

Good advice for young actors—and for aspiring followers of Jesus Christ, in whom we put our trust, to whom we can give ourselves completely and unreservedly. By grace, Christ will direct us not to a path we can know ahead of time, but through a process of losing ourselves in love that will result in joy. Don't miss out. This is the role of a lifetime. Act now. Follow him.

—*John Van Nuys*

God's guiding light

Thy word is a lamp unto my feet and a light unto my path.
When I feel afraid and think I've lost my way,
still you're there right beside me. Nothing will I fear as long as you are near.
Please be near me to the end.

— AMY GRANT AND MICHAEL W. SMITH, "THY WORD"

This familiar and loved contemporary song, based on Psalm 119:105, assures us that God is our guide, our path, and our light. In him we find comfort and security, knowing we are headed in the right direction. He helps us when we stumble and lifts us up again.

Last night I ventured up the hillside to my neighbor's property to examine their massive landscaping project. I failed to take a flashlight. You can guess what happened; I stumbled, tripped, stepped on teetering rocks from the old stone wall, and nearly fell into a big hole. Construction diggers and backhoes were all around. Fortunately I didn't hurt myself.

Wandering around in the darkness, through the woods at night, is dangerous—much like meandering through life without God's light to shine before us. As a director for the Christian Association of Youth Mentoring, I work with churches to help young people across the country who are often very lost. Frequently, these teens are fatherless or have an incarcerated parent; at a minimum, they are confused. Many have no faith and are in desperate need of being found. Experiencing the change in a person's life when they accept Jesus Christ is astonishing—a light of hope in an unimaginable dungeon of decay. Please pray that these hurting and abandoned young people will find the constant light and love of Jesus.

Jesus is the way, the truth, and the life, if we but trust and believe. —*Carl Kinkel*

Fasting and feasting

Many people give something up for Lent. That's fine, but when we get rid of one thing, we usually put something else in its place. Here are a few suggestions of things to give up this Lent, together with possible replacements:

Fast from shrieking at the children; feast on listening to them. Fast from feeling unappreciated; feast on appreciating others. Fast from the excessive use of alcohol and tobacco; feast on treating your body as its Creator intends. Fast from making snotty remarks; feast on saying "Please" and "Thank you." Fast from sleeping in on Sunday mornings and from doing things on Saturday night that make you want to sleep in on Sunday mornings; feast on worship. Fast from spending money on indulgent pleasures and frivolities; feast on giving it away to others. Fast from frowning; feast on smiling. Fast from judging others; feast on self-examination.

Fast from putting off things you'd rather do tomorrow; feast on doing them today so that when tomorrow comes, you won't be tempted to put them off until the day after tomorrow. Fast from doing the thing you do repeatedly and compulsively; feast on using that time to pray, sing, dance, or rest. Fast from worry; feast on contentment. Fast from striving for the things you need and want; feast on giving others the things they need and want. Fast from getting angry about what others do, say, and think; feast on reforming the things you do, say, and think.

Fast from envy; feast on thanking God for making you the person you are, for the good life you have been given. Fast from wallowing in guilty feelings; feast on the fact that although you are indeed guilty, Christ has died for you, and that's all a guilty person needs.
—*Richard H. Schmidt*

On the journey

It was my first day on a new job, one that meant leaving a familiar city and friends and family.

It was a decent first day on the job as those things go: everyone I met was polite and helpful, and everything was ready—my office with a new desk and chair—for my arrival. After a round of introductions and a few meetings to orient me, I came back to my office, shut the door, pulled out some of the family pictures I had brought with me, and began arranging them on my desk. This was when the tears came, tears for the losses that even good things can bring.

"To see thee is the end and the beginning. Thou goest before me and carriest me. Thou art the journey and the journey's end." A Christian philosopher named Boethius wrote these words in a time of great societal chaos and loss.

This was not what I was experiencing, of course. I was not in the midst of the kind of upheaval that comes with war, political strife, or economic chaos. In many ways, I was fortunate—to have a new job at all, to have a new desk to put pictures on. And yet, even I, with all that I had to be thankful for, needed the reassurance that in the losses and changes of life—whether big or small—that God is the end and the beginning, that God ever goes before us, that God is both the journey and the journey's end.

Where in your life do you need the reassurance that God is the journey and the journey's end? What difference does this reassurance mean to you? —*Melissa Skelton*

Touchstones

So teach us to number our days that we may apply our hearts to wisdom.

—PSALM 90:12

How do we go about doing the work God has given us to do? How do we order our days? Today's world is so full of conflicting needs, conflicting goods, and endless possibilities. How do we choose the next right action, and then the next?

Perhaps these questions are not so new. For centuries, beginning with Saint Benedict, monastic communities have lived by what is called a "rule of life." Hardly a "rule," it is more of a framework for faithful, abundant living. In religious communities, the rule includes general guidelines for the life of that community, as well as areas such as hospitality, prayer, and study.

As an associate of a monastic order, I follow a rule of life that includes a commitment to practices such as prayer, worship, giving, and study as well as other priorities such as health and relationships. I have also formulated an individual rule that includes things specific to my life situation and commitments: parenting, household, care of the earth, simplicity.

Of course, life often is so busy and out of balance that I don't have time to think about my rule(s), let alone follow them. My condensed version of the rule is what I think of as touchstones: Every day, I try at least to "touch" on prayer, writing, physical exercise, giving, housework, garden work, close relationships, and simple kindness. Often, these are feeble attempts—for example, when emptying the compost counts as "gardening" and a quick email is all I can do to keep up with a friend. But, these touchstones help keep me grounded. They help me order my days. —*Nancy Hopkins-Greene*

Genesis 50

Joseph forgave his brothers, but not without making them grovel a little bit. If you've read the last few chapters of Genesis or seen the musical *Joseph and the Amazing Technicolor Dream Coat*, you know that Joseph toys with his brothers when they don't recognize him. He accuses them of being spies, even though their only reason for coming to Egypt is to find food in the midst of a famine. He accuses them of being thieves by secretly putting the money they brought to buy grain back into their sacks before they leave for home. Eventually they all wind up bowing before him, just like he saw in the dreams he had told his brothers about—the dreams that filled them with enough rage to throw Joseph in a well, sell him into slavery, and then claim to their father that the boy had been eaten by a wild animal.

That's a lot to forgive. But notice how Joseph waits to make himself and his forgiveness known. The brothers must somehow admit their fault, atone for it, and, yes, even grovel. Joseph forgives from a position of strength. He cannot be harmed any longer.

Forgiveness works best when it comes from a position of strength. If we forgive a person who harmed us, who still has power to harm us, and probably will continue to harm us, all we have done is put ourselves in danger. Better to get out of harm's way, be on sure footing, and then forgive. It does not mean that those we forgive will grovel (probably not). But forgiveness can be a powerful act, when done from a position of strength. It was incredibly powerful for Joseph and his brothers.

—*Stephen Smith*

Pontius Pilate is alive and well

Some say Pontius Pilate deserves a better press. "I find no case against him," he said of Jesus (John 19:6). Pilate spoke the truth, so why should the creed say Jesus "suffered" under him?

Yes, Pilate spoke the truth. Jesus was guilty of no crime, and that's what Pilate said. Standing in the presence of the One by whom all truth is weighed, Pilate said there was nothing criminal about him. It is as if a bachelor said of a young woman that nothing about her would make her a bad wife. Such words shouldn't be confused with "Please marry me."

Pilate kept his options open and covered his posterior. He risked nothing. His remark was safe, cold, calculated, detached, non-committal. Pilate is often pictured as washing his hands while saying, "I am innocent of this man's blood." I prefer to picture him holding his finger into the air to test the wind. Pilate made suggestions, offered compromises, threw up trial balloons. But he challenged no one. He showed no courage; he was the ultimate "law and order" man. Justice, truth, and integrity gave way to keeping the peace at any cost.

Pilate's disciples are many. They speak the truth dispassionately, without conviction. Their Jesus is a popular Jesus because he demands nothing. He is an intellectualized, bland, sanitized, gutless Jesus whose function is to bless the spiritual inertia of people who won't make a commitment. Dispassionate endorsement of Jesus is the same as rejecting Jesus. Our options are only two: to surrender our hearts and wills to him or to refuse to surrender. There is no other ground. Accept him as Lord or don't—but it will not do to "find no crime in him."
—*Richard H. Schmidt*

Risking for God

Martin Luther once said, "Sin boldly, but rejoice in the love of God more boldly still." I think he was onto something, because Jesus wasn't one to play it safe. So many times he could have taken the easy way out, but never did. Even to the point of dying on the cross.

God expects the same of us, as is clear from the Parable of the Talents (Luke 19:12-27). The person who buried his talents in the ground—because he was so afraid of what might happen if he lost them—is rebuked, and his talents are given to someone else. But the person who risked his talents is rewarded, many times over.

Now, granted, the risk paid off in this case, but I bet he still would have been rewarded even if he'd lost the talents. God wants us to risk everything we have in his service. He wants us to reach out to others, to bare our soul, to boldly do what we believe we are called to do. He wants us to run the risk of making a mistake, always trusting in his infinite love for us.

As night falls, I usually take a moment to reflect on my day. I used to identify the mistakes I made, in order to ask forgiveness for them and make some amendment of life. Now, instead of asking myself what I did wrong that day, I ask what I risked today, in the service of God. —*Robert Macauley*

Spring, interrupted

After a long, cold Midwestern winter, we long for the coming of spring, for warmth and flowers and sunny days.

Spring is fickle, though, teasing us with a few unseasonably gorgeous days in late February, blowing hot and cold in March, seeming to settle down in April, and then tossing off a late snowstorm, just to keep us on our toes.

It's hard to know just when to send your winter clothes to the cleaners; life here does build character in that regard. But a springtime snowfall, unlike its wintry counterpart, carries the reassurance that however deep the white stuff, it won't stay long.

We sometimes expect the weather to conform to the printed calendar, to follow a set program. We sometimes expect our lives to do the same, for our careers, school, work, for love, family life, and health to sail along a prescribed bump-free arc. But there are usually, along with unexpectedly good times, some switcheroos and infelicitous curves thrown our way when we least expect them.

This is where it helps to have a working faith, like having a well-fitting all-weather coat within easy reach. Both shelter and protect us; both give us comfort when the winds blow sharply.

Those winds may still blow cold in April, but they won't last forever. —*Sarah Bryan Miller*

Knit together in love

Knit together. If you knit, as I do, you know how strong a knitted project is. You cannot break or tear it. Once knit together, it stays knit unless you cut it with scissors. But if you made an error a few rows back, you may have to carefully undo your knitting.

Saint Paul says that we who believe in Jesus are "knit together in love" (Colossians 2:2, King James Version). Other Bible translations say "united in love." That's a weaker expression, especially for a knitter who knows.

However, the New Revised Standard Version (NRSV) gets it right in Psalm 139:13, where it says: "You knit me together in my mother's womb." I love that image. I think of all the little bones, tendons, and skin cells growing together into the persons they will become and I'm thankful.

Right now I am knitting a baby gift for one of my nieces soon to become a mother. I call it "Gramma's Baby Bag." It's for a newborn, only usable for two or three months, but useful and practical. The yarn must be soft and machine washable. With a hat to match, it makes a nice gift. Babies like it because it's warm and soft and it feels like the safety of the womb. Parents and grandparents like it because it makes it easy to carry the baby, no legs and arms going in all directions, just a cuddly, comfy baby to hold.

I belong to a knitting group called the Knit Wits. We meet at our church twice a month and we are currently making prayer shawls for those who are homebound or ill. Many of you may belong to similar groups. Thanks be to God for knitting us together and for our knitting together. —*Lois Sibley*

Stay awake with me

Then [Jesus] said to them, "I am deeply grieved, even to death; remain here, and stay awake with me."

—MATTHEW 26:38

On the night before Jesus died, he went to the garden of Gethsemane. He took three of the disciples along and asked them to stay awake with him. Three times he went off to pray, and each time he returned to find the disciples sleeping.

Reading that passage, it's hard to imagine anyone falling asleep even once—let alone three times—on such a momentous night. Yet there is a lesson here for all of us, because in the face of great suffering, it's easy to close our eyes and "fall asleep." We want to escape pain. Like the disciples, we want to be spared suffering.

It takes courage to stay awake with someone who is going through difficult times. It takes dedication to enter into that suffering and accompany that person on a grueling journey. Yet that's exactly what Jesus asked of his disciples that night, and he asks of us now. "Bear one another's burdens," he commands us (Galatians 6:2). Stand by the people you care for, even when—*especially* when—they're going through a time of trial.

"Remain here," Jesus says, "and stay awake with me."
—*Robert Macauley*

The stone

Were you there when they rolled away the stone?
—African American Spiritual

The Gospel of Mark records that Jesus' body was placed in a tomb after his death on the cross. The tomb was hewn out of rock and sealed with a very large stone. Everything was final. Jesus' life was over. The grave was closed. There was the stone. It was so large that when Mary Magdalene, Mary, and Salome went to anoint Jesus' body on the Sunday after his death, they wondered who would roll away the stone for them. But when they arrived, the stone was already rolled back, and Jesus' body was gone. A young man dressed in a white robe told them Jesus had been raised from the dead (Mark 15:46—16:6).

Sometimes on Good Friday we sing the hymn, "Were you there when they crucified my Lord?" (*The Hymnal 1982*, #172), which asks, "Were you there when they nailed him to the tree? Were you there when they pierced him in the side? Were you there when they laid him in the tomb?" Some versions of that hymn include a final verse that sings for Easter: "Were you there when they rolled away the stone?" It's a song of victory.

The stone is not confined to Jesus and the tomb. The stone can be anything that threatens dead weight and finality in our own lives. The stone can be disappointment, loss, fear, unresolved grief, or deep sadness. The stone can drain all our energy and joy, and leave us with a feeling of futility. But the stone isn't the end of Jesus or of our hope. We rise with him, every day, and roll away the stone.

—*Rob Slocum*

Exsultet

One night each year—and one night only, at the Great Vigil of Easter—we hear the "Exsultet," a beautiful song of rejoicing (for that is what the word means) that dates back possibly to the fifth century:

"Rejoice now, heavenly hosts and choirs of angels…Rejoice and sing now, all the round earth…Rejoice and be glad now, Mother Church…" (*The Book of Common Prayer*, page 286).

Lifting my voice in the ancient chant, I reach the line that sends shivers down my spine: "How blessed is this night, when earth and heaven are joined and man is reconciled to God."

Reconciliation to the one who created us, to our Lover who refuses to turn his back on us, who reaches out to us, time and again, never abandoning us, always loving us. It happens *this* night, this one special night, when God reached down into the bowels of death and grabbed back his only begotten son, destroying death and giving us new life.

We sing the "Exsultet" in the darkness, remembering again that moment when God's promises were fulfilled, praying that God's promises never end.

"Earth and heaven are joined." In that one moment, the gloom that descended upon us on Good Friday, the fear and trembling and hopelessness and despair are lifted and we can sing again in great joy.

"How blessed is this night." I live for this night each year. I yearn for it, almost cry for it. Please, I think, please, let this holy night come again. Please, I beg, please, let us be reconciled one more time. Please, I cry, please, let the Risen Lord's light shine anew!

I need the holiness, desire the reconciliation, crave that light in my life. I need to sing: *Rejoice now!* —*Lauren Stanley*

Why do you look for the living among the dead?

It is the third day. Dawn is just breaking, and in the dim half-light the women have gone to the tomb with spices to tend to Jesus' corpse. They find the stone rolled away and the body gone. Two men in dazzling clothes materialize beside them, and ask this timeless question: Why do you look for the living among the dead?

We're looking for life in all the wrong places. The gurus of our age spread a vast array of lifeless idols before us—materialism and consumption, striving and competition, power and social position, exhibitionism and brutality masquerading as entertainment. We will not find life among these emblems of sin and death.

"Grant us," we pray in an Easter collect, "so to die daily to sin that we may evermore *live* with him in the joy of his resurrection." By the power of God, sin and the death of the cross give way to the abundant life Jesus promised. We find life in God's good gifts, in home and hearth, families and friendships, learning, work, the boundless riches of creation.

Most of all, above and beneath and beyond all, we find life in Jesus Christ, who meets us on the Galilean shores, on the Emmaus road, and right here in these twenty-first century times.

Christ is risen! Why would we look for the living among the dead?

—*Betsy Rogers*

Nothing comes without cost

Once I worked with a general contractor, a man named David, on the renovation of a library. David had suggested an idea that would save money and enhance the functionality of the new building. Because of a subcontractor's mistake, however, this same good idea ended up resulting in a smoldering fire that damaged most of the volumes in the library's rare book room.

Months and many insurance claims later, David and I met to work through billing on the project. After a while, beleaguered, he turned to me and said: "Melissa, what I've learned in this process is that no good deed goes unpunished."

I thought to myself, "Yes, there's something true here. A person has a bright idea and it backfires; someone tries to help someone else and people get hurt; Jesus comes with a message of peace and ends up getting nailed to the cross."

But later I thought: "The word 'punishment' can describe how it feels, but it's neither a description of what the cross of Christ is about nor is it a description of what happens when we extend ourselves and suffering comes to us as a result."

For me, it's more like this: no engagement and bold offering comes without the shedding of our own blood. No vocation worth having, no relationship worth being in, no cause worth dedicating ourselves to comes without an offering of our life's energy, poured out of us with some pain and heartbreak accompanying it. This offering, this pouring out of who we are for something or someone else, is the holy act we call "sacrifice."

Where are you being asked to pour yourself out?

What is the suffering you will likely discover and experience as you do this? —*Melissa Skelton*

Zumba!

One day at my health club I heard really loud music, clapping, and much shouting in a large exercise studio. It was the Zumba class, and maybe thirty people were dancing and exercising their way around the room in a wild circle of energy. It was a hip-swaying, elbow-pumping, loud-whooping, fast-stepping parade. They were alive. They were happy. They were jumping. They were fun. They were moving like people with something to celebrate.

King David certainly knew how to celebrate. When he brought the ark of God to Jerusalem, he "danced before the LORD with all his might." But Michal, a wife of David, looked out the window and saw him "leaping and dancing before the LORD," and despised him. She thought his behavior was vulgar. But David was undaunted by her criticism (2 Samuel 6:12-21).

Unfortunately, I have seen Christian worship that was more in the spirit of Michal than of David. When I was a child, my family attended an Episcopal parish that was rather reserved. I remember watching the adults returning to their pews from communion. Their expressions tended to be fixed, somber, even grim, as if they had completed a necessary but somewhat unpleasant task. I didn't know what they were being given at the altar, but I figured it must taste really bad!

We can lose sight of common prayer as a time to celebrate God's love. We have good news. Lord, open our lips. We lift our hearts to the Lord. Christ is risen, and he calls us together by the Spirit to share abundant life. Alleluia, sing to Jesus! Rejoice! In him we have forgiveness, hope, mission, and glory. We have much to celebrate. We can move it! —*Rob Slocum*

From failure, freedom

It was Easter Sunday and I was distributing communion. I was tired, totally burned out. "I have nothing left to offer these people," I thought.

It all started in January. The patriarch of our parish had finally succumbed to cancer. His funeral was one of five I did in the course of three days. Five in three days. How did the church and I pull that off?

Then, that very next Sunday, the oldest member of our church collapsed in the pew during the reading of the Gospel. Paramedics were called, and she turned out to be fine, thank God. But a few minutes later, as I climbed the pulpit steps, my sermon blew off the pulpit and onto the floor. A young man in the front pew went to retrieve it for me, but I said, "Leave it. It hardly seems relevant now." I gave an impromptu sermon about God being with us even when everything looks bleak. As I stepped down from the pulpit I vowed to myself, "This church is not going to die on my watch!"

I threw myself into my work. I was always at church. I visited every potential new member. I joined several service groups to increase our visibility. I developed what I thought was an incredible Lenten study program and even advertised in the local paper. At the same time I neglected my family, my exercise and prayer routine, and my diet.

By Holy Week I was exhausted. And on Easter I was handing out communion saying, "The Body of Christ, the Bread of Heaven," all the time thinking, "I have nothing left to offer them."

Suddenly the incongruity of my words and thoughts hit me. "This is *nothing*?" I asked myself, looking at the Bread. I then realized that what I had to offer was not all that dogged over-functioning, but simply proclaiming the presence of Christ in our lives. I began concentrating more and more on that while working reasonable hours, and the church grew. —*Stephen Smith*

Prisoner of love

Surely he has borne our infirmities and carried our diseases; yet we accounted him stricken, struck down by God, and afflicted. But he was wounded for our transgressions, crushed for our iniquities; upon him was the punishment that made us whole, and by his bruises we are healed.

—ISAIAH 53:4-5

One of our county judges is a member of my congregation. He has a reputation for fairness and is a generous, good, and godly man. Nonetheless, it is his difficult duty to preside over cases involving serious crimes. Dispensing justice, he has set many free. He has also sent many to prison for decades.

When our new county jail was finished, local charities "arrested" suspects, holding them overnight in the new cellblock. The next morning, after a community breakfast celebrating the donations generated as "bail" for their release, all were freed.

My parishioner, the judge, agreed to be "jailed." And so, for one night he assumed the place to which the crimes of the guilty consign them.

The Bible tells of another good man assuming the place of others, the worst place of all for the whole of guilty humanity: the cross.

Forsaking privilege, God in Christ incarnated holy love from Bethlehem to Calvary to assume our place, living to show us the Way, teaching to give us the Truth, and dying to usher us into the Life that is without end. By being a prisoner of love, the God we know in Jesus Christ made a prisoner of death, forever freeing us to live for him.

Such is the saving love of Jesus Christ, who is our Judge and our Redeemer.

May our selfless love for others match his sacrificial love for us. —*John Van Nuys*

The empty tomb

Bible stories didn't merely happen many centuries ago. They also reverberate down through the centuries and in our own lives. Thinking of the Easter story that way finally made it real for me.

Easter had long been a difficult holiday for me, partly because as a priest I was exhausted from all the extra sermons and worship services during Holy Week, and partly because the story of the empty tomb seemed to me to border on fantasy. And even if I could accept the empty tomb literally, what difference could the resuscitation of a corpse two thousand years ago make for me today?

My problem, I now see, was that I began with the empty tomb. The place to begin is with my own experience. Although I have not been crucified, I too have seen my dreams smashed, heard mocking words from people I trusted, and ached with loneliness and failure. My shriveled soul has lain in the spiritual tomb. My death was that of an ego-driven self that battled for control. I fought to preserve that life, and when it ended, I felt all was lost.

But what seemed like the end was really the beginning. God called me out of the tomb and into a new life of joy and contentment I could not have imagined before. This doesn't depend on my understanding or acceptance of a long-ago event. Rather, my own life validates the ancient story. The story of the empty tomb is also my story. It has become an archetype of God's victory over evil and death, a lens through which I now view everything. I don't have to worry about the interpretation of the empty tomb, because with my own eyes I have seen the empty tomb.
—*Richard H. Schmidt*

The opening door

Jesus breathed on the disciples and said to them,
"Receive the Holy Spirit."

—JOHN 20:22

The disciples gather in a house on the evening of the Sunday after Jesus' death, and they lock the doors for fear of the Jews (John 20:19). It is a reasonable precaution. They are identified as Jesus' closest followers, and he has been brutally executed by the religious and political authorities of the day. It is easy to foresee that they might face the same brutal treatment, and they are afraid. The disciples are marked men in a very dangerous situation. They are hiding out. They are laying low.

I can imagine the disciples inside the house as they listen anxiously for outside sounds of an angry mob or approaching soldiers. But then the risen Jesus appears and stands among them. He wishes them peace. He shows them his hands and side, and again wishes them peace. Then he sends them into the world, as the Father sent him. Jesus breathes on his disciples, giving them the Holy Spirit and empowering them to forgive sins (John 20:19-23).

Never again do we see the disciples hiding in a room for fear of anybody. They receive the Holy Spirit from the risen Jesus and know the fire of love. They're sent with a mission. The world around them is absolutely as dangerous as before, but they are changed. Inspired by the Holy Spirit, they find the heart and courage to unlock the door and bring the gospel to the world. The Holy Spirit is visible in their changed lives as they walk through an opening door into a world of new possibilities. —*Rob Slocum*

Rendering unto Caesar

*Give to the emperor the things that are the emperor's,
and to God the things that are God's.*

—MARK 12:17

This seems an appropriate reading for income tax day in the United States: the story of Jesus telling the Pharisees to "Render unto Caesar what is Caesar's, and to the Lord what is the Lord's." Yet to appreciate the wisdom of Jesus' comments, you have to go back and look at the question he was asked, and how he answered it.

The Pharisees started off by buttering Jesus up—"Teacher, we know that you are sincere," they said—and then they tried to trap him. "Should we pay taxes?" they asked, knowing that no matter how Jesus answered the question, he'd be in trouble with somebody.

So Jesus simply didn't answer the question. He knew what was in their hearts, and he answered the question they *should* have been asking, not the one they did ask. Rather than a simple "yes" or "no," he thrust the responsibility back on them. "Give to God the things that are God's," Jesus said. So if everything belongs to God, then we have to give everything to God. Not just our money, or our words, or our time. Everything. Our very hearts and souls.

The next verse says that the people were "utterly amazed at him," as well they should have been. Not only did he see through their ploy, but saw right into their hearts. —*Robert Macauley*

God's embrace

My spiritual director, a wise and wonderful Roman Catholic nun, encouraged me some months ago to find a visual image to help me pray. "A waterfall, perhaps, or a candle," she said, "or anything that helps you enter into God's presence."

Immediately, without any conscious thought on my part, I was given an image that is more visceral than visual: a powerful sense of embrace, of being held in God's arms, "love to the loveless shown that they might lovely be" (*The Hymnal 1982*, #458).

How this image, when I use it, transforms my prayers! Like most of us, I expect, I have people in my life whom I find frustrating or difficult. (I imagine they find me frustrating and difficult, too.) Sometimes they make me really angry, and I find myself thinking about them too much, having furious conversations with them in my head.

But when I feel myself in God's arms, enveloped by God's love, the next thing I know these other people are there with me! At first I cringed a bit at such close proximity, but if I too reach out my arms I find myself filled with peace and an overwhelming sense of love's healing power.

The processional cross in our parish bears an image of the *Christus Rex*, Christ the King, arms flung wide to welcome the whole world into God's embrace. Behind the figure of Christ stands the cross itself, a symbol of suffering but of embrace as well, its arms also extended to gather the world into the arms of God. And there, in that embrace, we're held against the beating, sacred heart of Jesus. There God's all-encompassing love, which reaches through the cosmos, enfolds each one of us as a precious child. —*Betsy Rogers*

Come, Holy Spirit, come

Years ago our telephone rang as we ate supper with guests. Excusing myself, I took the call. A young boy's voice asked for "Dr. Duvall." I told him he had the wrong number.

He called again, asking for the same person, then again. Finally I said, "Is something wrong? Why do you need Dr. Duvall?" He replied, "My Mommy is sick. She is lying on the bathroom floor, and I can't get her to wake up."

I asked if his father or other grown-ups were there, and he said no. His father and mother had gone to a party, and his father was taking the babysitter home and then going somewhere else. I asked if he knew his address and he did. He stayed on the phone while we found parishioners who lived on that street. I got the boy's number and told him I would call him right back. Then I called and asked the parishioners to go to the boy's house. Today I would call 911 on a cell phone, but neither was available then.

The parishioners were able to rouse the mother and stay until the father returned. She had taken a drink at the party, and then an allergy pill at home, a dangerous combination. She had passed out.

A few days later the chagrined mother called to apologize for her son's calls. I complimented her on the young boy's pluck in trying to get help. She was lucky the medicine was not stronger.

Looking back, I see the Holy Spirit at work. Why did the boy call Dr. Duvall rather than their physician? Why did I ask what was wrong? How did we find someone to help right down the street? The Holy Spirit does good work. —*Nancy R. Duvall*

Airborne

Flying to Los Angeles from St. Louis, in the unwonted luxury of a window seat in first class (real food! comfy seats! leg room!), favorite music in my ears, the geographic variety of the continent is laid out before me.

First came recognizable territory. We sped southwest over Missouri; then, abruptly, we were over Oklahoma, with the oddly geometric shapes—perfectly round green circles, perfectly square yellow blocks— left by modern irrigation techniques giving a jarringly surreal note to the landscape.

That gave way to New Mexico's sere brown beauty, beige deserts rising to meet rough mountains still topped with snow in mid-April. The country's crumpled backbone defies the occasional slanchways line of a railway or the abrupt curves of a switchback road; the mountains are continually arresting to the eye with their patterns of light and shadow in the angled rays of early evening.

Are we over Arizona now? The states here are arbitrary oblongs with borders drawn by rulers rather than natural features, and it's hard to tell. The view ahead offers a distinctly Southwestern palette: a deep blue sky gives way to a strip of bright yellow that fades into oranges and reds, giving way to near-purples and then to the beiges and browns of the arid mountains below. The Grand Canyon opens up in layers of mauve and lavender.

The folds of the mountains are fading, made visible by streaks of snow that soon disappear in the dimming light. Their painterly beauty changes with the sun's angles, growing subtler by the minute. The distance diminishes into night, and the lights of the great city fill the horizon. God's world keeps turning toward the next bright day. —*Sarah Bryan Miller*

The cross

...here is God, whose arms of love
aching, spent, the world sustain.

—THE HYMNAL 1982, #585

Christians encounter lots of cross images—in stained glass and on altars, on vestments and jewelry and steeples. These can be wonderful reminders for faith, but we can forget their meaning. The cross can easily become a decorative ornament or a trinket.

Jesus died a horrible death on the cross. But his resurrection brought the best out from the worst. The cross was the instrument of Jesus' self-offering, the ultimate expression of God's love for us. The way of the cross is the way of both ultimate sacrifice and our victory. It demands everything and makes everything available to us. It's how we drink the cup that Jesus drank and share his baptism (Matthew 20:22-23).

The cross is the place of intersection. Death and life come together at the cross, and life prevails. Sin and obedience come together at the cross, and obedience prevails. Hate and love come together at the cross, and love prevails. God's saving desire, intention, and action come together in Jesus' sacrifice for us on the cross. William Porcher DuBose states in *The Ecumenical Councils* that the cross is the way God lost and found himself in humanity, and the way we lose and find ourselves in God.

At its most basic level, the cross is just the intersection of two pieces of wood, one vertical and one horizontal. Living the way of the cross embraces the vertical and horizontal in our lives. Loving God "above" draws us into deeper relationship with others "below," as loving others draws us to serve and know God more fully through them. —*Rob Slocum*

Anselm

Tomorrow is the feast day of Anselm, archbishop of Canterbury at the end of the eleventh century. I remember well the day I discovered Anselm, while sitting under a tree on a crisp, fall afternoon, studying for a class.

"God is that than which nothing greater can be conceived."

I read those words of Anselm and felt a thrill go through my body. Suddenly, I was all aquiver, like a puppy dog filled with joy at finding someone who loves it, its whole body wiggling from the tip of its nose to the tip of its tail.

"God is that than which nothing greater can be conceived!"

At last, I had found a definition of God that made sense. At last, I had words to put to my tenuous thoughts.

"God is great." "God is love." "God…" All my life I had struggled to put into apprehensible words what I knew in my soul. Now, sitting under a towering oak, breathing in the earth and the leaves and the turn of the season, I was breathing in God as well.

It was a moment of stark clarity for me, as though God on high had descended not *next* to me but *into* me, opening me up to the limitless being that God is, filling me with all understanding, as Jesus filled the minds and hearts of the disciples on the road to Emmaus the day he was raised from the dead.

This was more than a *Eureka!* moment. This was *God.*

Every year, as Anselm's day approaches, excitement builds within me. I feel as though I am going to find, just around the corner, that mystical moment again. I yearn to experience it anew.

Oh, hurry up, tomorrow! You can't get here soon enough!
—*Lauren Stanley*

Called to prayer and action

"There's gonna be a meeting, come on, old fashioned meeting. Meeting on the old Campground," the gospel group sang to open a community meeting at the hospital about an upcoming health and hospital levy.

God is not confined to churches, those lyrics instruct us. During the opening prayer, the pastor told us that this levy—for safety net funds to treat people who are indigent and others who are either uninsured or underinsured—is right and righteous. Someday, he said, there will be a meeting at the Campground at the end of our lives. What will we say we have done for others?

What role are you going to play in making our community a better place?" the pastor asked. "Made up my mind to serve God til I die," affirmed the gospel group in their second song.

We need time to meditate, time for being quiet, listening, accepting God's love, and loving others. There is an ambience of private prayer, individual reflection, and emotion. God is encountered as a spiritual director.

But let's not forget the communal aspect of Jesus' message: "cease to do evil, learn to do good; seek justice, rescue the oppressed, defend the orphan, plead for the widow" (Isaiah 1:16-17). Jesus would have also known Jeremiah 1:16: "I will utter my judgments against them, for all their wickedness in forsaking me; they have made offerings to other gods, and worshiped the works of their own hands." And in Revelation 22:12, John reports Jesus saying "my reward is with me, to repay according to everyone's work."

God calls us to both contemplation and to action, as individuals and as members of a community. What role are we going to play in making our community a better place?
—*Noël Julnes-Dehner*

Living in the bright immensities

And have the bright immensities received our risen Lord,
where light-years frame the Pleiades and point Orion's sword?
Do flaming suns his footsteps trace through corridors sublime,
the Lord of interstellar space and Conqueror of time?

The heaven that hides him from our sight knows neither near nor far;
an altar candle sheds its light as surely as a star:
and where his loving people meet to share the gift divine,
there stands he with unhurrying feet; there heavenly splendors shine.

—THE HYMNAL 1982, #459

Faith is filled with paradox. Jesus is fully human yet fully divine. We are called to walk in righteousness yet live out compassion, to be wise as serpents yet innocent as doves. This wonderful hymn expresses one of the most baffling of paradoxes: our transcendent yet immanent God.

Here is Jesus, striding through the vast immensities of the cosmos, illuminated by all its flaming suns, sovereign Lord of time and space.

Yet he is *here*, too. He is here most especially in the eucharist, where his loving people meet to share the gift divine. He is here also as I write at my computer, visit with friends, work with clients, shop for groceries. The sovereign Lord of time and space stands beside me in the wonderful moments when I marvel over dwarf lake iris blanketing the forest floor or rejoice in my family. He is here in the hard moments, when I'm overcome with remorse at some careless thing I've done or ache with grief over illness or loss. Everywhere! Every moment!

As I fumble along, struggling to become the person God created me to be, here stands Jesus with unhurrying feet, and the heavenly splendors shine around us. —*Betsy Rogers*

Hope for the day

I wake up sometimes with a feeling of heaviness: too much to do, grief or concern for a loved one weighing me down, or simply feeling the weight of the world. Slowly, in my rambling writing (and with a little help from my first cup of coffee), hope and possibility seem to emerge. I finish most of my daily journal entries with a simple intention for the day ahead: "Let it be good."

In an interview on the National Public Radio (NPR) show *Speaking of Faith*, author Barbara Kingsolver discussed her book *Animal, Vegetable, Miracle*, which addresses concerns over our food supply, climate change, and the degradation of the earth. Asked how she keeps up hope in the midst of it all, she replied, "I need to consider hope to be a renewable option. If I run out at the end of the day, well then, when I get up in the morning I put it on with my shoes."

I, too, like to think of hope as a renewable option. We all live through cycles of hope and hopelessness, times when things seem heavy and dark, followed by lightness and light breaking in. Our liturgical year does this too. Every year, Good Friday is followed by Easter. Hope dies and then it is restored.

Our world can be so full of conflicting images: excessive materialism and greed coupled with great generosity, feelings of despair amidst glad tidings, messages of "peace on earth" while our country is at war. In Christ we celebrate light coming into a sometimes dark world. Each of us has our own grief, our areas of darkness and hopelessness in our lives and in our days. But let us trust that light is coming, that hope *is* a renewable option. —*Nancy Hopkins-Greene*

The good shepherd

The Lord is my shepherd.
—PSALM 23

On our farm, we raised sheep. What would a lamb's perspective have been, growing up under my father's care?

We cut off baby lambs' tails because wooly tails retain waste, which attracts flies, which results in damaging larvae. But lambs knew only the pain, attributable to my father and me. Later, we weaned adolescent lambs from their mothers—from the one constant to which they were attached for protection and sustenance. Lambs must transition from milk to grass, but I still remember their plaintive cries for mother.

Grazing feeds growth—and causes intestinal parasites. So we regularly wormed the sheep by dispensing a bolus down unwilling throats. Then as winter approached, we segregated the mature females from the rams—fragile lambs untimely born in the dead of winter die easily, whereas those born in warmer, spring weather usually survive. Again, something our sheep did not understand when their strongest wish was refused. Except for spring shearing to remove their thick winter wool, our sheep probably perceived our care only as pain.

When we experience pain and feel abandoned by God, maybe some of what is going on is blessing that we cannot yet recognize. Spiritual director Margaret Guenther counsels, "When in doubt, I always assume God is at work." When you are struggling or doubting or at the end of your rope wondering "Lord, I'm doing all I can here. Where on earth are you?" it is a good bet to trust that God *is* indeed at work—in veiled ways you may not yet perceive or understand, but certainly in gracious ways you can trust are loving.
—*John Van Nuys*

The wisdom of whatever

You can't conceive, my child, nor I nor anyone,
the appalling strangeness of the mercy of God.

—GRAHAM GREENE

My prayers have taken a certain turn in recent months. Increasingly my supplications tend toward "Whatever, God." Not spoken in a flip, slangy tone, but with the growing recognition that I am in no position to dictate terms to the God of the Universe.

The "Whatever, God" prayer has entered my repertoire as a substitute for the extremely specific demands I've been known to make of God. The big picture about what we need, what is best, is not, I've decided, for me to know in great detail.

But I'm beginning to perceive this spiritual myopia as a gift. By not being allowed to see too clearly, we're required to trust. Were we to have the whole, big show of our lives laid out before us, how smug we humans would become.

Perhaps God gives us clear vision—God-eyes—in small moments, in little doses because it's all we can handle. With near-sightedness we're required to get close, nose-to-nose like lovers. We work to eliminate hunger by serving hungry people on Tuesdays. We model loving-kindness by treating gently those who drive us crazy. Our blurry, temporal vision keeps us both engaged and in need of frequent spiritual sustenance.

As I open my eyes on late winter mornings, the big Norwich maple in our backyard is outlined by the rising sun. Without my glasses, the bare branches are indistinct, but I have faith that the leaf buds are present and will burst forth on a fine spring day of their choosing. —*Heidi Shott*

Playing the game

Some people maintain that life is a game. It does seem to me that cancer treatment is much like a board game: you throw the dice, you land on a square, and you deal with whatever you've been handed that turn.

Unlike, say, Monopoly, where you might have to go directly to jail or pay an exorbitant rent when you land on the wrong square, the rules of Chemo may hand out mouth sores or constant nosebleeds, an aversion to salty foods or to coffee, flu-like symptoms, or just chronic fatigue. Whether or not to play is not really an option.

My most recent round dealt me a case of anemia that kept me in bed for days. The queasies are always just beneath the surface, like the bass line in the soundtrack of a horror film; sometimes it's more obvious than at other times, but it's never far away. This game is definitely not for wimps.

Chemo is more than a game, of course, and it's getting results. The progress in shrinking the tumor is, in my oncologist's word, "astounding." I have exceeded expectations.

I don't face either the good news or the difficult aspects by myself. I have the help of loving friends and of a host of medical personnel, of neighbors and colleagues, and I have the love of God to sustain me. It's all a blessing, the prayers of others wrapping around me as comfortingly as my mother's arms when I was little.

That support gives me the strength and courage to continue the game, tossing those dice, and accepting whatever square I've landed on. It's tough, but I'm not playing alone—and it's a game that, with God's help, I will win. —*Sarah Bryan Miller*

A harvest of hope

Harvest Hope is a large operation serving eighteen counties in my state. It collects food in large amounts and distributes it to many places where hunger is rampant. Other communities have similar operations that serve those who have lost jobs and lost hope. As a family we pledge to Harvest Hope's work, and my husband serves on the board. I donate food and other needed things, religiously.

For many reasons we do this, as you probably do, too. I knew people were hungry in our city, state, and world, but several years ago I heard a simple story that peeled the blind spots from my eyes and made need personal to me.

A young family had come to the food pantry, filled out the necessary paper work, and received a week's worth of food. The father kept his eyes lowered, ashamed to have to ask for help, ashamed because he could not provide for his family.

When they left the building, he helped his little brood into their car and then came back to ask for one more thing. Without his children there to hear him, he asked, "Do you have any soap? We don't have any, and I have a job interview this week and I would like to be clean."

Yes, we had soap, which we gave him. Yes, we now include soap, toothpaste, toilet paper, and other personal items when we give. If you can't buy food, you can't buy these things either.

How can I live my comfortable life if others have nothing? Even with all the comforts in the world my heart would be heavy, my conscience tattered. I cannot fix the whole world, but I can bring soap so that fathers do not have to be ashamed in front of their children.
—*Nancy R. Duvall*

Not this morning, NPR

Not this morning, NPR.
Not the news of violence in Darfur or the cyclone in Burma,
Not the news of the primaries or the latest presidential gaffe,
Not even the news of the rescue of coal miners or the birthday of a poet.
No, instead—the poetry of dogs barking, their first woof of the day,
The rescue of spring light coming in through an open back door,
The news that a cup of tea and an old bathrobe bring.
Not this morning, NPR.
No, instead—this morning.

I wrote this one spring morning when I decided not to do what I normally do. Instead of beginning my day with the buzzing of National Public Radio (NPR) in the background, I turned the radio off and tuned into the sounds and sights that were immediately around me.

It was an experience that redeemed my day from the very beginning, buying it back from the business that usually preoccupies me and giving me the blessing of the here and now.

Sometimes we need to let go of the news of the day as we ordinarily understand it so we can tune into a news that doesn't just inform us but grounds us to ourselves, to God, and to the world right around us in the moment. This news takes us from hearing about something to the experience of living here and now.

Spring invites our attention to the news of the here and now because spring brings new sounds, new light, and new bodies sprung from our many winter layers. Spring is the time of God's renewal of the earth, a witness to the new life right before us.

What is the news right around you? What are you experiencing right now? —*Melissa Skelton*

Looking up

The other day, I got caught in a traffic slowdown on the interstate. Normally this irritates me, but for once, instead of fuming, I decided to open my sunroof and look up at the sky.

The first thing I saw were planes taking off and landing at the airport up ahead. I admired the angle they presented as they sped toward the clouds. I imagined myself on one of them, going somewhere exotic and restful (desert island?) or interesting and beautiful (Gothic cathedral?).

The next thing I saw was a red-tailed hawk circling overhead. The sun caught its fanned-out flight feathers and they glowed orange as it changed direction, hunting.

And then I just looked at the fluffy clouds. I remembered how when I was little, we kids thought that angels sat on those clouds and that God used a cloud like a gentle magic carpet to move around in heaven. And then when we were bigger and knew that clouds were vapor, we were disappointed; angels or God would surely fall through misty vapor. (And thus we learned to hold differing theological ideas in tension.)

Sitting there, I realized that I don't look up enough. I usually have my eyes on the road, on the sidewalk, on down-to-earth things. And I often feel weighted down. Could the two be related? Maybe. Anyway, it felt good to watch things (created, generated, innovated things) moving in all kinds of ways across the blue expanse and to allow myself to be in awe of the universe, and its Creator, again.

I need to lift up my eyes more often. —*Penny Nash*

Giving light

No one after lighting a lamp puts it under the bushel basket,
but on the lampstand, and it gives light to all in the house.
—MATTHEW 5:15

My friend Becca Stevens is changing the world. Aware of prostitution in her city, Becca tirelessly labored to create Magdalene House, a free, two-year residency program where women can recover from violence and addiction, receive vocational training, and leave the street for good. To fund Magdalene House, the women produce and market eco-friendly bath and body products under the name Thistle Farms. Becca rightly says that "love is the most powerful force for change in the world." For her labor of love, Becca has received numerous awards. Her faith truly shines.

Another friend of mine labors in the same city with a light that shines just as brightly, but obscurely. Hers is a hospice ministry. Her presence is to remind those who are dying that God is with them, that God's everlasting arms cradle us all from this life to the next in love.

In our baptism, we are commissioned to labor with Christ in sharing our God-given gifts. None of us has to do it all, but each of us can do something. Each of us has something unique to contribute to further Christ's peaceable kingdom.

Whether you are recognized or obscure, celebrated or anonymous, your life can and does make a difference. As the late Presbyterian theologian William C. Placher wrote: "The way we best show our love to the whole world is to love with a particular passion some little part of it."

As you provide wax and wick, the Holy Spirit will provide fire—and give light. —*John Van Nuys*

Magnolias

My daughter, Claire, attended Converse College in Spartanburg, South Carolina. The perimeter of her campus was lined with magnolia trees. I remember visiting her toward the end of her senior year, and she said the magnolias drop their leaves when they bloom. There's nothing wrong with the magnolia leaves, but there comes a time for the tree to let them fall to the ground.

New life and creation can be costly and require sacrifice. Shortly before his death, Jesus explains to his disciples that "unless a grain of wheat falls into the earth and dies, it remains just a single grain; but if it dies, it bears much fruit" (John 12:24). The life of the plant follows the death of the seed, as our new life in Christ follows his sacrifice.

Sometimes we need to let go of something in order to engage our own life and creativity. And the thing we let go may not be bad in itself. It may even be a good thing, in a way, but perhaps not the best thing for us at the time. To say yes to one possibility may require saying no to any number of other things. Saying yes to an invitation to faith may mean saying no to some older patterns of behavior. Paying attention to the movement of grace may require saying no to any number of attractive distractions that are in the way.

Blooming can be a very costly process, when we drop our leaves.
—*Rob Slocum*

Empty and obedient

Let the same mind be in you that was in Christ Jesus, who, though he was in the form of God, did not regard equality with God as something to be exploited, but emptied himself, taking the form of a slave, being born in human likeness. And being found in human form, he humbled himself and became obedient to the point of death, even death on a cross.

—PHILIPPIANS 2:5–8

Philippians is a brief book, only four chapters, but it can be life-changing for those who take Paul's words seriously.

I remember our friend Bob, who often recited these words with both humility and passion. He wanted to be like Christ, and he lived out his days trying to be the person Christ wanted him to be. Bob taught the adult Sunday school class, and we all appreciated his guidance as we tried to apply the words of scripture to ourselves, where we lived, and what we did in that community.

How do we empty ourselves, humble ourselves, become obedient even to the point of death? Jesus did that for us, and for all who believe. It's pretty amazing.

We had some good discussions with Bob and with one another. I don't know whether others from that class remember, but I do. And I thank God for small group Bible studies. They are a gift to those who attend and appreciate the pleasures of learning together. They help our churches grow. —*Lois Sibley*

Bread of heaven, cup of salvation

In my Father's house...I go to prepare a place for you.
—JOHN 14:2

We entered his nursing home room to find him sprawled sideways across the bed, legs hanging down, head against the wall, mouth caked with dry saliva, and an adult diaper his only apparel.

As we approached, my husband, who was his cousin and dear friend, murmured a hello and moved to cover him, telling him a lady was present. He could not have cared less. All he wanted was one thing—to stop his treatments for kidney failure. He had had enough—years of spending the days with tubes running from his body, with no hope of being well again.

Though all of us knew that stopping dialysis would result in his death within weeks, we told him we would back him in this decision. Then he asked for one more thing—Holy Communion. He did not want to die without being blessed with the sacred Body and Blood of Christ. We had brought no kit containing wine and bread, but decided that although my husband, a priest, could not turn water into wine, Christ could. A soda cracker, the only bread available, would serve as the bread of heaven.

The three of us had this simple and profound communion together. We were filled with love and compassion; he was filled with relief and peace. We sat and talked quietly with him, telling him how much he had meant to us, so much that one of our sons is his godchild. He said little, but seemed comforted and relieved that we had come.

As he tired, we slipped out. He died two weeks later, at peace with his Lord and going to his real home at last. His Lord had prepared a place for him. —*Nancy R. Duvall*

Surely it is God who saves me

I have been experiencing hard times of late. I lost my job, I am uncertain of my future, and I am not convinced that I am cut out to be the person I thought God was calling me to be.

Most days, I can handle these hard times. They are but passing phases. Simply because I don't understand what is happening, or why, does not mean I am a bad person, or that I am unwanted—or worse, uncalled.

But there are days when the darkness threatens to overwhelm me, when I want to withdraw so that I cannot be hurt further. It is on those days that I hear, in my head and in my heart, Isaiah's song: "Surely it is God who saves me; I will trust in him and not be afraid. For the Lord is my stronghold and my sure defense, and he will be my Savior" (Canticle 9 in *The Book of Common Prayer*, Isaiah 12:2-3).

These are not mere words written by a prophet of old. This is a prayer song, one I sang in seminary that has lifted me ever since. When I sing these words—I never simply say them—the darkness lifts and I find joy in my life.

Yes, I am unemployed, but that gives me time to respond to the needs of others, family and friends who need someone to be with them or to simply listen as they battle their own darkness. Yes, I am struggling with how to live out my call...but then a call comes and I am summoned to preach, to teach, to pray, to celebrate, to baptize, to bury.

Surely God does save me. When I trust in God, I need not fear, for God defends me and lifts the darkness and I bathe in the light again.

—*Lauren Stanley*

Encountering God

I think most people care more about what's in our heart when we say or do something, than what we actually say or do. I know that from my preaching. When I've spun together some really nifty words that I think are quite profound, my listeners are left unmoved. But when I speak right from the heart, no matter how repetitive or clumsy I am in my expression, people value what I have to say.

The same goes for God, I think. There are lots of flowery words we can use in speaking to God, and those of us who've been around church long enough know what we're *supposed* to say. What matters more, though, is what's inside of us, what's leading us to say something to God in the first place.

That's clear from the encounters Jesus had with people. The people Jesus welcomed did all sorts of crazy things to reach him: lowering friends through open roofs, climbing trees, reaching out to touch the hem of his garment. They were a ragged bunch, united not by their eloquence but by their desperate need to be near Jesus. He didn't have much use for flowery words; instead, he valued honesty and candor.

So I don't think we should feel embarrassed to come before God when we don't know how to say what's in our hearts. God already knows what's in our hearts; he just wants us to come to him.
—*Robert Macauley*

Early morning on the porch

I often rise before dawn and sit quietly on my porch as the blackness slowly turns to gray. I listen to the night sounds—birds singing (birds are about their business long before the first hint of dawn), the wind in the leaves, and the haunting jingle of the wind chimes.

Some time later, I watch as the sunlight breaks through the branches of the trees and reaches the spot where I sit. This time of year, the green of the leaves is sheer and feathery, so that the sunlight almost shines through them. By summer, the leaves will have matured and the darker, heavier green will block out the sunlight. On this particular spring day, I watch as the dew on a spider web in the nearby azalea bush catches the early morning rays. It shimmers and shakes in the wind, the sunlight on it seemingly dancing and alive. I enjoy the beauty of the night and the beauty of another morning.

It is easy to believe in a good God, easy to pray, easy to feel at peace when you're sitting on a quiet porch watching the dawn. Such moments are a gift from God, and those privileged to enjoy them should thank God for them. The real test, though, comes later in the day, when the dawn is long past and we're dealing with the problems, fears, and questions of people, including our own; when we look at our long lists of tasks and realize we will not accomplish most of them; when we're called on the carpet; when we're staring at questions that lack obvious answers and decisions that could go either way.

Thank you, Lord, for the sunrise on the porch. Stay with me, please, through the rest of the day as well. —*Richard H. Schmidt*

Touched by grace

When I was thirteen, we found a stray dog: a female mixed collie breed with soulful brown eyes. Our family already owned a dog, so we could not keep this one.

We took out an ad in the paper to see if we could find her owner. No response. After a time we ran a second ad which read, "Found: Gentle Female Collie Mixed Breed. Free to a good home."

Within a few days a man and his young son came to see us. As they got out of the car, the boy was already letting his dad know that he was not interested in the dog we had found because he wanted a puppy.

Over the continuing protests of the boy, the father began suggesting that the boy do things with the dog: give her some water, offer her a treat, throw the ball and have her fetch it. This went on for at least half an hour as the boy continued to talk about how much he wanted a puppy.

Time passed, and we began to wonder.

And then the father said to his son: "What would you name this dog if she were yours?" The little boy stopped, got quiet, and a serious look came over his face.

"What would you name this dog if she were yours?" the father repeated.

"Sweetheart," the little boy said.

That's when we knew. That's when we knew that while we rarely get exactly what we think we want, there are moments of grace when something or someone comes along, touches our heart, and asks us: "Will you give your life to me?"

What or who is asking you to give your heart?

In saying "yes," what expectation will you need to let go of? —*Melissa Skelton*

The pathology report

The phone rang just after noon on Sunday. It was my surgeon, a man as kind as he is skillful: "Your pathology report found its way to my office over the weekend," he said, "and I didn't want to make you wait any longer for the results."

I suspect he also wanted the pleasure of personally delivering the unalloyed good news that the cancer was dead and gone, so thoroughly departed that only microscopic traces of the tumor remained in tissues that once harbored five deadly centimeters of pure ugly, aggressive malignancy. The tissue margins were clear. The lymph nodes were clear. The chemotherapy had worked, and all the struggles of the last six months were worthwhile.

My oncologist has used words like "astounding" and "amazing" to describe the tumor's response to treatment right from the start. The chemotherapy worked, but I believe there's more to it than that.

The other thing working on the tumor from the beginning was prayer: the prayers of family, friends, and colleagues; the prayers of my own parish and my father's; prayers offered by members of other churches, synagogues, and religious communities; the prayers of online friends and people I don't know.

My mother used to say that she could feel it when people prayed for her. I feel it, too—a kind of lightening and buoying up, a reassurance of the love, faith, and concern of others.

Attempts by researchers to study the effects of prayer on the sick have, unsurprisingly, yielded mixed results, and I do not pretend to know why some prayers are answered and others don't seem to be. For now, I am simply grateful for the knowledge and skill of my doctors and nurses, and for the mercy of God in this miraculous gift of healing. —*Sarah Bryan Miller*

A tiny healing hand

In our parish, parishioners often ask for prayers for healing at our regular Wednesday morning eucharist. After communion, still gathered around the altar, we'll pray for those who ask, laying hands on that person if we're standing close or on another person if we can't reach. From one person to the next in our little cluster of worshipers, we connect to the one seeking prayers.

A few years ago a young mother and her toddler often attended this service. Little Emma was an alert and eager participant. She'd brighten at the sound of the bells, join in the "amens," and clap as the smoke from the extinguished candles rose toward the ceiling.

One day we gathered around a woman who had asked for prayers. My hand rested on the shoulder of another whose hand lay on the petitioner. Soon I felt another hand, a tiny one, on my own shoulder. Looking around I found Emma, not yet two, perched on her mother's hip, eyes closed, joining in the laying on of hands.

Skeptics might scoff, suggesting that she was just imitating what she saw others doing...but I think not. I think at some mysterious level Emma grasped that this touch is something we need, that we do for each other, as believers.

Who am I to say that Emma was not praying? Or that her prayers were not efficacious? In truth, I suspect that God's ear is especially attuned to the prayers of children, however primal they might be. Jesus himself tells us that unless we become like children, we will never enter the kingdom of heaven. Children in their very innocence have a natural connection to God. I felt that connection in Emma's tiny hand.
—*Betsy Rogers*

The grace of beauty

When all the news seems to be bad, when flagrant injustice dominates the headlines, when people are dying, when everybody seems to have lost any sense of what loving one's neighbor and doing justice and loving mercy and walking humbly with our God demands of us, when the world just seems irretrievably broken, and I am moved to tears of despair—I go looking for the beautiful.

Bees and flowers; baby snorts and giggles; water music.

Not as an escape, not as denial, but as a reminder that God is good. That when God created the world, God said, "It is very, very good."

God's ways are not our ways. The ways of the world are the way they are because we are human, and, just like Jesus said, we need to repent. We need to be converted, over and over again.

And so I look for beauty to convert me. To remind me that this life is a beautiful life, that God's gracious gifts are all around us, that God loves us all. I look for beauty to save me from sinking in the mire that I'm into up to my neck, to save me from the ugliness that threatens to wash over me altogether. To help me remember that sometimes I am the one who lets myself sink in the mire when I discriminate, dismiss, deride, and otherwise "act ugly," as my mother used to say. To be convinced that the God who made cocoa beans and waterfalls and bees with yellow pollen pouches on their knees loves the people I think are hateful blockheads just as much as God loves me. —*Penny Nash*

Mirror Lake

I recently spent a couple of days at Yosemite National Park and joined other hikers, climbers, and pilgrims in reaching the top of Half Dome. It was an exhilarating experience, standing on top of that rock overlooking so much beauty and with a deep sense of satisfaction for having reached the summit.

The next day, we took a couple of shorter hikes. One was to Mirror Lake. I had seen pictures of this lake and photographs of the mountains mirrored in its waters. My recollection was that there was a great view of Half Dome reflected there. Still swelling with pride over my climb the day before, I arrived at the lake only to find the water level down and the waters murky. I looked in the direction of Half Dome and there was nothing. Mirror Lake seemed to be nothing but a muddy pond. We took pictures and walked on.

When I got home and downloaded my photos, I was surprised to see that one of my pictures of that lake had a beautiful scene of another mountain mirrored in it. I had been so disappointed not to have the perfect view of "my" mountain that I had missed the fact that the view was to be had in the opposite direction.

So it is often in our spiritual life. We can so easily have our set notions of where God is to be found that we miss God's presence in other places—often in the opposite direction. I remind myself today to keep my eyes open for the holy in all parts of my life. Who knows in what places—or people—I will find a reflection of God?
—*Nancy Hopkins-Greene*

Sharing the light

We recently sang "This little Light of Mine" in our worship service, with the younger children leading. The familiar verses were sung, and then I opened it up to suggestions from the little children, who always surprise me. A young energetic boy blurted out, "Shine all over the galaxy!" So we sang, "Shine all over the galaxy, I'm going to let it shine," to the joy of both the congregation and the Holy Spirit.

God works through people in unexpected ways. On several occasions I have seen the complete transformation of entire families through the evangelism of just one person. Often it is a youngster. God then continues to expand his love, and these families invite other families and friends to church. Neighborhoods, towns, and cities are changed from the initial action of the Holy Spirit working through one willing person!

Jesus said, "Go therefore and make disciples of all nations, baptizing them in the name of the Father and of the Son and of the Holy Spirit, and teaching them to obey everything that I have commanded you" (Matthew 28:19-20). We are commanded by the full authority of Jesus Christ to go into this world and shine. We are told to spread the word to everyone, everywhere. We're to bring the good news to those in darkness and to be bold and unafraid in our quest.

This is the complete transformational love of Jesus. In our lonely and troubled times we cling to the promise that he is our light. We will never walk in darkness!

So, my friends, today let your little light shine all over the galaxy!
—*Carl Kinkel*

Baby shower

It's been a long time since I've been to a baby shower; I'm in the place between my having children and my children having them.

So it was both an honor and a novelty to be invited to a shower given for a fellow singer, Kate, held outdoors on a beautiful made-for-entertaining day. Kate was well and generously showered by friends and family, and it was instructive to see how some baby gadgets have evolved and others stayed essentially the same.

The baby is coming at an awkward time. Kate's husband Kevin is still in law school, and she works in a field not noted for overgenerous compensation. They've moved in with her mother, to be near their families and caregivers, but their little house has yet to sell in a difficult market, and both job and school are a long commute away. It must surely be a strain.

But babies seldom do anything on our particular schedules (note: the first lesson of parenting), and this is a family solidly grounded in faith and rooted in love. However awkward the timing might be, this child will be swaddled in love and embraced by a large, close cast of aunts, uncles, cousins, grandparents, and friends—a child who will grow up with parents committed to their faith.

My prayer for them is that they may have a sense of joy, but know that weariness is normal; to have a sense of calm, but understand that it's okay to lose it completely from time to time; to realize that all the mistakes they will inevitably make have been made many, many times before, and usually without lasting trauma; and to walk on in the light of God's deep love, whatever comes their way.

—*Sarah Bryan Miller*

Pampered, promising, proven, pooped, passed

Those who want to save their life will lose it, and those who lose their life for my sake, and for the sake of the gospel, will save it.
—MARK 8:35

The human lifespan has a very predictable arc consisting of five phases: pampered, promising, proven, pooped, and passed.

When you are young, you are *pampered* figuratively and literally. You are given the opportunity to learn and grow into the person God created you to be. Then you are *promising*. You have potential, and the world is eager to see all you can do. When you've accomplished some things and enjoyed some success, you are *proven* and are counted on to deliver. Eventually, you become *pooped*, still capable but increasingly freighted with fatigue—and (hopefully) deepening wisdom. Finally, at life's end, you are *passed*—into the next world where you will pray for the rest of us making our way through the five p's of life.

Psychologist Erik Erikson viewed each juncture in life's journey as a crisis or question. For folks in their middle years, the choice is stagnation or generativity. Do we focus our attention on ourselves and stagnate in the mirrored pool of narcissism? Or do we give ourselves away in love to children or to a cause in other-focused care and creativity?

Giving ourselves away in love is the essence of our true nature in Christ. Irrespective of life stage, slough off your servile adherence to the false trinity of Me, Myself, and I. As you live for Christ you will discover the promised life that is pardoned, pure, peaceful, and perennial—in short, perfect. —*John Van Nuys*

Me and the black fly

One magnificent Saturday in May, the temperature hit 85 degrees on the coast of Maine.

Poking around the yard, I enjoyed a few blissful minutes until the first black fly arrived. The Bane of Spring hovered around my hairline, extracting droplets of A Positive. Then the surface of the millpond flickered as a mackerel struck. Down below the dam, where the fish are thick, the osprey and eagles fed from above.

Black flies, mackerel, and eagles. My blood and my neighbors' blood is what feeds this remarkable ecosystem. In May we rush from our homes, feed the black flies who, heavy with our donation, skim the water to be eaten by mackerel who are, in turn, eaten by eagles and osprey eager to feed their young.

What's a bit of pain and an unsightly red welt when I can help feed the eaglets? It's a small price to pay to live amid this natural beauty. By letting myself be chomped, I can be a living sacrifice—a little of my life given freely will support a little of theirs. Of course the sacrificial life, particularly the blood kind, has fallen a bit out of fashion over the past couple of thousand years. But in this setting, it represents a yielding, deferential way of life that does not much diminish me as a giver but rather offers my small oblation up to the wider world.

As Christians we are called to a sacrificial life. Sometimes a small gift of time or treasure will yield so much more than we could hope or imagine. Sometimes a small sacrifice will snowball into blessings that we will never, ever know. —*Heidi Shott*

Glaucoma and other life surprises

Because glaucoma is hereditary, I have been aware that I might eventually lose my sight. Glaucoma is pressure in the eyes that causes the nerve from eye to brain to die. Frequent pressure testing, eye drops, and finally surgery are the road I have traveled for thirty years.

Several years ago the pressure in both eyes went from good to bad. Surgery was performed and pressure in one eye reduced, but the other eye closed the drain with scar tissue. I use drops in that eye every day. So far, so good.

In my anxiety, I began to write poetry to express my feelings. First I wrote of the desperation I felt at the prospect of becoming blind. Then my plea was for God to help me deal with the situation, which will continue as long as I live. Lastly I was able to write of my hope and realization that God is in charge of what happens next and will help me deal with it.

Perhaps you have an ailment or trouble. My hope is that you will find the same hope I did as I worked through this time in my life. I find that poetry is helpful in getting down to where my feelings are.

A portion of a poem I call "Feed Me" follows:

O Lord, my God, place before me
   for heart and mind to see
your love and blessing.
Let me bravely bear my body's burdens,
   and if my eyes fail, enable me still to see
thy kindness and goodness encircling me.
Let me feed on Thee, Lord, and I will be blessed.
   No matter if darkness enfold me,
     You are my Light and your Love lights my way.
     —Nancy R. Duvall

We do not walk alone

The Ascension of Jesus into heaven is one of the stranger occurrences in the Bible. The idea of this day—the fantastic notion that Jesus ascended into heaven—can seem distant from our faith in a scientific age.

We should not let questions about the physics of the day interfere with our understanding of its meaning. Before he departed, Jesus blessed his followers and trusted them to carry on the work of being loving, incarnate in a broken world. Jesus' words to his disciples as he was leaving are recounted in Matthew 28:20. He says, "I am with you always, to the end of the age."

Today, two thousand years later, that is still true. Jesus asks us to carry on his work—sharing God's love, spreading the kingdom, and inviting people into closer relationship with God. It's a big job. We cannot do it on our own.

We need God to do the work that we are given. When we read the newspaper or look at our world, it's not hard to see the need for God's love. Perhaps we know fear in our own lives—fear of the unknown, fear of an uncertain economy, fear for our safety, fear of changes too vast to comprehend.

Fortunately, we do not face this world alone. We have God, and we have one another. As we gather in church or in prayer, we are reminded that in Christ we are one mystical body, together seeking to carry on God's saving love for the whole world. As we enter a world that can seem scary, let us go forth knowing that Jesus has blessed us to do the work that God asks of us. —*Scott Gunn*

An unexpected gift

It was a Bible. The Rev. Don Little, a retired priest, gave it to me before I went to seminary. I used it in at least one class, and I put special tabs on it before my ordination exams. But I left it behind when I moved from a parish where I served for about ten years. It was in the library, and I forgot it. Years later, a parishioner was looking for a study Bible and the priest invited her to take one from the library. She picked the Bible I left behind, and appreciated the markings and notes in it. After a while, she realized it was my Bible and sent it to me with thanks. I was amazed. It was an unexpected gift.

The gifts we share can become the gifts we receive. We reap what we sow (Galatians 6:7). Some people say, "What goes around comes around," and it does seem that we shape our own destiny by our actions. Jesus advises in the Sermon on the Plain that the measure we give will be the measure we receive (Luke 6:38).

As people learned from Mahatma Gandhi, we can be the change we want to see in the world. People may follow our lead, for better or worse, with or without awareness of what they're doing. The world will be a quieter place if we are gentle, and it will be a more frightening place if we are cruel. As we offer ourselves, we may discover that we're living in a world of abundance and find unexpected gifts to offer and receive.

The Bible I received and used became an unintended gift of its own, and then returned to me with thanks as another gift.
—*Rob Slocum*

In the net

When I was in seminary I had a homiletics professor who liked to challenge the theology that appeared in our sermons, asking us embarrassingly pointed questions about what we really believed.

One person in the class had preached a sermon on Luke's version of the Beatitudes. The preacher had decided to focus on the last section of the passage, the part exhorting its listeners to engage in bold Christian behaviors. And so the sermon focused on all the things we each need to do as Christian people: hard things like loving our enemies, praying for those who abuse us, and turning the other cheek.

After listening respectfully to the feedback we gave our classmate, our homiletics professor couldn't contain himself any longer.

"Listen, people," he said, "This is not a pull-yourself-up-by-your-bootstraps religion. The purpose of a sermon is not to exhort others to earn their way into a relationship with God, even through laudable behavior. No, the love of our God in Christ is like a net stretching across the universe, and in our baptism—no, even before that, at our conception—we are gathered into that net. It isn't possible, no matter what we do, to earn our way into that net. And, I believe, it isn't possible, no matter what we do, to fall our way out of that net."

When I get lost in my life or become confused by the ins and outs of theological or ecclesiastical debate, I go back to this—to the net of the love of God that I did not earn my way into and that I cannot fall my way out of.

Where in your life are you in touch with the net of God's love? How can you be this net for others? —*Melissa Skelton*

Prisoners of hope

For ten years I visited a man on Death Row, until he cheated the executioner and died of a heart attack. I don't know whether John was guilty or innocent. I do know that somewhere along the road—he said it was during a year's solitary confinement before his trial—he had a manifestly genuine conversion experience.

John loved Jesus and took his Christian responsibilities very seriously. He organized Bible study and worship. He listened with real concern to his fellow inmates, and he knew their wives, children, and parents by name. And he prayed, like a monk in the desert, for matters large and small, local and global. He prayed for me, my husband, my aging mother, my coming-of-age children. He prayed for the Christians in Sudan, for victims of earthquakes and hurricanes and wars.

To enter Death Row, to pass under the sign that says "Condemned Unit," is daunting, but one of the surprises that awaited me there was that—despite the drab little cubicle, the deafening noise, the cuffs on John's hands, the hovering guards—it all seemed oddly *ordinary*.

I was a suburban housewife with a graduate degree, and an Episcopalian. John was a high school dropout, a convicted child murderer. And a Baptist! But what linked us together—our common humanity—was greater than what divided us.

Those of us on "the outside" are not so different, after all, from those in jail. We often dwell in prisons of our own making, walled off by fear or prejudice, scorn or pride.

But God has made us prisoners not of sin but of hope. Like Lazarus (and John), we are unbound and set free to love, to hope, to serve, to learn and grow. Thanks be to God! —*Betsy Rogers*

"English, por favor..."

Neli and her almost-four-year-old son Maxito came from our companion diocese of Guatemala to visit two of our parishioners who are on the companion diocese committee. They came for a week. It was winter and Maxito wanted to see snow. He certainly was not disappointed, as we had much snow while they were with us.

On Tuesday evening, the committee had supper at the church with our guests. Some of us had provided warm winter clothes unavailable in Guatemala, a car seat, and a few toys and books.

Maxito loved his snow boots and wore them from the moment he saw them. And he loved the teddy bear, took it to bed with him, and carried it everywhere, including to church that evening. He ran around the fellowship hall in that after-dinner joy and excitement we often see in small children.

At one point, Neli tried to quiet him by reading from the board books that we had given him. I used to read those books to my grandsons and they were familiar to me. I was surprised to discover that one of the gifts to me that evening was watching and listening to Neli read those same books to Maxito in Spanish.

I smiled when she asked him to count the animals behind the flap and he said, "*Uno, dos...*" Her response: "English, *por favor*," and he quickly said, "One, two..."

I enjoyed hearing her read in Spanish about Pooh's search for his honey pot, and Thomas's train trip. I learned once again that mothers and their sons are not so different, whether they live in Guatemala or in the United States of America, in Africa or in the Middle East. God loves his people wherever they live. —*Lois Sibley*

Pray as you can

There are a lot of different ways to pray and to worship. Many of us searched long and hard for a place where we felt at home; some are still searching for it. Sometimes people will tell us how we *should* pray, or how we *should* worship. Perhaps we see folks who seem clearly at home with a certain style or tradition, and we wish we were, too. But we're not, so we keep on searching.

"Pray as you can and not as you can't," Dom John Chapman once said. Those are some of the wisest words I've ever heard, because we're all individuals, and what works for one person may not work for the next. Jesus certainly knew that, because when he instructed his followers how to pray—in the words we now call the Lord's Prayer—he didn't give many specifics. He didn't tell them what time of day to pray, or in what posture, or in what direction. He didn't tell them to go on at length, or to include lots of specific words or actions.

Instead, Jesus told his disciples to praise God, to trust that God's will be done, to ask for their basic needs, and to be willing to forgive, even as they were forgiven. The only other thing he told the disciples to do was pray in secret, so that they wouldn't be tempted to show off for others.

Keep it simple. Don't show off. Come as you are. Pray as you can. If we can just remember a few simple rules, we'll eventually find our way to a place where we can pray, and worship, and flourish.
—*Robert Macauley*

Free cats?

I once visited a New Orleans veterinarian who had a sign in his office window: "Free Cats." It was true. The waiting room of the office had a large container, almost like an aquarium without water, and inside were the free cats. Actually, they were kittens, maybe a dozen or so of them, and they were free for the taking. My first calico, "Patch," came from there. We could have gotten more if we wanted—our pick of the litter.

But there are actually no free cats. Any new cat from the vet would require shots and an exam. And, of course, once the new cat came home there would be daily food and water and care. Only a very unworthy and irresponsible pet owner would neglect the free cat. A true owner would love the cat and take care of the cat. The cat is free, but not cheap.

Like grace. God's love for us is unconditional and God's gift is never earned, manipulated, or forced. The relationship comes to us through God's initiative, but it invites our response. Grace comes to us freely, just as we are. But if we accept it, grace will not leave us just as we are.

God's love, like all love, invites us to give back. In the Lord's Prayer we pray, "Forgive us our sins, as we forgive those who sin against us." Love makes us grateful stewards who offer ourselves generously. "Loving puts us on our knees," says a Ghanaian hymn, "serving as though we were slaves" (*The Hymnal 1982*, #602). If we refuse to give back, we haven't really known the gift. We don't get it. But as we receive, we can respond more and more fully in love. —*Rob Slocum*

Times and division

I came to bring fire to the earth, and how I wish it were already kindled!
—LUKE 12:49-56

Every spring when redwing blackbirds return to Indiana to build nests and hatch their young, those nests offer all-you-can-eat buffets for any buzzard gliding silently overhead. Buzzards look for anything to eat, dead or alive, and there is no easier meal than a flightless baby bird.

It would be easy—except for the mama and papa blackbirds. These six-inch-long blackbirds fearlessly attack the marauding turkey buzzards that have six-foot wing spans. The blackbirds' parental protectiveness drives them to relentlessly dive-bomb the slower moving buzzards, repeatedly diving and pecking until the looming threat is banished.

I think that fierce, parental protectiveness is the kind of driving life-force in Jesus when he says, "I have come to bring fire and division. I have come to sort things out for good!" Sobering words if you are a buzzard. But saving words if you are a baby blackbird.

Out of love, Jesus is determined to exile all the principalities and powers of death. In so doing, God will complete the work of creation by finishing the separation of darkness from light. Such truth makes me tremble—and it makes me want to get moving.

When God's kingdom comes, a sorting out will take place. All that is good will be lifted to God's bosom. All that is antithetical to life will be banished. It's high time to rid ourselves of the world's deadly ways. Time to banish from our hearts all greed, anger, and vengeance. Time to embrace God's gracious ways of compassion, forgiveness, and mercy. Let Christ's saving life arise in you today.

—*John Van Nuys*

Proof enough

how should tasting touching hearing seeing
breathing any—lifted from the no
of all nothing—human merely being
doubt unimaginable You?

—E. E. CUMMINGS

One evening last spring our friend Tom, a biologist, hosted a peeper hunt.

After five minutes down at the marsh's edge, we'd found a lot of big spiders but no frogs whatsoever. "I can hear them, but I can't see them," Lucas, my five-year-old partner, said, earnest but exasperated.

I realized that the only way I was going to get close enough was to kneel in the water. One plunge and my left leg was soaked. My flashlight probed nooks in the marsh grass for the evidence of just one of the gajillion tiny amphibians making this racket. Obviously they're here, so why do I feel compelled to see one? How cold and wet must I become before I'm rewarded with proof?

I switched off my light until I heard a call just inches away. On with the flashlight, a quick grab, a plop. My light picked up a tiny peeper in the murky water, froggy-kicking out of sight.

How powerful is this need to see with our own eyes, to feel, to taste, to hear, to smell. It's not a far leap to liken this human requirement for evidence to how we demand such proof from God.

Occasionally we are gifted with moments that give us license to believe the unbelievable. They embolden us to make choices that the world deems foolish. They feed us enough in the way of faith to last until we return to be replenished, week after week, year after year. —*Heidi Shott*

God waits for us

The church calendar today commemorates Augustine of Canterbury, considered the founder of the English church in the late sixth century. To visit Canterbury is to be steeped in Augustinian lore. He converted first King Ethelbert of Kent and then thousands of Britons; he founded the original Canterbury Cathedral and St. Augustine's Abbey; and his throne, the ancient marble Chair of Augustine, sits today in the cathedral's sanctuary.

For all his pioneering reputation (and hard work and faithfulness), Augustine was not the first to bring the gospel to England. Roman soldiers had introduced Christianity centuries earlier, and Ethelbert's Queen Bertha was herself a French Christian who worshiped at St. Martin's Church, already some centuries old when Augustine arrived.

The word of God reached England long before Augustine. It seems God is always there ahead of us, waiting.

This prevenience of God is as true for us in prayer as for Augustine in England. God awaited Moses in the burning bush. He called Jeremiah even before he was born. "Before they call," God told Isaiah, "I will answer."

Mystics of every hue know this truth. "Beneath every 'O Lord' of thine," the thirteenth-century Muslim poet Rumi heard God saying, "is many a 'Here am I' from me."

We might think we initiate prayer and summon God's attention, but how our prayers are changed if we remember that God is already there ahead of us, waiting for us. Then those long lists of petitions become less central. Humility and gratitude seep into our spirits, and we know that our prayer is in truth just our reply to the ever-present voice of God, speaking in our hearts.

—*Betsy Rogers*

Not a holy vapor

Unlike God the Father (whom many adults envision as a kindly old gentleman with a beard) and God the Son (who actually appeared among us), God the Holy Spirit may seem vague, a kind of Holy Vapor.

The Holy Spirit is God in our lives, right here and right now. The manifestations of the Holy Spirit at the first Christian Pentecost were indeed spectacular. But most of what the Spirit does is so commonplace that we take it for granted. Think of the sun, ninety-three million miles away. But it is also in some sense right here in our garden, warming our faces and brightening everything about us. Because the sun appears so regularly, the marvels it produces seem unremarkable to us. So it often is with the Holy Spirit.

The Holy Spirit is God around us, among us, within us. It is God acting as glue, repairing our divisions and binding us in love to one another and to himself. It is God possessing us and enlivening us as the wind possesses and enlivens the flute. It is God subduing and breaking our rebellious wills, then pouring balm upon our wounds and massaging our aching joints until he has healed and recreated us. It is God falling upon our parched souls as soft, refreshing rain. It is God flooding our dulled senses with his gentle radiance. It is God holding us in his lap and singing sweet melodies into our ear as he rocks us. It is God within us, dancing with our feet, laughing with our lips, embracing with our arms. It is God living his own life and enjoying himself in us.

Perhaps the reason we don't notice is that we're looking for fireworks and windstorms. —*Richard H. Schmidt*

Windmills

I once drove past a large open field in Indiana, and was surprised to see it converted to a "wind farm." A row of large windmills (actually wind turbines) extended as far as I could see, and their blades were spinning in the wind like a squadron of giant airplanes. These windmills provide clean energy. Of course, the wind "blows where it chooses," as Jesus says to Nicodemus (John 3:8), meaning the Spirit and everyone born of the Spirit. We cannot know "where the wind comes from or where it goes." But we can recognize patterns in the wind's frequent movements and be ready to respond. We can find a good place for a windmill.

God moves freely, but grace consistently reveals divine love and fulfills God's promises. We can count on God. Before his death, Jesus promises his disciples that he will not leave them comfortless, or orphaned. He will come to them. They will live because he lives (John 14:18-19). And we will continue to find him whenever two or three are gathered in his name (Matthew 18:20). These are dependable promises, and they invite our response. Grace moves us to choose in faith, but we must choose. We can locate ourselves where the wind blows.

Yves Congar, a Dominican, offers an image for his Christian vocation in *I Believe in the Holy Spirit*. He will sing his own song, like an Aeolian harp whose strings vibrate and sing with the breath of God. He will "stretch and tune" his strings so the Spirit can "make them sing a clear and tuneful song of prayer and life."

Grace brings our gifts to life, but we must do our part. We can let the wind turn us. We can make ourselves available. We can tune our strings. —*Rob Slocum*

The only path I know

Do not be conformed to this world, but be transformed by the renewing of your minds, so that you may discern what is the will of God —what is good and acceptable and perfect.

—ROMANS 12:2

This is the verse I have printed on my business cards, so that all who meet me know right away who I am: a person who refuses to conform to this world, a person seeking to discern the will of God, a person who is desperately seeking to do good.

It is a huge burden I have placed upon myself, for it would be so much easier, many days, to go along to get along. It would be easier to simply do what others do, for then others would not spend so much time telling me, "You're bucking society. You are going against the grain."

But I do not know any other way to live. I have been caught up by Paul's injunction, thrust into a way of being that does not conform with society's expectations, and in being caught up and thrust there, I set myself apart.

"You are a person who goes to bed angry every night that the kingdom has not come," a friend once said.

"No," I said, "I am not angry. But I am frustrated that we are not doing enough."

So I go off on my own path, often choosing to zig left instead of zagging right as others expect of me. I am not deliberately trying to be different. I am only attempting to do my best to be as faithful as possible to God's will.

It is not an easy path, and I often do not know where it will lead. But it is the only path I know. —*Lauren Stanley*

"I beat ya!"

I never knew his name. The first time I saw him was in the parish hall. He was shoving cookies into both his mouth and his pockets.

He became a regular at coffee hour. We learned that he was a homeless veteran. He was not only welcomed to coffee hour, but also to church. He took his time about attending services.

Someone found that he needed medical attention. They took him to the Veterans Hospital where he had a complete checkup. Soon he was living at the hospital, and parishioners took turns bringing him in his wheelchair to church.

One Sunday morning I found him sitting by me. I nodded a greeting and he smiled. I don't think he could follow the service. But he did know one prayer.

When time came for the Lord's Prayer, he raced through it as the rest of us said it together. He was so fast that he finished way ahead of me, and then with a twinkle in his eye he said, "I beat ya!" Somehow that prayer had stuck in his muddled mind.

As months went by, his health began to fail and he could no longer come to church. Some of the men went to see him, bringing him cheer and what many others did not have—visitors.

When he died, we buried him in the church cemetery. An old soldier had transformed from a homeless bum to a man who was cared for and cared about. He gave us much more than we gave him. He reminded us that the prayer says "*Our* Father"—and that includes everybody.

Every time I say the Lord's Prayer I think about that "I beat ya!"
—*Nancy R. Duvall*

Pay attention

Consider the lilies of the field.
—MATTHEW 6:28

I am going about my business in the kitchen—unloading dishes, wiping down countertops, getting ready for dinner—when all of a sudden my two-year-old daughter pipes up "Bird!"

I instinctively glance over to see what she is looking at, only to realize that she doesn't see a bird; she hears one. I am distractedly, even frantically, trying to get things done, oblivious to what is around me. My daughter, on the other hand, is paying attention to all that is around her, taking it in, learning from it, enjoying it.

It is, I think, a spiritual practice we all need to work on, this art of paying attention. It is far too easy, in the craziness of life, to miss out on the moments, the glimpses of God that are scattered throughout our days in the beauty of creation and the people that we encounter. When Jesus was on earth teaching people, he always pointed to ordinary things: bread and yeast, fig trees and mustard seeds, birds of the air and lilies of the field. We have to pay attention to these things, to notice them, in order to learn the lessons Christ is trying to teach us now.

Take time today to engage in the spiritual practice of paying attention. Listen to the birds of the air. Notice the lilies of the field. See what they tell you about the grace and glory of God.
—*Melody Shobe*

Walking in God's will

Teach me the way I should go.
—PSALM 143:8

This is a longing my daughter has been feeling for months now. The school district budget requires cutting six teaching jobs, including hers. After ten years in a lovely school with a fulfilling job, she is searching for another. It's painful for her, her sons, her students, friends, fellow teachers, and supervisors at the school. And for us. We have lived near each other for the past twenty-five years, helped each other, comforted each other, encouraged each other.

Oh, we can still do that, wherever they go, but it won't be the same. Ten minutes away by car will become a much farther distance, I'm sure.

"I remember the time past," writes the psalmist (143:5). And we do. There are many happy memories: soccer games and sleep-overs, swimming at the Y pool, sharing tips and plants from our gardens, picking raspberries together in the backyard, watching the boys in their school programs and church pageants and piano recitals. It was great. Thank you, Lord.

And yet, our first concern is to be in God's will, whatever and wherever that may be. So my daughter searches the Internet for the right job, sends out her resume, goes through interviews, and we pray. "O LORD, make haste to answer" (Psalm 143:7). That is our prayer and yet, we are trying to wait patiently, knowing that God's time is best, his plan is best, and in his will is where we want to be.

So many people are looking for jobs or making decisions about new directions in life. If you are among them, may you also "wait patiently for the LORD" for his best will for you. —*Lois Sibley*

The saxophone

Come, thou fount of every blessing, tune my heart to sing thy grace!
—*THE HYMNAL 1982*, #686

My son Jacob is a jazz musician who plays the baritone sax. The "bari" is a large saxophone, and it sounds as he blows through the mouthpiece and fills the instrument with his breath. Then he plays the keys and creates amazing music. But no matter how skillfully he plays the keys, the music stops if his breath stops. His breath is in the music and makes it possible.

In a similar way, God's life is in us. Before we choose to obey or cooperate with God, before we seek to know God or discern the divine will—God is with us. In Christ, all things hold together (Colossians 1:17). Without God's presence, the music of our lives would just stop. We would not be. God's initiative makes our initiative possible. We can say yes to God because God continues to say yes to us.

God's creation isn't done. Creation isn't a completed one-time event. It continues to unfold in us and all that is. Our existence is a coming-into-being that begins with God and continues through God's presence.

God breathes in us. God is closer to us than we are to ourselves. We may play the keys of our life with all our skill, but every sound begins with the breath of God. —*Rob Slocum*

On the Trinity

The Nicene and Apostles' Creeds are basic to the Christian faith: We believe in one God, Father, Son, and Holy Spirit—the Trinity. But what, exactly, is that?

The Trinity is not an easy doctrine. It states that there is one God, but in three Persons. God is the Creator of all, the Father; God is the Word made flesh, the Son; and God is Wisdom and Love, the Holy Spirit, the Comforter.

Saint Patrick famously explained it by holding up a shamrock, a plant with three distinct leaves that is still of one substance. In combining two molecules of hydrogen and one of oxygen, what results is always of the same substance, whether manifested as flowing water, frozen ice, or water vapor. A human being is still the same individual, the same essence, whether perceived as child, or parent, or spouse.

While the word "Trinity" does not appear in the Bible, the New Testament is shot through with references to the three Persons of God, from 2 Corinthians to the gospels of Matthew and John. Most of all, it's the only logical way to reconcile the essential Jewish understanding of God—"Hear O Israel, the LORD is our God, the LORD is One" (Deuteronomy 6:4)—with our understanding that Jesus and the Holy Spirit are God as much as is the Father.

It's how we keep our monotheism intact while acknowledging God's multiple aspects. The human mind cannot fully comprehend the Creator who conceived and made the unspeakable vastness of the universe, but we can understand that God cares for us, loves us all enough to dwell among us as one of us, and gives us comfort in our confusion and distress. —*Sarah Bryan Miller*

Who needs a vacation?

Let's face it, the concept of "vacationing" with young children is an oxymoron. There's nothing the least bit relaxing about schlepping around the country with toddlers in tow. Perhaps a more accurate name for such family endeavors would be "traveling chaos." I specifically remember morphing into the guy I used to laugh at in airports: trudging through Concourse B like a beast of burden heavy laden with car seats and strollers and diaper bags with nary a skycap in sight.

It's hard enough to take a vacation these days. Smart phones, laptops, the Internet, and general availability by cell phone all conspire to make even the most remote spot a mere office satellite. Technology has become the world's longest umbilical cord connecting overachievers and workaholics back to the office. For many people "vacation" simply means working from somewhere else.

Yet we all need time off to engage the profound sabbath time that our souls crave. Time off—true time off, not merely the outward appearance—is essential to our physical and spiritual well-being. Without it relationships suffer, creativity dwindles, perspective is warped, and life becomes an obligation rather than a joy. Sabbath time allows us to set aside the cares of our lives in order to focus on our relationships with God, with one another, and with ourselves.

These three ultimately are what life is about—everything else is tangential. Time away allows us to regain the perspective that allows us to lead more healthy, productive, and joy-filled lives.

If even God rested after creating the world, I think we can all get away with some guilt-free vacation time. —*Tim Schenck*

If you could have just one wish

God doesn't often take the form of a genie rising out of a bottle, but he apparently did so at least once. In 1 Kings 3, the Lord appeared to Solomon in a dream and said, "Ask what I shall give you." Solomon gave his answer. It pleased the Lord, and the Lord granted Solomon's wish.

Solomon, who had just become king of Israel, asked for "an understanding mind to govern your people." I expect the reason Solomon's answer pleased the Lord was that it showed that Solomon knew who he was and asked for what he really needed. A king needs wisdom to govern.

But we are not kings—what do *we* need? The other day I watched a series of fifteen-second television commercials during a program break. Each commercial was spoken by an off-camera voice that sounded likeable and authoritative and gushed with excitement. Anything those voices said would have sounded appealing to me. Each voice urged me to buy a product. The products were a deodorant spray, toilet paper, a car, an airline ticket, a financial planning service, a feminine hygiene product, and a pseudo-food (no nourishment, no calories). The tone of the commercials suggested that by buying and consuming these products, I'd be excited and joyful, like the voices on the commercials.

Probably not. I know better than to believe television commercials. They peddle what they cannot deliver, and if God granted me one wish, as he did Solomon, I wouldn't ask for the sort of empty husks hawked over the airwaves.

But what would I ask for? To ask wisely requires both a knowledge of ourselves (Solomon knew he was king) and a knowledge of what we need (Solomon knew he needed wisdom). What would you ask for? —*Richard H. Schmidt*

Gifts of the Spirit

*Now there are varieties of gifts, but the same Spirit; and there are
varieties of services, but the same Lord; and there are varieties of activities,
but it is the same God who activates all of them in everyone.
To each is given the manifestation of the Spirit for the common good.*

—1 CORINTHIANS 12:4-7

I finally put up some bird feeders in the yard last week and then sat on the front porch to see how long it would take the birds to find them. After about thirty minutes, two chickadees began darting toward the feeders, grabbing the sunflower seeds with their beaks and then darting back into the trees. Later on a walk I noticed how many different birds were now in the neighborhood: chickadees, yes, but also robins, purple finches, flickers, doves, crows, starlings, and jays.

While differences are a delight in the animal world, they can be difficult in the human world. We love our chickadees and our finches and our flickers, but we don't always take equal delight in our own differences in gender, race, personality type, age, ability, life experience, sexual orientation, economic level, or nationality. Our ignorance about these differences, our fear of them in others and in ourselves, is the root of much heartache and strife.

But God, it seems, delights in variety and diversity in creation. And God, it seems, uses variety as a way of creating and sustaining a world where each different creature plays a part and contributes to the common good.

What is the unique difference you bring to the world?

How do your differences contribute to the common good? —*Melissa Skelton*

Loved into being

It is the beginning of the wedding season, when people come together in joy to celebrate the joining of two people's lives. One of the readings most commonly used in weddings is from the first letter of Paul to the Corinthians.

"Love is patient; love is kind; love is not envious or boastful or arrogant or rude. It does not insist on its own way; it is not irritable or resentful; it does not rejoice in wrongdoing, but rejoices in the truth.... Love never ends....And now faith, hope, and love abide, these three; and the greatest of these is love" (1 Corinthians 13:4-13).

We are created in love. Because God did not need us, God *loved* us into being. But do we remember to *live* in love?

It is on those days when we are irritable, when life is not going our way, when we feel abandoned or downtrodden, that we most need to recall being loved into being. For when we remember that God loves us, perhaps—at least on our better days—we will remember that God loves every other person just as much.

When I preach at these weddings, I say:

"Remember Paul's words this day. Remember that love lived out intentionally is hard. Remember that envy and boastfulness and arrogance and rudeness and resentment are not part of love. They are the things that break down love—if you let them. Do not let them. Remember instead the love you have for each other this day, the joy, the elation you are feeling. God loves you more than this. If you remember this kind of love, if you try to live in this kind of love, your marriage will be a blessing to each of you, to God, and to all of us."

—*Lauren Stanley*

Unintended mercies

My husband was holding services at a lovely little town in our diocese. I was on the church porch overlooking the lawn when I noticed a couple examining the monuments there. It began to drizzle and impulsively I called out to the couple, "Come to church. Get out of the rain."

They replied, "We are not dressed for church."

I called, "It doesn't matter. We are having a special service and you will enjoy it!"

Wonder of wonders, they did come in and stayed for the service and reception. I did not pay any special attention to them or ask them to sit with me.

Two years later we were in St. Louis where my husband was leading a storytelling conference. After the service that ended the conference, he told me a man was waiting to speak to me. *Me?* I found the man and asked how I could help him.

He said, "Mrs. Duvall, you probably don't remember me, but two years ago my wife and I were on sabbatical and stopped in a small town where your husband was holding services. It started to rain and you invited us to church. We enjoyed it so much we went to church every Sunday as we traveled.

"I wanted you to know how much we appreciated your inviting us in and tell you that no one else even spoke to us as we attended the other churches around Florida."

I was floored—that no one had spoken to them and especially that he had made the effort to tell me how much it meant to them to be made welcome. I had done such a simple thing.

What is simpler than "Hello" or "Welcome?" Those are magic words that stir the heart, especially when accompanied by a smile. —*Nancy R. Duvall*

When God says no

I've heard it said that God always answers prayer but that sometimes the answer is "No." "Pray without ceasing," the apostle Paul tells us (1 Thessalonians 5:17). That's a tall order. Some folks have taken those words literally, like the author of the spiritual classic *The Way of the Pilgrim*, who strove to say the "Jesus prayer"—"Lord have mercy on me, a sinner."—over and over again throughout the day, until it began to pray *through him*.

Most of us, though, pray at defined times, like before meals, at the end of the day, or in church. And a lot of our prayers involve asking God for things: for healing, for wisdom, for comfort. And God, ever faithful, listens to and answers all our prayers. But sometimes the answer is "No."

That can be hard to accept. It might feel that God wasn't listening. "I told God what I needed," we might say, "but my prayers weren't answered." What we're really saying is that God didn't give us what we wanted. There could be a lot of good reasons for that: it might have been bad for us to get it, God had something better in store for us, or there was a valuable lesson to be learned in not getting it. Yet for all those potential explanations, it can still be hard to get "No" for an answer.

At the same time, though, it is a wonderful opportunity for trust. It's easy to praise God for granting all our wishes; it's harder to trust that God loves us—and listens to us—when we aren't given what we ask for. Yet that's the essence of faith. —*Robert Macauley*

Blessings beyond imagining

It is more blessed to give than to receive.
—ACTS 20:35

Our parish sponsors an annual mission trip to Honduras to volunteer at a home for impoverished boys. One year the director of the home shared her dream of starting a musical group in which the children could perform around the country. She was convinced this would help the boys improve their sense of pride and self-worth. The challenge was that instruments were too expensive. A member of our group immediately offered to pay for the instruments.

The band was formed and the results were as expected. The boys were full of pride as they performed music, sharing their talents and gifts. One day the band played at a home for abandoned girls. One of the girls in the audience could not take her eyes off one of the boys in the band, to the point that it made him uncomfortable. After the concert, she immediately approached him and began questioning him: "Where are you from?" "What is your name?" "What was your mother's name?"

He answered all her questions, and then she looked at him with tears in her eyes and said, "You are my brother."

I often think of that moment and the many times people around the church said "yes" to an opportunity to give. Because all those opportunities were embraced, the blessings were many—far more than we could have ever asked for or imagined. When Jesus said, "It is more blessed to give than to receive," he was urging us to give of ourselves because when we do, we find ourselves standing in the kingdom. Right here. Right now. —*Jason Leo*

Sowing beautifully

The one who sows sparingly will also reap sparingly,
and the one who sows bountifully will also reap bountifully.
—2 CORINTHIANS 9:6

The Apostle Paul, writing to his fellow Christians in Corinth, is very clear: Do not be stingy in your giving, your work, your life, for God is not stingy with you. Be bountiful as God is bountiful.

But for a brief moment, I do not read *bountifully*. Instead, I read *beautifully*: He who sows *beautifully* will also reap *beautifully*. I am stunned: "What a delightful thing to write...to sow *beautifully*!"

I revel in the sentiment, because it sums up so well all the people who participate in mission and ministry around the world, all that so many are doing together to share the gospel with people far away, whom they do not know and probably never will meet.

Yes, I think, this indeed is a *beautiful* thing that all of us do when we work together in the service of the Lord, and Paul is so very good to write this and remind us.

Of course, then I read the passage again, and see that Paul has *not* written *beautifully*, he says *bountifully*, and I think, "Well, yes, that indeed is what our partnership in the gospel is; it is *bountiful* as well."

But I couldn't get away from the image of sowing *beautifully*. That thought sets off in my mind's eye a kaleidoscope of people, a dancing mosaic of all those in Sudan and Haiti and Honduras and every parish where I have preached, every community where I have taught.

I see in my mind's eye those who have given, and those who have received, and as each face flashes across the screen of my mind, I see God's creation, and it is *beautiful*.
—*Lauren Stanley*

Lessons from the garden

I am not an outstanding gardener. I'm a few rungs above my mother, who was famed for her brown thumb, but no one comes to me for advice on how to make plants flourish.

For that, I turn to my friend Linda and to Bill the Landscaper. Bill's team has gradually transformed my yard with knockout roses, butterfly bushes, and other attractive vegetation whose names I cannot recall, but which meet my criteria of visual appeal, easy care, and not being favorite deer munchies.

Linda, whose house testifies to her good taste, has a real gift for putting together appealing outdoor flower pots for each season and chooses varied plants that go well together. There's usually something vertical and something horizontal that will drape itself over the sides.

In the early spring, we went with pansies. They flourish when it's chilly, but when summer heat and humidity strike, Linda tells me it's time to switch.

This is where I have problems. I love pansies, with their sweet cheerful faces; I hate to yank them up while they're flourishing. It gives me a pang to see them still vibrant but trashed. It just seems heartless somehow.

Instead, most years I end up leaving them in place until they fail in the summer sauna that is St. Louis. That seems heartless in a different way. This year, I listened to Linda.

Sometimes our good intentions lead us astray; sometimes we let sentiment overcome good sense, and not just in the garden. It's a gift to know when the time is right to make a change, or to have friends who are willing to give us a gentle nudge in the right direction.
—*Sarah Bryan Miller*

New shoes

Our three-year-old grandniece Caitlin had new shoes. She was thrilled. Bursting with excitement, she fairly danced along as she and her parents took a walk in the park. Spotting a perfect stranger across the grass, she sang out joyfully, "I have new shoes!"

The excitement of newness is at the heart of our faith. "See, I am making all things new," Jesus tells us (Revelation 21:5). We are a new creation. In Christ, God takes all our old tatters and weaves them into something splendid and new. He takes our tired brains and weary hearts and aching bodies and fills them with new life. When our thinking falls exhausted into ruts, he grants us fresh insight and dazzling vision. When the old solutions no longer work, he gives us a new way forward. When change shakes us to our bones, he walks with us till we see his world in a new light.

Sometimes I don't feel new: I feel creaky and wheezy. Sometimes I don't really want to feel new: I'm attached to the old. Sometimes I'm afraid that I'm simply past the point of renewal: too old or too tired or, heaven help me, too indifferent.

But then the scales fall, if ever so briefly, from my eyes, and I catch a glimpse of life as God means for us to live it, in the breathtakingly beautiful world he has given us. New strength courses through me. I am renewed!—and filled with hope and joy. "Your old men shall dream dreams," Joel prophesies (Joel 2:28; Acts 2:17), and it's true.

In those moments even I feel like singing out to perfect strangers. We would do well to emulate Caitlin's irrepressible joy in response to God's renewing power at work in us. —*Betsy Rogers*

Angels amongst us

Manoah did not know that he was the angel of the LORD.
—JUDGES 13:16

Do you believe in angels? I'm not talking about decorative figurines or the smiling cherubs of greeting cards. Angels are divine spokespersons. Do you believe God speaks to us through other beings? Do you believe in the kinds of angels who appear in the Bible?

There are two kinds of angels in the Bible. The first is impossible to mistake for anything else—a knock-you-down, in-your-face confrontation with the supernatural; the angel Gabriel, for example, in Luke 1. Such angels usually say, before they start in on their message, "Don't be afraid!" They say that because people are terrified of them.

The second kind of angel is like the ones Abraham and Sarah (Genesis 18) and Manoah saw. They are usually mistaken for something else. Many people have met angels and didn't know it (Hebrews 13:2). Not only do such angels not frighten us, but we may hardly give them a thought. They may seem silly or crazy or rude. We are particularly likely to discount what angels tell us if it's something we'd just as soon not hear.

Be attentive, for you never know through whom the Lord will speak to you. It probably won't be through a heavenly being with wings and a halo. Maybe it will be through your child. Or your spouse. Or your boss. The postman, the cab driver, the person next to you in the checkout line, the politician you dislike, the homeless person on the street. Or that irritating, irascible jerk in the next office. Even your worst enemy. Perhaps everyone we meet is a potential angel, bearing a message from the Lord, if we have ears to hear and eyes to see. —*Richard H. Schmidt*

Entertaining angels

I have a colleague who is a single mom and a minister; her child is elementary school aged. One night, the two of them went out to eat dinner, and when they had finished, they learned that someone—some anonymous person, some angel—had already paid their tab, including the tip. The waitress told my colleague that she was sworn to secrecy about the identity of this angel.

My colleague shared this story on Facebook and said that in addition to making her day/week/month (she was just starting her first job out of seminary and money was tight), this experience made a huge impression on her son. They embarked on a discussion about doing good deeds, especially doing them in secret, expecting no recognition or reward. The discussion was good, but she felt it was the experience that made the real impression. She expressed her gratitude for this anonymous example of Christian love to all of us, her Facebook friends, because she could not express it to the gift-giver face to face.

We are admonished in Hebrews 13:2 to "not neglect to show hospitality to strangers, for by doing that some have entertained angels unawares." And surely when we do that, we experience blessing. We know that it is more blessed to give than to receive; children are reminded of this every year at Christmas. But oh, what a lesson for a young child to learn through experiencing such hospitality himself or herself, by being on the receiving end of someone's generosity unexpectedly and for no discernible reason!

Sometimes angels entertain *us* unawares. —*Penny Nash*

Incident at White Rock Beach

It was a nice little neighborhood beach, a few blocks from our house, and we loved to swim there each summer. White Rock Beach was named for a white rock about halfway along the length of the beach. There were marshes behind it all the way to the railroad tracks. Our beach was snuggled into the end of Mill Cove, and as the tide went in and out, we spent many hours there.

New sand was brought and dumped each summer, paid for by our community association. There was a large millstone on the beach on which we used to sit.

One summer, a man whose house was back across the tracks, not even in our neighborhood, wanted that millstone on his property. The neighbors were upset and determined to keep "our" millstone. Years ago, the mill had been near the beach and the millstone had been part of it. It became a big argument, and my mom was in the midst of it.

One day a truck came to take our millstone to that man's property. My mom said, "No way. It's ours. You cannot have it." And she sat herself down on the millstone to stay as long as necessary. Someone called the local newspaper, and soon a reporter and a photographer came. They talked to her, took her photo, and left. She stayed. The truck finally left.

The next day our mom's photo was in the *Ledger* and everyone in our neighborhood was talking about it. We were amazed. Our quiet, peace-loving mom involved in a big protest? For her, it was justice. She was determined to save our millstone. And she did. The man gave up.

So what does God require of us? "To do justice, and to love kindness, and to walk humbly with your God," as Micah claims in 6:8. We saw our mom do that. —*Lois Sibley*

Bite your tongue

In the 1980s I served on the board of the Presiding Bishop's Fund for World Relief. The name has now changed to Episcopal Relief & Development. Sometimes it takes years to simplify names so that people understand right away what they mean.

During one of the General Conventions I was asked to give a talk about this organization to the young people in attendance. They had a special meeting place, and I was to speak at 10:00 p.m. because that did not interfere with other scheduled activities.

I arrived a few minutes early and found a room full of couches which were full of young people, who also sat on the floor and anywhere else they could find. I was allotted a chair, for which I was grateful. At my feet sat two boys, and as I began speaking they continued to talk.

I was irritated. It was distracting and rude, I thought. Several times I paused, but they kept talking. I finally decided just to ignore them and finished what I had to say about the work of the fund.

The first question I received when I asked for comments was from one of the boys at my feet. He was an American and told me the other boy was from Central America. The American had been translating everything I said, and his friend was so excited at what he had heard that he now wanted to know more about how his country could be helped.

Talk about the Holy Spirit holding my tongue! I was so grateful that I had not lashed out at the boys for being rude. Sometimes the Holy Spirit lets you know that you don't know it all. Bite your tongue until you have the facts. —*Nancy R. Duvall*

Prepare, then let go

There is only so much you can do to prepare for surgery.

Yes, you can follow the directions you're given for what you should and should not eat or drink before the date of the surgery. You can arrange your calendar to create an open schedule after the date, time to do nothing but recover. You can even visualize certain moments related to the surgery as a way to prepare yourself.

But even with all of this mental and physical preparation, nothing prepares you for the actual and specific experiences you have: the fearful anticipation and dread you feel when the nurse says to you, "Now you're going to feel a little stick;" the helpless awe you feel when you first look upon the stainless steel glory of the operating room and the bed, narrow as a shelf, on which you will lie during the surgery; the swift darkness of the anesthesia; the intense, delicious taste of the saltines and the apple juice in the recovery room after a day of fasting.

Yes, we can and do prepare ourselves in so many ways for the big moments of our lives, moments that excite our anxiety, our expectations, our dread, and even our joy. But we cannot (and should not) try to prepare ourselves for everything that will happen.

For life, like God, is new in every moment, appearing before us, peculiar and surprisingly gracious in ways we could never have guessed or prepared for. And we are invited, after all our preparations, to let them go and to stay attentive to these surprises.

What are you spending time and energy preparing for? What can you do to allow for surprises along the way? —*Melissa Skelton*

Waken the dawn

Wake up, my spirit; awake, lute and harp;
I myself will waken the dawn.

—PSALM 57:8

I am not a morning person. I would rather stay up all night than get up at oh-dark-hundred.

Except on those mornings when I read this verse and my heart and soul leap for joy. *I* will waken the dawn...not someone else, but *me!*

In the movie *City of Angels*, starring Nicholas Cage as one of many angels who watch over the earth, there is a scene in which all the angels "assigned" to Los Angeles gather on the beach and turn eastward to the rising sun. They lift their faces heavenward and experience such obvious joy, such life-giving harmony with God that I have decided: *This is what I will do when I get to heaven.*

No, I will not be an angel—theologically, that is impossible. What I *will* do, I have decided (as though this were up to me!), is sing in the morning choir. Like the angels in the movie, I will lift my face to God, and I will waken the dawn with song and prayer and thanksgiving to God, who knit me together in my mother's womb, who has created me marvelously, who has loved me from before time began, who loves me now and who will love me until the ages of ages.

I will fill the dawn with my song of eternal gratitude so that all of creation will know of this love and rejoice in it as I do, so that each day will begin with this love and be blessed by it.

I am not a morning person.

But I am willing to become one, if I can be the one who gets to waken the dawn. —*Lauren Stanley*

Rust and sin

How is sin like rust? My first car was too far gone to bother scraping and sealing, so I supplemented the floorboards with cardboard and duct tape and limped along until I could afford a new car. When metal is exposed to the elements, it begins to oxidize and lose its integrity. Left untreated, that metal becomes totally corrupted and loses its created purpose. Sin works the same way.

It's unpopular to talk about sin, but it is a part of each human story. Just because we are human, even though life begins with a God-given wholeness, we're exposed to the cultural systems, the environment that creates little spots of corruption on our person.

When rust blooms you can use a little elbow grease and steel wool to get it off. When one of those sins like anger, envy, lust, or pride blooms to corrupt a life, if you are paying attention and confess it, it is not so deadly. But like my metal floorboards, the damage will come right back unless you change the environment or somehow treat or condition your life. If you never address the damage or you choose to be exposed to corrosive elements by engaging in behaviors that corrupt and destroy the creatures of God, you can bet you'll fall apart. Then you will no longer serve the purpose for which we humans are created, which is to delight in and generate God's goodness and blessing.

The blessed truth is that our total disintegration is prevented by accepting Jesus Christ as Lord and Savior. His love is the power that removes our impurities. We have only to cooperate with that grace as it works in our lives to transform us from brittle iron to brilliant gold, an incorruptible mineral that radiates God's glory.
—*Ruth Lawson Kirk*

The eighteenth camel

There was a wealthy man who lived in the desert with his three sons. When he died, he owned seventeen camels. His sons were confused when they read his will, which left half his camels to the oldest son, a third to the next oldest son, and a ninth to the youngest son. They couldn't agree about what to do, because none of the numbers worked for them. They began to fight.

Finally a wandering sage came along on a camel, and he offered a solution for their dilemma. He added his camel to the father's estate, and that changed everything. With eighteen camels, it was easy for the oldest son to take his half with nine camels. The next son easily took his third with six camels. And the youngest son took his ninth of the camels with two. That left one camel unclaimed, the sage's camel, and he rode away on it! He removed himself (and his camel) when they were no longer needed. He didn't hesitate to get involved, and he didn't linger when his job was done.

Jesus warns his would-be disciples that "Foxes have holes, and birds of the air have nests; but the Son of Man has nowhere to lay his head" (Luke 9:58). He became deeply and lovingly involved with the people he served. But he never settled in one place. Like the sage with the eighteenth camel, he offered what he had in a way that changed everything, and then he departed, taking nothing for himself.

Effective ministry can look very much like the gift of the eighteenth camel. It helps to set things right so life can thrive, and then it gets out of the way to let that happen. —*Rob Slocum*

Fortune cookie theology

The New York Times feature "Schott's Vocab" notes developments in our evolving English language. Readers recently were invited to share original aphorisms. Some memorable ones included: Never taunt a person in a taped-up car. All politics is loco. Celebrate a marriage, not the wedding. Given a 50/50 chance to insert a grounded plug correctly, you'll be wrong 90 percent of the time. Don't believe everything you think. Even if you don't decide, you've still made a choice. Boys are stupid; girls are crazy. A lost item is always found in the last place you look. What you don't know can't hurt you, so the ignorant are completely safe. Many a truth is said through false teeth. Everyone eventually quits smoking. There's never a cop around when you're obeying the speed limit. 'Tis better to have loved a short woman than never to have loved a tall. Writing with a broken pencil is pointless. The older you get the more dead people you know. There is always a choice.

Journaling during an especially hellish time, I found myself writing: "God will work *it* out. Or God will work *me* out. Or *both.*" That may sound like fortune cookie theology, but those thirteen words are absolutely true. As we patiently allow God time, God never fails to transform our brokenness, refashioning it by grace unto greater wholeness and life. As Paul more eloquently described this truth in Romans 8:28, "We know that all things work together for good for those who love God, who are called according to his purpose."

Those words may be small enough to fit on a fortune cookie-sized slip of paper, but when all hell breaks loose and you hear yourself saying "that's how the cookie crumbles," that larger-than-life truth will not break apart. Hang onto that truth as God hangs onto you in love. —*John Van Nuys*

Cicada summer

"Bugs, Mr. Rico! Zillions of 'em!"
—ROBERT A. HEINLEIN, *STARSHIP TROOPERS*

There are about 2,500 species of cicadas—those chunky, noisy, transparent-winged, harmless-but-annoying insects—in the world. This month, it sounds as though they've all moved to my neighborhood.

They emerged from the burrows in the ground where they'd spent more than a decade, pausing to shed their old skins on any available surface. Then they took to the trees, by the thousands, and to their mating calls.

At its best, the whir of the cicadas is a kind of quiet and almost vaguely comforting white noise. At its worst—which is most of the time—it's a high-decibel screech like a dentist's drill, a buzz bomb descending, the ill-pitched call of an insect love that not only dares to speak its name but refuses to shut up. Cicadas get louder as the temperature rises. It's been a hot few weeks.

When I go for my morning walk, the cicadas and I startle each other. They zoom from their trees and streak past my ear with what sounds like a shriek. They brush my arm, or my face. I jump; they fly off at disquieting angles. The end of their mating season cannot come too soon for my nerves.

The cicadas have a devilishly simple survival strategy: although birds and other predators have been gorging themselves silly since the emergence, there are so many bugs that nothing can eat them all. God gives all creation ways to survive and flourish; God makes all creatures appealing to someone else. The cicadas' song may fray our last nerve, but they are beautiful to one another, and in the sight of their Creator. —*Sarah Bryan Miller*

All or nothing

Jesus said to Peter, "Simon son of John, do you love me?"
He said to him, "Yes, Lord; you know that I love you."
Jesus said to him, "Tend my sheep."

—JOHN 21:16

Like him or dislike him—or maybe a little bit of both—the apostle Peter is an amazing character. Peter clearly wasn't into moderation: when Jesus washed the disciples' feet on the night before he died, Peter initially wouldn't let him do that, but once he understood the reason he asked Jesus to wash his whole body. It was all or nothing for Peter. One minute he loved Jesus so much he was willing to die for him, and the next minute he was denying he even knew Jesus.

For all of that, Peter is the rock on which Jesus built the church, which provides the rest of us with hope, and with a challenge. The hope comes from knowing that no matter what we've done wrong, there is always the possibility of redemption. The challenge is to be as passionate as Peter was, not caring what anyone thinks or what the consequences of our faith might be. When Peter did something, he did it all the way.

I think of this most often at Holy Communion. In my church we eat bland wafers and take polite sips from the chalice of wine. I can't imagine Peter doing that. He would have lopped off a huge hunk of bread and drunk deeply from the chalice, desperate for the eternal life that was promised there. He treated communion—and the rest of his faith—as a matter of life and death.

So as I kneel at the communion rail, I think of Peter, and reach out eagerly yet reverently, as if my life depended on it. Because it does. —*Robert Macauley*

Close to God?

Feeling close to God isn't a sure indication of anything. I know a man who loves to attend events where he feels so close to God that he seems almost fizzy when he returns. But I get the impression he cares more about fizzy feelings than about God. "I could just feel the Spirit!" he exclaims. I usually nod my head and say nothing because I am not his pastor or counselor and don't know him well. But if I felt it my place to guide him, I'd try to plant a bit of skepticism as regards mushy spiritual highs. The devil can create feelings as easily as God can, and he sometimes creates exactly the same feelings God creates. One who focuses on feelings is not focusing on God.

Similarly, feeling cut off from God is not a sure indication of anything. Years ago I nearly lost my faith in God. If there was a God, I felt entirely out of touch with him. Time and again I awoke in the middle of the night, my stomach in knots and my mind whirling with doubts and fears. I prayed Psalms 42 and 43 over and over with their repeated rhetorical question: "Why are you so full of heaviness, O my soul, and why are you so disquieted within me?" I begged the God in whom I no longer believed to pick me up, hold me, and restore me.

Looking back now, I don't think I was cut off from God. God was with me the entire time, prodding me, nudging me, waiting for me. It was actually a time of deep spiritual growth for me, a time when I learned to accept my weakness and to trust in God's power, whether I felt anything or not. —*Richard H. Schmidt*

As long as we shall live

Wedding day. Ivory silk bridal gown, antique lace veil, bouquet of white roses and hydrangeas. My daughter stands before me, radiant and beautiful, like a princess in a fairy tale.

Today she and her beloved will choose not only each other, but also a common path. Unlike fairy tales, it is after the wedding that true love begins. Life is hard and throws a lot at everyone. There is no perfect day when everything goes according to plan. Clothes will hug the floor, the boss will not be appreciative, and arguments about money will fly.

In the midst of real life, my daughter and her husband have a choice, the same as we all do: to trudge through life disappointed and dealing with one character flaw after another, or to walk on the path where life is a journey with the Spirit.

It is when we tread the latter that "you don't care" becomes an opportunity to listen to each other in ways you never thought possible. On this route you see gifts in each other that no one else does, and you say, "Go for it. I support you." You feel called beyond couplehood into communities of love and faith, to service in the world. Walking this way, when all of your children have chicken pox sequentially, you sit next to each other at the kitchen table and fall asleep, but only after you have touched your wedding rings together like superheroes getting superhuman strength—and you celebrate your miracle.

No matter our domestic situation, as long as we shall live, this is our choice: to turn toward the road of the world or to follow the path of the Spirit, a way of companionship, spiritual adventure, and joy.
—*Noël Julnes-Dehner*

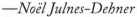

Flying

Once when I was flying from Louisville to Tampa, I found myself sitting next to a woman and her mother, who was ninety-five years old and making her first flight on an airplane. The mother was in the window seat and watching very carefully. We taxied to the runway, accelerated for a normal takeoff, and moved smoothly toward our cruising altitude. At some point the older woman leaned toward her daughter and asked, "Why did we stop?"

It was a reasonable question. The scenery outside the window was changing quickly as we sped down the runway for takeoff, but the airborne view of sky, clouds, and ground was relatively unchanging. There was certainly a sense of motion as we gained airspeed on the runway, but (fortunately) the ride in the air was very smooth. We were quickly gaining speed and elevation, but the perspective of our new altitude suggested otherwise. It seemed as if we weren't moving at all.

Sometimes we can be impatient when it seems that nothing is happening in our lives. The reality may be otherwise. It may be that much is happening and changing, but in ways we can't detect. A seed may be growing in the ground for some time before the seedling emerges. Prayers may be answered in ways we can't yet recognize. The kingdom of God is like a seed that grows secretly by night and day (Mark 4:26-27).

We may not recognize the signs of change as we engage our own "ascending" reality. New creation and possibilities may be unfolding in ways we can't detect. We may need to rest patiently and wait, until we see how far and fast we've moved. At some point we may realize we're flying. —*Rob Slocum*

Revelation at the Montréal Insectarium

In Canada one summer, we visited the remarkable Montréal Insectarium. It was my husband's idea, not mine. But what an experience awaited us!

This unusual museum exhibits hundreds of thousands of insect specimens from all over the world, displayed in cases and, in one delight-for-the-eye installation, butterflies on the wing. We wandered from room to room, astonished at the variety in size and shape, color and texture, habits and life cycles, habitats and ecological roles. One fascinating butterfly had one brilliant blue wing and one brown one! I couldn't help but imagine God at creation, saying to himself, "What next? How about...a walking stick!" Each one of these countless insects was unique and fascinating.

Nature is filled with this endless variety. There are 25,000 species just of orchids, most of them so amazingly intricate they could only come from the mind of an infinite God. It is marvelous to behold the interior of a columbine blossom or the indigo bunting's iridescent blue or the sequoia's towering majesty. The infinite variety of nature inspires awe and delight.

Yet we draw back from variety in our fellow human beings. Other races, other ethnicities, other religions, even other viewpoints inspire not rejoicing but fear, contempt, and rejection. We don't know how to relate to people who are different. We experience our differences as negative. Why can't we celebrate our own variety with the joy the orchids seem to take in theirs? And why can't we see beneath the variety the deep unifying realities that make us one—our yearning for love, for peace, for our families' welfare, for meaning in our lives, and most of all, the reality of God's embrace that would hold us all together, close to his heart? —*Betsy Rogers*

Singing in the reign

The Lord sits enthroned over the flood;
the Lord sits enthroned as king for ever.

—PSALM 29:10

I was terrified. We were to raft one of the world's top whitewater rivers—West Virginia's Upper Gauley River—the day Hurricane Hugo made landfall. There was more rain above us than river below us. Ours was the last raft to launch before they closed the river, an aquatic roller-coaster without tracks or brakes descending as pure chaos.

The Hebrew Bible scholar Walter Brueggemann states the psalmist's language of flood is code for chaos, reminding us that as God tamed the primordial, watery chaos in Genesis 1, so, too, God rules with power over world-threatening chaos today.

That's hard to affirm during a dissolving marriage or when the flood waters of change drown out cherished blessings like health, independence, family, and life. Nonetheless, we discover God's saving reign not apart from chaos, but during it. We find not the God we want, who will "miracle" everything away, but rather the God we need, who will preserve us in love for life.

Over the waters of your baptism, God declared, "This is my child. You belong to me. Now and forever. I will be with you throughout your life and through death and into life again. My Spirit is upon you, for you are my beloved. In Christ, your former self and sin is washed away; your new nature and future is at hand. Live it without fear. Rain falls on the just and the unjust. You will get wet in the troubles of this life, but above you my rainbow shines. My saving love shall prevail."

Despite the rain, God still reigns. Trust that and live.
—*John Van Nuys*

The ultimate test

When my oldest daughter was seven, she was desperate to learn how to ride a bike. Most of her friends already knew how, and she was feeling left behind. We tried having lessons here and there, but something usually seemed more fun, especially compared to learning something a little scary that she wasn't sure she could ever do.

One summer weekend we decided we were going to focus on bicycle-riding. We did long lessons in the morning and the afternoon, with some valuable advice from neighbors who'd gone through that before with their kids. (*Hint*: run behind the bike holding onto the seat, rather than alongside with a grip on the handlebars.) With each practice ride, my daughter was able to do a little bit more on her own, until I was spending most of the time running alongside her, just in case something went wrong.

Then it was time for the "ultimate test," as she called it. She had to ride from our driveway to the end of the street and back, all on her own, with no one there to catch her. I'm not sure who was more scared: me or her. I gave her pep talks and told her how great I thought she was. And then I asked her how she was going to pull this off.

"I just imagine the sound of your footsteps running next to me," she replied. "And that makes me feel safe."

I cried, of course, and also thought of how that describes the love of God: running alongside us, letting us push ourselves to our limits, always there to catch us before we fall.

And she passed her test with flying colors. —*Robert Macauley*

Crazy things for love

On a recent Saturday morning, our teenage sons in slumber, I was savoring a cup of tea on the deck when my husband stomped up beside me in florescent yellow scooter garb. "We could go to Moody's Diner for breakfast and the boys would never know," he declared cheerily.

"You want me to ride on the back of the scooter ten miles to Moody's?" I looked at this good man with whom I've spent my entire adult life and saw how much he wanted me to enjoy the scootering life. "Okay, but no splaying my body on the roadway."

The crazy things we do for love.

Sometimes trying to live a life of faith can feel like a crazy thing to do. We get preoccupied with the details of polity and protocol in our faith communities to the point when we are almost paralyzed. Yet the way and the truth and the life is spelled out for us so simply: Hello, people! Do justice, love mercy, walk humbly with God, fear nothing, love your neighbor, tell the truth, teach children kindness and respect, honor all people by seeing Christ in them.

Jesus was the master of doing crazy things for love. His love for us is so crazy it's hard to conceive of the sacrifice he demonstrated for humankind. The disciples and early Christians understood this particular call to love and acted without regard to the consequences by sharing the gospel to the ends of the known world. Miracles ensued and lives were transformed.

As followers of Christ, God expects us to do crazy things for love. Everyday, for everyone.

Though I expect scooter-riding is optional. —*Heidi Shott*

Unstuffed

There is something exhilarating about walking through airport security. While it's a hassle to have to snake through all the lines and pull my ticket and identification out to show the TSA agent, while it's annoying to have to get my little plastic bag full of liquids and my laptop out for security perusal, there's a moment after I've relinquished my bags, my purse, my shoes, my jacket, and my belt to the conveyer belt when I'm standing there barefoot that I feel, well, free—free of all that stuff—free of all that stuff and more.

I am a person who loves her things—the artwork hanging on her walls, trinkets picked up while traveling, books purchased over the years. But there are times, more often these days than not, when these things feel like so many burdens. There are also other less tangible things—painful memories, worries, anxieties—that feel more and more like too much weight to carry in my life.

Martin Smith, in an address he wrote for the College for Bishops in the Episcopal Church, said this: "Spirituality is a complex of practices and values concerned with the divine urge for our freedom. Spirituality is not a realm of concepts and ideals but is embedded in praxis, actual ways of practicing freedom. We need lots of practice to be set free."

What are the things, tangible or intangible, that cut across the freedom that God yearns for you to have?

What do you long to do with your freedom? —*Melissa Skelton*

Sailing

I love sailing. It can be a very spiritual experience. I am amazed that air—something invisible and weightless—can move a boat that weighs thousands of pounds. A sailboat can only maneuver when it's in motion, because a rudder only works when water is moving past it. And sailing is humbling because, unlike a powerboat, a sailboat can't go wherever it wants. A sailboat has to modify its course based on wind strength and direction.

There is one place that a sailboat can never go: directly into the wind. Come too close to the wind, and a sailboat loses speed and then maneuverability. It is dead in the water, what sailors call being "in irons." Theologians might call that being enslaved to sin and needing to repent (literally, "turn away") in order to get back on track.

For all the rich lessons sailing can teach, perhaps the most spiritual part of it is the feeling that comes from well-trimmed sails in a strong, steady breeze. The boat has adapted to the wind and shaped its sails to catch enough of it while letting the rest spill off. There are no harsh sounds, just the whistle of the wind and the rhythmic lapping of the waves. And perhaps the most precious part of the whole experience is the knowledge that it is temporary. Sometime soon—maybe in a minute, maybe in a few hours—something will change and an adjustment will have to be made.

But if the sailor listens to the wind and respects it, the next course might be just as glorious as this one, perhaps more so. And in the meantime, there's nothing to be done but savor the blessings of this life.

—*Robert Macauley*

Thankful, responsible freedom

I was in the Democratic Republic of the Congo in 1998, leading a work team of mission volunteers, when civil war erupted. Deep in the rainforest interior, we didn't learn about the rebellion until we were ensnared in it. Our vehicle was stopped by young, nervous soldiers with AK-47 rifles. They threatened our Congolese host who tried to explain that, no, we were not C.I.A. spies but missionary visitors. Eventually the soldiers were persuaded, and we were freed.

We flew back to the capitol, Kinshasa, thinking we were safe. Within hours the rebel army cut power to the city. The United States embassy soon called. All U.S. nationals were to be evacuated immediately.

By the time we reached the embassy, a large angry crowd had surrounded it. As our vehicle inched through chanting protesters toward the razor wire gate, I saw two Marine guards and beyond them the American flag. I breathed a sigh of relief. I knew we were home.

Today is a day for the people of the United States to reflect on our heritage, remember our freedom, and give thanks to God for our nation. When I had to flee a war zone, my country was there to protect me. And I need to constantly return that favor. We all do.

That African rebellion was about ousting a dictator. While I had been casual about voting before, I have never failed to vote since. Neither should you. In addition, we all need to stand by our nation when it is right and work to correct our nation when it is not. Ignoring the blistering invective and hate speech of the extreme left and right, we need to encourage passionate, reasoned, civic discourse. Our democracy is only as good as those who participate in it. God bless America. Let us all labor faithfully to live well our freedom. —*John Van Nuys*

Nuked

I have moved into the third and final stage of my cancer treatment. Five mornings each week I leave the house at a little past seven, drive to the hospital, and receive radiation treatment.

Radiation oncology is just down the hall from the chemotherapy infusion center, but the two are very different; instead of sitting for hours with an IV drip, I'm in and out in less than twenty minutes.

The machine that zaps me is the medical equivalent of a combination fax-phone-printer: It takes X-rays, sends the images to the technicians, and then delivers a dose of carefully calibrated, carefully aimed radiation to my breast.

I receive it while lying on a hard, narrow board, my head on a sort of padded doughnut, my arms above my head in special frames. My job is to lie very still, something that's easier if I don't think about it.

The radiation burns my skin and makes me tired. If I'd had it first I'd have groused about the side effects, but my attitudes about what's difficult have changed since chemo.

In a few weeks it will all be over. Meanwhile, hair like an infant's is sprouting atop my head, giving hope that I won't be bald forever; the beginnings of eyebrows have appeared, and my eyelashes are halfway back to normal.

"This time next year, it will just be a bad memory," say well-meaning acquaintances. Perhaps, but the cancer has changed me forever, physically, spiritually, and emotionally. I will never take my life and abilities for granted again, nor the lives of those around me. This life is a great gift from God. I intend to use it wisely. —*Sarah Bryan Miller*

The worthy poor?

For several years I joined with two dozen other people every Tuesday night at Christ Church Cathedral in downtown Cincinnati to serve dinner to two hundred or so people who live on the streets. I had gotten to know a number of these people, but I didn't pry into their personal lives unless invited to do so. No doubt many of those we served were homeless because of poor life decisions—they're where they are because of what they've done.

One of those we serve confirmed this to me one night. "I've got issues with these people," he said. "You would be appalled at what some of these people do. A lot of them are pimps and whores and they're on the streets because they spend everything they get on drugs and booze. Then they come here for a free meal. They know the system inside and out and they take advantage of everybody, including this church. I'm homeless myself, but I don't hang with these people."

That man expressed a sentiment I'd heard before, that we should screen the people who come to us for help and serve only the "worthy poor" so as not to be an "enabler" of bad behavior. But there's nothing in the Bible about distinguishing among people in need. Jesus told a story about a father who threw a banquet for his manifestly unworthy son, asking no questions about where the boy had been or what he'd done (Luke 15:11-32). We don't call it the Parable of the Foolish Father. And Saint Paul said to feed even our enemies (Romans 12:20).

Who is to say who is worthy and who is unworthy? And why should that matter? If someone is hungry, we are to feed him. Let God ask the questions. —*Richard H. Schmidt*

Three fears we all face

I remember a sermon in which the preacher said that we all have three fears: fear of the dark, fear of falling, and fear of dying. And we have to face these fears whenever they come to haunt us. I think he was right.

When we fear the dark, we should remember Jesus said, "I am the light of the world. Whoever follows me will never walk in darkness but will have the light of life" (John 8:12). There are many references in scripture to God as light. In our healing liturgy we say, "In your light, we see light," and it's true.

When we are afraid we're about to fall, we need to remember that Jesus said, "I am with you always" (Matthew 28:20). He is with us even when we fall. Last winter, I fell on a bit of ice. One of my fingers hit the ground and broke. I prayed much for healing, and it's healed now. It looks ugly and bent, but I can still type, knit, and play the piano, so I'm fine.

When we admit to our fear of dying, we should remember that Jesus said to his disciples, "...because I live, you will also live" (John 14:19). This verse and many others assure us that all those who believe in Jesus will be with him in eternity.

I love to read these verses to people because they remind us all of the promises the Lord has given us so that we need not fear anything.
—*Lois Sibley*

So many disasters— what's happening?

"You're a pastor," the woman says, worry tightening her voice. "What do you think is happening?"

She is referring not just to the latest natural disaster devastating a far-away land, but to all the disasters that have struck in recent years: earthquakes, tsunamis, torrential downpours, hurricanes, typhoons, massive floods. She wants me to explain, theologically, what is happening to this fragile planet, our island home.

I cannot give her a definitive answer. Oh, I do understand the science of these disasters; I can explain plate tectonics and high-pressure systems, wave motion and the eye of the storm. But I cannot tell her, theologically, why any particular disaster strikes at any particular time. All I can say is that we have damaged the earth. That we, in our recklessness, have not been the good stewards God calls us to be. That we have misheard God's command to Adam and Eve to "have dominion over" all that God made. I can preach that "dominion" does not mean we are allowed to mistreat God's gifts to us—that I believe God has *entrusted* to us all that God made, asking us to be good stewards, not through domination but through responsible, loving care for that which we have received. I can proclaim that we are to *love* the world, because it is part of God's very good creation, and that God loves all of creation, not just us.

But I cannot explain why this, why now. So I tell her: We need to pray. For those who have died and those who are injured, those who are homeless and those who are alone. We need to act: sending money, food, water, blankets, tents.

And then, I say, we need to take better care of God's gifts. —*Lauren Stanley*

First steps

Jesus saw Simon and Andrew fishing as he walked by the Sea of Galilee (Mark 1:16-20). Jesus invited them to follow him and "fish for people." They immediately left their nets and followed him. Jesus went a little farther and saw two more fishermen, James and John. The brothers were mending their nets in a boat. Immediately Jesus called them and they followed him. They became disciples. They left their father Zebedee in the boat with the hired men. He must have been shocked as he watched them go.

The disciples stepped away from their home, their family and friends, their livelihood and family business. Where would they go? Where would they stay? How would they support themselves? What would happen to them? There was no way to know.

The disciples were together with Jesus, and he called them to follow. That's all they really knew. Jesus asked without hesitation, and they responded immediately. They got out of the boat. They invested themselves and stepped into an unknown future, sacrificing their way of life and just about everything.

A child making her first steps may hesitate and stumble, but it's just the beginning of a new way to live. I have seen some first steps, and they are amazing to witness. First steps may be the hardest, but there's a new world to explore, and the next steps may be easier. As Lao Tzu wrote in *Tao Te Ching*, "A journey of a thousand miles begins with a single step." We all start somewhere as we take the first steps of a new beginning. It can be a journey filled with surprise. —*Rob Slocum*

Watching seagulls

Freedom, it has been said, is obedience to the element for which we were created.

One day I stood on the Green Bay shore, watching a powerful thunderstorm approach. The wind ripped past me. Waves crashed on the beach. The trees behind me thrashed furiously. The sky to the east was blue, but above the water it was a deep purple-black, punctured by lightning striking again and again. That moment, awaiting a storm, is electric, charged with energy, excitement, and a primal fear.

I looked up, and there were the seagulls, unperturbed, coasting peacefully on the updrafts. Clearly the approaching storm was not the least alarming to them. Serenely at home, working with the wind, they were obeying the element for which they were created. They were free.

Can we doubt that we were created for love? When we remember our mother's arms, our true love's caress, our best friend's understanding, our child's tiny hand gripping ours, we must know that love—God's vast, confounding mystery and very being—is the element for which we were created.

Love is sometimes frightening. It challenges our illusions of control. It demands an openness and trust that our wounded, withered hearts often find hard to summon. It means renunciation of our own narrow self-interest. It requires humility, an anomaly in our self-important age. But when we obey this element for which we were created, how it lifts us up! When in love we give up competing, we're free just to be ourselves. When in love we reach past fear or hurt or anger, we're free to revel in life's relationships. When in love we give up insisting on our own views, we're free to learn new truth.

Love sets us free within God's abundant life. Like the seagulls, we can ride the wind, unafraid. —*Betsy Rogers*

The freedom of failure

As a priest in the church, I remember the day I became irrelevant to the culture around me. It was at a wedding rehearsal in the early 1990s. The bride was a member of the church but the groom was not. I was leading the bride, groom, and attendants through the service when the groom asked, "Will we have books or papers up here so we know what to say?"

I responded, "I'll give you all your lines for the vows. Other than that, the only part of the service you will say is the Lord's Prayer."

"What's that?" asked the groom.

"You mean you don't even know the Lord's Prayer?" said the bride, while playfully hitting the groom with her fake bouquet made of a paper plate, ribbons, and bows. From the quizzical looks on the faces of some of the bridesmaids and groomsmen, I could tell he was not alone.

"How many of you have heard of the Lord's Prayer?" I asked. About half raised their hands.

"How many of you know it by heart?" Only the bride raised her hand.

The Christian Church is no longer at the center of American culture. While 38 percent of Americans told a Gallup Poll they go to church, another study that counts attendance revealed only 20 percent of the U.S. population attends church. Churches are now little more than a lifestyle enclave—and I find this very freeing. We no longer have to live up to what the culture expects us to be or thinks we should be. We can be ourselves. We can experiment, try new things, and joyfully experience the power of the gospel, kind of like dancing when you don't care if anyone's watching. And those who do pay attention may just catch the spirit and power of the gospel, and join in the dance. —*Stephen Smith*

We forgot what?

"The tent poles, I don't see the tent poles," I called to my husband, who was in our Volkswagen bus, unpacking our camping gear. We had just arrived at a woodsy campground for a few days of vacation.

The kids were helping us unpack. But with that announcement, we all stopped what we were doing and stared at each other in dismay. Then we searched through our bags, but the tent poles were definitely not there.

"I saw them on the garage floor, ready to be put in the car," said one of the kids. And we soon realized that they were probably still on the garage floor. Not a good feeling.

Fortunately, we were not off in the wilds, but just an hour from our home (thank God for small blessings). So my husband and the boys turned the car around and went back for the missing tent poles. The girls and I sorted through our gear while we waited, but there wasn't much we could do. We thought about supper and checked our supplies, eager for their return.

We had camped many times over the years, so this was unusual and unexpected for us. We thought ourselves experienced campers. We who waited wandered around the campground, checking out the washrooms, the swimming area, the announcements on the campground bulletin boards. We found some trail markers, read part of a book, looked for birds, and watched a squirrel, until finally the men returned with our tent poles.

We put up the tent, made supper, and gathered at the campfire to make s'mores and listen to stories before we crawled into the tent and our sleeping bags, comfortable and content in God's beautiful forest campground. Now that day is a story—we laugh about it and enjoy the memories. —*Lois Sibley*

A heavy weight

The poet William Stafford was a conscientious objector in World War II. In the collection of his writings on pacifism, *Every War Has Two Losers,* he says this about one person's effect on the world when adopting nonviolent ways of dealing with aggression or the threat of violence: "To hold the voice down and the eyes up when facing someone who antagonizes you is a slight weight—once. But in a lifetime it adds up to tons."

As a conscientious objector who spent time in a work camp where he encountered some who responded with antagonism to his choice, Stafford knew a great deal about the difficulty of the stance he advocates. Though I have no real equivalent experience, I too know that "holding the voice down and the eyes up" is a challenging stance to adopt in my life.

Why is this so challenging? Holding the voice down and the eyes up means steering clear of two impulses that are hardwired in all human beings—"fight or flight," the impulse to fight another in the face of challenge or to absent ourselves from the situation.

Jesus is the paradigm of one who held his voice down and his eyes up, one who neither fled nor fought in the face of antagonism and the human fear that he must have felt throughout his ministry and death.

What tempts you to fight or to flee?

What "weight" will your choice have if you choose to do either? If you choose to do neither? —*Melissa Skelton*

Sabbath

The sabbath was made for humankind,
and not humankind for the sabbath.

—MARK 2:27

The fourth commandment states that we should "remember the sabbath day, and keep it holy" (Exodus 20:8). For many of us that means going to church, but in biblical times the sabbath was a day of rest. People weren't supposed to do any work, and Jesus even got into trouble for doing noble deeds on the sabbath.

Jesus replied to his critics that "the sabbath was made for humankind, and not humankind for the sabbath." That means that the sabbath is good for us. It's not some arbitrary, outdated rule, but a concept that recognizes our need to rest and restore ourselves. We are not called to be productive each and every day; one day out of every week we are supposed to be grateful and dedicate time to appreciating the blessings of this life and the fruits of our labors.

It's hard to do that in the modern world—full as it is of email and kids' soccer games and overdue bills to pay—but it is worthwhile to carve out a sabbath each week. During that time no chores are done, no projects undertaken, no duties fulfilled. Instead, we spend time living the way God intended us to live: in communion with him and with each other.

A holy sabbath is not another task to accomplish, but rather a gift of rest and welcome. We would do well to slow down long enough to receive it. —*Robert Macauley*

Making the most of the second best

*My word shall not return to me empty, but it shall accomplish
that which I purpose, and succeed in the thing for which I sent it.*

—ISAIAH 55:10-11

It was the best sermon I never heard. In 1987, I took *Introduction to the Hebrew Bible* with Dr. Walter Harrelson. All of us were entranced by his wise teaching. We hung on every word. If he had given an altar call at the end of class, I think most of us would have gone forward.

It's odd what stays with you over the years. All I remember now of Harrelson's enthralling lectures is an off-hand comment. Lecturing on Nehemiah, Harrelson noted how first temple ornamentation was gold, but that renovated items were brass, adding, "I once heard an interesting sermon on this text entitled 'Making the Most of the Second Best.'" Then he continued his lecture.

Making the most of the second best. I thought of that after my divorce. I have thought of that grace-filled phrase many times over the years as I have encountered disappointment and setback.

Who gave that sermon that is still speaking to me? Does that person even remember giving it? I rarely remember anything I've preached. But, by God's odd grace, it seems that God's word does indeed accomplish more than we realize or imagine. So if you ever despair, wondering if your efforts for God matter or not, know that they do.

God is at work through your words, actions, and life lived for Christ.

Keep speaking the love of God in Jesus Christ. Leave the results to God's mysterious purpose and grace. Despite any evidence to the contrary, God indeed will have the last word.

—*John Van Nuys*

Humility

When I was a seminary student, one of my best friends was a Jewish student named Fred. Fred and I lived in the same rooming house, which was run by a vicious woman named Patty. Patty invited Fred and me to supper one evening. When we sat down, I was stunned to see that Patty had crumbled bacon over the salad. Didn't she know that Fred, a conservative Jew, could not eat pork? I looked at Fred. He ate the salad without blinking.

Then Patty served the main course. It was ham. The green beans accompanying it had been seasoned with fatback. The twice-baked potato had a strip of bacon on it. I realized that these were not coincidences or oversights—Patty had set out to embarrass and humiliate Fred. She sneered as she placed each dish before him. Fred ate everything, all the while conversing pleasantly.

When Fred and I retired to our rooms, I told him how mortified I had been at Patty's behavior and asked him why he had eaten food that I knew violated his conscience. "The law is a beautiful thing," he said. "Laws about showing respect for people take precedence over laws about diet. To have declined hospitality graciously offered would have been to insult my hostess. One must always be gracious to others. I was therefore bound to eat what was placed before me."

I marveled at Fred's humility. Not only had he cheerfully eaten what he did not want to eat, but he had described Patty's vile behavior as "hospitality graciously offered." When I get to heaven, I expect to find Fred there, probably in a more honored place than the one I'll occupy. If there's a problem with the fact that Fred isn't a Christian, I expect God will find a way around it. —*Richard H. Schmidt*

Buzz kill

I grudgingly admit that mosquitoes are God's creatures. I guess they fall into the "small" category of "All creatures great and small." But let's face it, God has done better work. From a scientific point of view, I suppose these flying leeches serve some purpose in the wider ecosystem, though I can't imagine what it is. "Here, take my blood, make my skin itch like crazy, and then leave me with a potentially deadly virus. Thanks!"

We all have pests in our lives. Some have wings and suck your blood, while others are just annoying and passive-aggressive. It's not unchristian to admit that some people drive us nuts. We all have crosses to bear—although let's not confuse the redemptive power of the cross of Christ with a whiny cousin.

How we treat the pests we encounter in this life says a lot about our character. Jesus tells us to love our enemies, but he doesn't say much about those who annoy us. It's hard to love the neighbor who mows his lawn at 6:00 a.m. on a Sunday morning or the lady who drives 48 miles per hour in the high-speed lane.

While mosquitoes are irritating, it's not as if we allow them to ruin our entire summer. We have coping mechanisms like bug spray and screen doors. In the same way, we can't let human mosquitoes ruin our lives. Coping mechanisms include praying for those who annoy us, breathing deeply, and keeping things in perspective. At least they can't give us the West Nile Virus. —*Tim Schenck*

Bring your heart when you move

We have moved to five states, seven cities, and eleven houses over more than fifty years of married life. I enjoyed each place in turn. However, it is nice now to be retired from hectic schedules. Retired is a relative term, and we still enjoy making new friends and having new interests. I don't think we will ever really retire fully, and that is probably a good thing.

Each place was a fresh challenge. I enjoyed working in new gardens and decorating new (to us) houses. Meeting new friends and finding places to exercise my interests and talents was exciting. The problem I always had was bringing my heart with me at the same time my body moved.

When I began to pray at church on Sunday for the people going up to the communion rail, I knew that my heart had arrived to where my body had been for a while. Loving and knowing people well enough to pray for them is a precious gift, and I am always grateful when I arrive at that place.

Every Sunday after taking communion, my heartfelt prayer is "Thank you, Lord, for feeding me again." In so many places, in so many settings God has fed me and fed my heart so that I may love not only those I have known for many years, but the newcomer behind me, the sick who are not in church today, my whole church family, God's world.

When you move, don't forget to bring your heart.

—*Nancy R. Duvall*

Of drunks and wrecks and liberation

Late one July night, as my husband, our two dogs, and I waited for a traffic signal to turn green, a drunk driver, asleep at the wheel, ran his pickup truck into the back of our car at fifty miles an hour. The good news was that Frank and the dogs were unhurt; the bad news was that I had a collapsed lung and spent the next five days hospitalized with a chest tube, IVs, and other unnatural appendages.

The drunk driver was, predictably, uninsured.

It didn't take Frank and me long to count our blessings. He and the dogs were fine. No cross traffic hit us as our car was shoved through the intersection. The accident occurred close to home after a long trip; it might have happened hours from anywhere, miles from a good hospital, where no one knew us and friends could not reach us. As it was, I received exceptional care and a shower of love from people close to me.

It took me rather longer to feel any mercy toward the other driver. But one day, sitting in a contemplative prayer group, I quite suddenly realized that I had forgiven him. I experienced this not as my own action but as God's gracious gift, right then and there. Of course there would be consequences for this man, but I was surprised and gladdened to realize that I was no longer angry. Were I to speak with him, I hope I could simply express a heartfelt desire that he might know and grow into God's love and yearning for his life.

A wise friend in the prayer group smiled when I shared this realization. "You have been freed," he said.

Freedom! Is this not the mind-bending, heart-bursting truth of forgiveness? —*Betsy Rogers*

Compost

I call myself a gardener, though I am more of a backyard farmer. I do enjoy my perennial flowers, but most of my time and energy go to my berries and vegetables. And, through this, I have become a passionate composter.

I've decided that composting is a great metaphor for the spiritual life. It speaks to many dimensions of our life with God. First of all, like a compost pile in the middle of winter, there is often much going on below the surface that we cannot see. Times that feel dry or dead can actually be times when God is at work within us. Each of us also has parts of ourselves that need to die so that new things can be born. Things in our lives that were good, like leftover scraps of delicious food, can become old. And—like compost's nitrogen and carbon mix and the necessity for water and air—we need to find balance in our lives.

Compost is even a metaphor for the cross. As we see in Jesus' death and resurrection, death sometimes needs to happen for new life to emerge. And, perhaps even more importantly, compost reminds us that we are not in control. We do what we can to enable the process of decomposition: we put in the brown and green materials, we turn it regularly and make sure it is watered. But then our job is simply to wait, to wait as our waste becomes treasure ("brown gold," as passionate composters call it.)

Quite simply, compost happens. In the same way, we can put together the necessary ingredients: a regular practice of prayer, life-giving hobbies and friends, meaningful work, and care for our families. But, in the end, we are not in control; God provides the growth. Often all we do is watch and wait.

—*Nancy Hopkins-Greene*

Sure footing

A construction worker on a roof may need to step on a plank to get from one place to another. At some point the worker makes a judgment about the plank. Will it hold, or will it break and cause a terrible fall? The worker's thoughts about the plank may be hypothetical at first. But if the worker chooses to trust the plank, the decision is no longer abstract. It can be a matter of life or death. When the plank holds (and we hope it will!), the worker knows the truth about the decision and the plank.

This image is drawn from theologian and philosopher Austin Farrer, who also likens a faithful person to a mountain climber depending on the rope of an experienced mountaineer. The mountaineer's help is not engaged until the other climber's weight is on the rope. The relationship becomes effective when the lower climber depends on the rope.

In a similar way, we may consider many interesting opinions about God and the meaning of faith. We can analyze and compare these ideas, and discuss them with others. That's fine, but we don't really know the truth of our theology until we invest ourselves. A would-be swimmer may read many books about swimming, but will only know their real value by diving into the water and beginning to swim. We must live faith—literally depending on God—to know faith.

Jesus died on the cross for our salvation. He could have devoted that Friday afternoon to an interesting and helpful discussion of faith with his disciples, but he put his weight on the cross and trusted God. His resurrection came through the actual cross. We engage his new life as we commit ourselves through decision and action. —*Rob Slocum*

Mary Magdalene

Today is the feast day of Mary Magdalene, the first woman apostle, the faithful servant who walked with Jesus, who watched him die, who watched as he was laid in the tomb, who first saw him raised from the dead, who first told the story of his resurrection.

She is one of my role models, because she risked it all: she broke all the rules, in order to be faithful. Following Jesus meant risking her reputation—in her world, women were chattel, belonging to their fathers or husbands. She followed Jesus anyway. Witnessing Jesus' crucifixion put her in physical danger—the Romans routinely executed family and friends of those they condemned as criminals. Mary Magdalene watched anyway. Confronted with Jesus' death and the seeming end of her dreams, the seeming dashing of her faith, she refused to stop believing. She went to the tomb anyway—and found the Risen Lord. Risking ridicule and disbelief, she first proclaimed the Good News of God in Christ Jesus: He is risen!

Over the centuries, Mary's reputation has suffered among those who felt threatened by her. With no proof, religious leaders have called her an adulteress and prostitute. With great imagination, novelists have taken the little we know of her and distorted it. Her witness has been disputed and derided. She was, after all, merely a woman. Women, too many have said, cannot be faithful bearers of the message.

But this one clear fact remains: Mary Magdalene was a brave— and incredibly faithful—disciple of Jesus. I pray that as a disciple two thousand years later, I can be as brave, as faithful, as Mary Magdalene.
—*Lauren Stanley*

No peace without forgiveness

Desmond Tutu wrote a book called *No Future Without Forgiveness*. In it he explained what he and others had been doing to free the people of South Africa from apartheid. It's an amazing story, hard to read without shock and tears. But I'm glad he wrote it. We need to know. His book is important these days when communication is so easy but conflicts between peoples and nations seem to arise continually. Jesus told his disciples, "Nation will rise against nation" (Matthew 24:7). It's happening all around us.

On a personal level, we all have disagreements with others. There may be hard feelings, verbal abuse, even physical abuse, and we are separated from those who were once close to us. If I were to write a book about such happenings, I think I would call it *No Peace Without Forgiveness*.

If we do not forgive, our inner selves are miserable. We cannot be happy when separated from friends, family members, neighbors, or other church members. Our fellowship is broken and we grieve inside. Lack of peace in our hearts can affect our health and our plans for the day or for the future.

At many places in scripture, we are urged to "seek peace and pursue it" (1 Peter 3:11). We must forgive those who hurt us, and, I suggest, as quickly as possible. Then we may discover we are at peace in our hearts and ready to go on.

If you are in that situation, maybe today is the day you should call that friend or visit that neighbor. Talk it out. Pray. Forgive. And be friends again. The Lord will give you peace, as he promised: "My peace I give to you" (John 14:27). —*Lois Sibley*

Laying down burdens

"Come to me, all you who are weary and carrying heavy burdens, and I will give you rest," Jesus says. "Lay down your burdens," Jesus directs. "Why are you carrying around all this stuff?" Jesus asks, with some exasperation.

"I don't know," I reply, "but I am. And it's heavy."

This is a regular conversation Jesus and I have. Jesus is always the one who starts it. I am always the one who realizes that I have been carrying something around I need to let go of only after I get that reminder. Fortunately, this verse (Matthew 11:28) appears all over the place. A church downtown displays a mosaic of Jesus speaking these words on their wall facing the street. I pass it frequently. I see these words in *The Book of Common Prayer* when I am reading and say them when celebrating the Rite I Eucharist. I hear them spoken at odd times—"odd" in that I realize these words are what I need to hear at those times.

Why do we carry so much stuff around with us? Guilt and shame, mostly (especially!), but also anxiety and worry about things over which we have no control. Grudges. Perfectionism. Prejudices. Things that weigh us down and keep us from being free to love God and neighbor—not to mention being free to love ourselves.

I guess I can say that my penchant for loading myself up does afford me multiple opportunities to experience the sweet relief of laying stuff down. How about you? Repeat after Jesus: "Come to me and lay your burdens down." —*Penny Nash*

Prayerful spaces

My liturgy professor in seminary had a favorite saying: "The space always wins." What he meant was that you shouldn't have a black tie wedding on a beach, or a come-as-you-are wedding in a grand cathedral. Of all the elements in a service, the physical space is the one thing you can't change. You just have to adapt to it.

I frequently think of his words when I enter a prayerful space. It need not be a grand cathedral; it may not be a church at all. It could be someone's home, or an office building, even a restaurant. There are just some places where prayer has so long and fervently been practiced that it literally becomes a place of prayer. It's as if everyone who enters that space is bathed in the prayers that have been offered, and is invited to contribute prayers to that space.

I wonder if looking at prayer that way might expand our spiritual lives. Prayer then is no longer an act isolated to one moment in time; rather, it is a practice that changes not only the hearts of the people praying and those whom they're praying for, but the hearts of the nameless people who will one day enter that space. And what a gift those prayers are to those unsuspecting yet needy souls who encounter a blessing where they may have least expected to, and who as a result are invited into a deeper relationship with God. —*Robert Macauley*

Out of the nest

Hummingbirds are a curious blend of the awe-inspiring and the appalling: tiny beauties that weigh less than a nickel and seem to defy the laws of physics with their speed and grace, their wings beating too fast to see—on average about sixty times per second for the ruby-throated birds who summer here—and their fascinating, beyond-agile maneuvers.

And then there are their aggressive impulses: hummers fight off their fellows, and one in my yard recently went after a bewildered fledgling finch who mistakenly thought a hummingbird feeder might be a pleasant place to perch. The dogfights are spectacular, but their atavism is counterproductive. With plenty of nectar (two feeders, seven apertures, no waiting), more than enough to provide many times their usual ten calories per day per capita, why waste the energy?

Most creatures are programmed to hoard. We, who have reason and philosophy to support a policy of generosity, still fight the urge to hang onto all available resources. Jesus famously told his followers to love their neighbors as themselves, but the Golden Rule has become a constant for lip service in civilized human societies, too rarely observed.

In these days of economic anxiety, we easily revert to the hoarder model, cutting back on our giving and sharing. Jesus again: "Look at the birds of the air; they neither sow nor reap nor gather into barns, and yet your heavenly Father feeds them. Are you not of more value than they?" (Matthew 6:26).

It hasn't registered with the hummingbirds, but we have faith that tells us that there's plenty of nectar to go around, and our Lord's assurance that God's love and generosity will never fail us.
—*Sarah Bryan Miller*

The community of St. Dismas

The first Kairos prison retreat was held in a medium-security prison in southern Alabama more than twenty-five years ago. Kairos is a three-day ecumenical prison ministry where the people who lead it are locked inside with the prisoners and present the gospel to those who have had little chance to know it.

At the first Kairos at this prison, prisoners heard, for the first time in some cases, that Jesus loved them, that those outsiders with them loved them, that there was a chance for them to be at peace, even in a cell and sometimes with no parole coming up.

One huge man, who had come reluctantly, got to his feet and told the group, "I have always been big, and I was expected to be mean 'cause I was big. This is the first time anybody ever told me they loved me." Tears rolled down his cheeks, and down many others.

Clergy, active and retired, began visiting the prison weekly. They baptized inmates and got the bishop to confirm them. Prisoners were paired with churches near their families and prayed for regularly, helped to find jobs when they were released, and were sent church bulletins.

Faith and determination grew, and the inmates asked to become a mission congregation, right there in the prison. The name they chose for their congregation was St. Dismas. Since they could not attend diocesan convention, others carried their pictures on banners up the aisle and read their letter asking that they be made the newest mission of the diocese, a community of intercessory prayer for others. Their wish was granted, and the convention exploded in applause.

Dismas is the legendary name of the thief who died on a cross next to Jesus, asking to be remembered in heaven.
—Nancy R. Duvall

Lord, you have searched me and known me…

The Jerusalem Bible gives Psalm 139 the heading "In praise of God's omniscience." But this psalm speaks of a particular kind of knowledge that God has. God knows us—me!—inside and out. Nothing I can think or feel or want or say or do or fail to do is hidden from him. He has searched me out and known me. He knows my thoughts, my ways, my journeys, my resting-places, my "sitting down and my rising up."

Sometimes I don't want God to know me quite so well! Sometimes I want to flee from his presence, but no matter if I climb to heaven, or descend to the grave, or seek out the uttermost parts of the sea, God is not only there ahead of me but leading me, his right hand holding me fast. Perhaps the darkness will hide me? But no, "darkness is not dark" to God, "darkness and light are both alike."

Being so totally known, all my secrets bared, is unnerving.

It is also magnificently freeing. Since Adam and Eve first fumbled for fig leaves, humankind has tried to cover up the things of which we are ashamed. We wear masks to show the face we choose to the world. We pretend to possess power and strength that is not ours, but God's. We hide what we don't want the world to see. We act the roles we think we want or should, when in truth the only role worth having is not a role at all, but our reality as beloved children of God, made in his image.

No more masks, no more pretense, no more hiding, no more playacting: this is the wonderful liberating truth of Psalm 139. We can forget the fig leaves and rejoice that God knows us through and through, and loves us. —*Betsy Rogers*

Live long and prosper

Zacchaeus, hurry and come down; for I must stay at your house today.
—LUKE 19:5

Few people still believe in predestination anymore. Theologically, the concept is largely abandoned, but psychologically it is embraced as gospel truth: who we are is set by the time we become toddlers; our psycho/social development from birth to age three determines who we are for life.

But as the Bible repeatedly reminds us, people can and do change.

His career, marriage, and life on the line, country singer Waylon Jennings went to the Arizona desert to get clean. There, for the first time, he noticed his young son Waylon, Jr., nicknamed Shooter, scribbling in a coloring book. Taking Shooter on his lap, Waylon held the boy as he colored away for about forty-five minutes. "I'd been on so much cocaine for so long, I'd never been able to sit still that long. Watching my boy, holding him, I decided to never touch cocaine again. And I never did."

Don't write off others—or yourself. If outlaws like Zacchaeus and Waylon Jennings can change, you can, too.

Leonard Nimoy, who portrayed the *Star Trek* character Spock for over forty years, said: "Writers come and go. I am the only constant. If a new writer says Spock's home planet of Vulcan has three moons, I have to remind him that, no, it does not. The actor is the guardian of the character." So, too, you as a moral actor are the guardian of your character. Your present course of action is not predestined. Your choices determine who you are and who you will become.

If you, like Zacchaeus, are ever up a tree, know there is a way to come down and get on a different path. Jesus invites you now. Choose life. —*John Van Nuys*

A lesson from the big book

The morning after I returned from a ten-day trip for work that culminated in the loss of luggage and eyeglasses, my son suggested we go hiking.

Ahead of me up the trail, he talked a mile a minute over his shoulder about everything that had happened while I was away. He waited for me next to a big rock, tapping his Teva on the dry leaves of the path.

The woods were quiet with a lovely stream trickling down a ravine beside the trail. The summit, grand as ever, set us high above a vast lake. Open ocean peeked between the hills. But how red-faced, hot, and sweaty I felt. I opened my bottle to squirt water along my brow and rub my face. Salt dripped into my mouth. Suddenly I felt well and happy and refreshed.

On the way down, we walked along without talking. I thought of how much better I felt here in these airy woods, the blue sky above my head.

I thought of how Philip Newell, in his small treasure about Celtic Christianity, *Listening for the Heartbeat of God*, cites the ninth-century theologian John Scotus Eriugena. Eriugena called scripture the "little book" and creation the "big book," which we can read to divine the grace of God that surrounds us.

I thought of how good the water felt splashing on my hot face. I delighted in this winsome, changing boy who walked before me, bearing my burdensome pack. I thought of how near-sighted I am and how grateful for this enormous, world-sized book laid out before us all, its type as tall as trees. —*Heidi Shott*

Ho hum

I can't seem to concentrate on anything today. The air seems stuffy inside and sultry outside. Even the trees are droopy. Shouldn't I arouse myself and do something—something constructive, something educational, or something fun or silly, but something? I could read a book or write a letter. I could exercise or tidy up my desk. I could put away the clean dishes taking up space in the dishwasher (as I am taking up space in this chair). I could drink a glass of tea or cup of coffee, but that would mean getting up and walking into the kitchen. No, I'll just stare out the window and think of things I might do. Later. Maybe.

Did you experience times like this, Lord? The gospels never say, "Jesus lost interest in everything and sat around bored all day." But then, they wouldn't say that; it's not the sort of thing an evangelist would write down to report to posterity. I'm thinking, Lord, that you might have had days like this because the rest of us do, and if you experienced human life fully, then listlessness would have been part of it. Surely no one, not even the Son of God, can be at the top of his game all the time. But I suspect that when the languid times crept over you, you found a way to give them to your heavenly Father, as you gave everything to your heavenly Father.

Since I am doing nothing right now, Lord, enable me to do nothing faithfully. Take this listless moment and make it a holy moment. Sanctify this nothing, and when the present moment passes, sanctify the next moment as well, whatever I may do. Or not do.
—*Richard H. Schmidt*

Sanctuary

Do you ever go into a church when it's not Sunday morning worship? Even though I work on church property, seldom do I wander in to sit in quiet and soak in the blessedness of the sacred space. When I do I am moved by the beauty and the peace I find.

When I travel I visit churches. In well-known cathedrals that are tourist attractions there is usually a chapel set aside for prayer, but I also seek out smaller churches and sit in the stillness. My senses absorb the essence of faithful generations in their practice of worship. I make no requests of God, yet God provides. The beauty I see expands the beauty of holiness in this soul seeking God.

The sense of God's peace surpasses my human understanding. Those few minutes in sacred stillness influence the quality of the rest of the day. This happens whether the holy space and time is in a church or high in the hills watching the sun and clouds.

The words of the psalms encourage the sojourner. Psalm 46:11 reminds us how important it is to be still and know that God is God. Psalm 103:22 reminds us to bless the Lord in all the places of his dominion. The ongoing challenge is to carve out time, even a few minutes in the day, to place oneself in some part of God's beautiful creation and dwell in the infinity of God's blessing.

Where is your sanctuary for today? —*Ruth Lawson Kirk*

Removing calluses

After three months in Sudan, I return home and go for a pedicure. The woman taking care of me cradles one of my feet gently in her hands and exclaims at its roughness, the result of walking in sandals through dust and dirt and animal waste.

"Where have you been?" she asks in wonder. "Your feet are so...*rough!*"

"I have been living in Africa," I say, "out in the bush. It's rough there. We had very little water, so I couldn't keep my feet clean."

I had tried to keep my feet in decent shape overseas. I had used rocks and sand to scrub them and put lotion on them to soften them. But even so, my feet are a disaster—ugly, rough, dirty. They are, I know, a challenge for this young woman.

She sighs and sets to work, scrubbing away the ingrained dirt, filing off the calluses, rubbing in lotion to restore softness to my soles.

As she labors, as I revel in the love with which she is showering me, I imagine that this is what it feels like to have Jesus wash my feet. I imagine Jesus scrubbing away all the dirt of my life, making me clean again. I imagine Jesus filing away the calluses of my heart, removing its hardness. I imagine Jesus lovingly massaging my soul, restoring its softness. I am convinced that Jesus never simply rinsed his disciples' feet. On the night before he died, Jesus got down on his knees so that he could physically demonstrate what true love felt like.

Nearly an hour later, the woman working on my feet pronounces her verdict: "There. Now they are all clean," she says. "Come back soon. I'll be waiting."

I hear Jesus whispering as well: "Come back soon. I'll be waiting." —*Lauren Stanley*

Just visiting

Last Sunday, visiting another church, I arrived about five minutes before the hour and sat at the end of one of several empty pews near the front.

Two minutes later, a woman came in from the far aisle, looked at me a little bit askance, then sat a couple of seats over. A minute after that, another one came in, this time from the center aisle. "Excuse me," she said, with a touch of frost in her voice, "may I get in here?"

Rising, I realized that I'd committed the essential faux pas of church visiting: the sin of sitting, innocently but still guilty, in someone's Regular Pew. I debated moving. But would that look as though I didn't want to sit with them? What is the proper church etiquette in these situations? I stayed put.

I stayed put, but there was an undertone of discontent vibrating faintly in our pew throughout the service: My presence in their usual spot disrupted their routine.

We are territorial creatures and creatures of habit. I like to sit on the aisle near the front. I do it because my mother always sat there, as did her mother and grandparents, going back to the days of the rented family pew.

Who knows how long my ladies have held down their particular spots? On reflection, I should have smiled brightly and said, "Oh, is this your regular pew? I'm sorry—let me move."

As it is, it's a gentle reminder to me of biblical injunctions, from Genesis through the gospels, of the requirement of hospitality. My brief discomfort is something to keep in mind the next time I'm the one confronting another in a spot I consider my own, and to welcome everyone I meet. —*Sarah Bryan Miller*

The offering plate

We often had children sitting with us in church, and it was hard for the little ones to sit quietly. They had books to look at, crayons and paper to color on, but they got fidgety. We sat near the back usually, just in case a child had to be taken out and so people around us wouldn't be distracted.

I remember one morning when our children were especially active. It was time for the offering plate to be passed. Just as the usher gave it to me, Janie, not seeing the plate coming, jumped up and accidentally hit the plate. It fell crashing to the floor, and coins were soon rolling all around on the wooden floor under the pews. There were many smiles while people leaned down to help us pick up all the money and envelopes that were scattered under several nearby pews. The usher was laughing, but trying not to. The organ was playing so that covered some of the noise, but it was definitely disturbing in our part of the church. I know I was embarrassed, and little Janie was also.

I often remember that as I watch other parents and children in church. And I remember that Jesus wanted the children near him. The disciples tried to shoo them away, as though they were a disturbance, but Jesus said, "No, let the little children come to me, do not stop them; for it is to such as these that the kingdom of heaven belongs" (Matthew 19:14).

It's important for our children to be with us in church as we sing, pray, listen, share the Lord's supper together, and see babies and children baptized. Are we not all beloved children of the living God?

—*Lois Sibley*

A blessed childhood

*It is easier for a camel to go through the eye of a needle
than for someone who is rich to enter the kingdom of God.*

—MATTHEW 19:24

I'm often amazed at the wisdom that comes from unlikely places, at unexpected times. Some years ago I was doing some volunteer work in Tanzania and ended up having breakfast with a British doctor doing the same. There's something about being taken out of your comfort zone—and exposed to great suffering—that breaks down barriers and lets people share more candidly than they usually do.

He and I talked about our formative years. His were spent in a working-class neighborhood in London. He went to public schools, wore hand-me-down clothes, and sometimes there wasn't enough food for his family, so his parents went hungry to let the kids eat their fill. I, on the other hand, grew up in a wealthy suburb of New York. I went to private schools, traveled to Europe with my parents, and wanted for nothing.

I'll never forget what he said to me, as if it were the most obvious thing in the world.

He said, "I am sorry you didn't have the blessings I did, growing up."

What he meant was that, unlike me, he hadn't been encumbered by material possessions. He saw self-sacrifice on a daily basis. And everything he'd achieved in life had been through hard work and, ultimately, by the grace of God. —*Robert Macauley*

Transfigured

He was transfigured before them.

—MATTHEW 17:2

Today is the feast of the Transfiguration. Jesus' appearance to three of his disciples on the mountaintop was an event they remembered for the rest of their lives, a moment of searing clarity when they confronted Jesus' identity as Son of God in stark, incontestable terms. It was as if that truth slapped them in the face. What may have been a vague, undefined awareness now blazed before their eyes, stunning and explicit. Everything suddenly became clear to them. Of course they remembered it in later years. You would have remembered it, too.

I've often wondered about the other nine disciples who were not treated to the vision on the holy mountain. Clearly, such moments are not granted to everyone, not even to everyone among the faithful. Did the three tell the nine about the Transfiguration immediately? If so, did the nine have any idea what they were talking about?

"Mountaintop" moments still occur—charismatic experiences, visions, direct encounters with the divine. Scholars call this phenomenon mysticism, and it isn't limited to Christians. But mystical encounters do not occur to everyone.

No one knows why some people receive a divine revelation and others don't, but this is like everything else in life—people's experiences differ. For someone who wasn't there, it's hard to share in the excitement. When someone who has an experience I have not had tells me how marvelous it was, I want to say "I'm sure it was great—can we talk about something else?"

The important thing isn't who sees what, but what we do about what we see. —*Richard H. Schmidt*

The art of being still

A few years ago, after a wonderful week of scuba diving on coral reefs in the southern Caribbean, I spent the last morning of our trip swimming off the dock of our hotel.

Swimming on the surface, thirty feet above the terrain I had recently dived very close to, I recognized certain distinctive coral heads, a large prickly West Indian sea egg, brilliant purple stovepipe sponges, delicate, translucent vase sponges, and different species each of parrotfish, angelfish, damselfish, and butterflyfish. I recognized them from thirty feet above only because I knew them intimately from close at hand. As a scuba diver I had learned to be still and observe the minutiae of the reef life by using breathing to control buoyancy. I had learned the fundamental rule: be still, don't intrude.

As I paddled around in the gorgeous turquoise, it occurred to me that if one part of God's glorious creation—the ecosystem of the tropical coral reef—is so amazingly complex and fragile, doesn't it follow that other parts of creation—the family, the congregation, the church—each would be just as complex? Think of how nuanced and complicated the corporate life of any group of people is. Yet, if we're on the outside, how easy it is, with a bit of distant observation, to feel we have captured the nut of a place in the palm of our hands.

It's human to be dismissive of people with whom we don't agree or with whom we have little in common. I don't know how to change that, but scuba diving provides some good lessons: control your breathing, be still, watch carefully, and, for God's sweet sake, don't open your mouth. —*Heidi Shott*

On the way

Two of Jesus' disciples, walking to Emmaus later on the day of the resurrection, were joined by an unexpected companion. The disciples were sad, talking about everything that had happened when their Lord died, and at first they didn't recognize Jesus. As they walked, he interpreted the things that were said about him in the scriptures. It was late in the day when they approached the village. The disciples persuaded him to stay, and recognized Jesus as they shared bread (Luke 24:13-31).

We are all travelers, and the road can be a challenging place. Even if we don't encounter bandits or highwaymen, we may lose our way and get lost. We may miss our connection and find ourselves stranded. Our luggage may fly away to an unexpected destination. We may wonder where to find needed services, or even the next exit. The road can be threatening and disorienting. Our availability to others and the unknown may be more than we bargained for when we started. On the road we face our need.

But the road can be a place of discovery as well as vulnerability. Jesus finds the disciples on the way to Emmaus, between their point of origin and destination. They meet as dusk approaches, so they stand literally between light and darkness. In these gathering shadows, Jesus reveals the meaning of the scriptures and his suffering. He discloses himself to them. Their hearts burn within them as they talk with him on the way (Luke 24:32).

Our travels make it possible for us to step into something new. We may find that Jesus meets us in the dusky places of our need and reveals himself to us. If the experience of the journey makes a difference for us, we'll be new people when we arrive.
—*Rob Slocum*

Splintered tillers

We were sailing on Lake Michigan's Green Bay, on a gorgeous sunny day. Headed south, into a strong wind, we were tacking back and forth across the breeze. The hull smacked hard against high waves, and the boat heeled over under the wind's force. The wind was strong enough that it took real effort to come about, to turn the boat to the opposite tack.

Usually my husband skippers, but I had taken the helm while he stretched out in the sun. It was time to tack to port, so I pushed hard on the tiller. I felt an odd twinge against my palm, and then, with a resounding crack, the tiller snapped in two. I was left, stunned and completely at a loss, holding a short piece of splintered oak. The boat turned in the water and started sliding north with the waves...toward the unfortunately named Death's Door strait (truly!).

Frank quickly started the motor and got us headed back in the right direction. There are times when we're grateful for the iron sail.

But that single moment stayed with me: that instant of realization that the control we think we have is an illusion. Whether at work or in our families or neighborhoods or churches, we can strain against the tiller and try to make things go our way, and for a time we might think we've succeeded. But very soon we find that we're not in charge; God is. The flimsy implements we use—our words, our passionate exhortations, our agendas and organizational models and plans and power plays—are just so many splintered tillers. God will work his purpose out, and our lives only really find fulfillment when we sail with the divine purpose, not across it. —*Betsy Rogers*

Incarnating the kingdom

Then I saw a new heaven and a new earth.

—REVELATION 21:1

My son and I never miss the Indiana State Fair. He likes the rides; I like the animals; we both like the food. It is always a hot, noisy, fun time. But in a quiet corner of the fairgrounds, fairgoers are invited to rest a bit in another world at the Pioneer Pavilion, where nineteenth-century Indiana comes alive. Women in long skirts and aprons stitch quilts, dip candles, and prepare food. Men in straw hats and bib overalls run coal-fired machines, cutting logs and threshing wheat. Draft horses circle, grinding sorghum. Blacksmiths pound red-hot horseshoes. An entire world is brought to life to show how Hoosier life once was.

As the church, we are to bring Christ's way to life to show everyone how God's life is. Pointing out exhibits grown from differing seed varieities, the legendary civil rights activist Clarence Jordan, of Georgia's Koinonia Farm, wonderfully said that the church is to be "a demonstration plot for the gospel." As the advance guard of the kingdom, we are to demonstrate to the world the new variety of life that God is sowing, growing, and bringing to harvest.

In a selfish world haunted by scarcity, we are to demonstrate generosity by trusting in God's abundant grace. In a vengeful world, we are to witness to Christ's heavenly way as we forgive seventy times seven. In an eye-for-an-eye world blinded by hate, we are to be peacemakers, incarnating reconciling love.

The good news is that God's world is here. You are part of that arriving kingdom as you incarnate Christ today, demonstrating and sharing his love for all. The glad dawning of God's new day is at hand. —*John Van Nuys*

On the porch

It was so brutally hot, for so interminably long, that it just did not occur to me to go out on the porch.

Through weeks of temperatures in the 90s and low 100s this summer—with humidity to match—I went from the air-conditioned house in the air-conditioned car to the (nominally) air-conditioned office, and if my friend and I took our morning walk, it was at our usually-cold-weather-only destination, the air-conditioned mall.

The porch remained a haven for the cats: screened and roofed, offering a fine selection of sunbeams for lazing and a first-rate observation post for bird-and bunny-supervision. The heat doesn't seem to be an issue for the felines in the family. Iris the Orange Menace, in particular, likes to keep her paw on the pulse of our small slice of suburbia: no weather wimp she.

What sent me out was the arrival, ninety minutes early, of the cleaning team, a four-woman scrubbing, dusting, mopping, vacuuming tornado. There was nowhere in the house for me to work, and I was on deadline. I retreated to the only place I could go—the porch.

And stayed there. The weather had turned; the day was delightful, with a soft breeze and soft temperatures to match. With the phone and the laptop, I had an instant office annex, screened by blooming roses, enlivened by goldfinches and hummingbirds.

Sometimes we just need a little push to send us out of our ruts. Sometimes there's a change in the weather, and we're too focused to notice it. When that happens, the arrival of a helpful tornado at a seemingly inopportune time may be the best blessing we can have.
—*Sarah Bryan Miller*

Angle of vision

Everything we see or think about, we see or think about through some sort of lens. We are not always particularly aware of our lenses, and our lenses naturally change over time—"when I was a child, I thought like a child..." (1 Corinthians 13:11). They change just by virtue of our own selves changing.

We also are capable of deliberately choosing a lens through which to view the world, or at least a particular situation. We can choose to see through the eyes of another. We can choose to see another point of view. But it takes courage to do so.

Wouldn't it be nice to go through life with our lenses arranged like a kaleidoscope where we could make a slight turn and easily look at things differently? Where we could see the same experiences or "facts" rearranged? We could always be ready to view a situation or a person or an idea through multiple lenses.

Instead, we cling to our own point of view so tightly that we cannot see that there may be other points of view. Others may have lenses that are quite valid and valuable, but often we feel that there can only be one way to see something—and those who see it our way are right and those who do not see it our way are wrong. Sometimes we judge others' lenses as inferior and say, "When you get older, you'll see it my way and then you'll understand." As if "you" don't actually have any understanding now.

Mea culpa, I am so guilty of this. Lord, today, give me eyes to see as others see. —*Penny Nash*

A growing vision

If you have faith the size of a mustard seed, you will say to your mountain
"move," and it will move, and nothing will be impossible for you.

—MATTHEW 17:20

A friend of mine was the founding priest for a new congregation. The property had been purchased, and he took a friend who was a visiting missionary from a foreign country to see it. They stood in the field that the congregation had just purchased, and my friend shared his vision with his visitor. He talked about the construction of a small building that would serve as the first worship space, and said that after some years they hoped to one day build a large church building that would accommodate many people.

The missionary looked at my friend and said, "Your vision is an insult to God. Build the big building now. Invite large crowds of people now." He shook his head and said again. "Your vision is an insult to God."

The priest was somewhat taken back, but the man's words got him thinking. He shared his experience that day with the congregation, and it got them thinking too. Before long, their plans changed and a really big beautiful building was designed and built, and the congregation grew in number and spirit beyond all their expectations, and the kingdom came a little closer.

Over time my friend became regarded as a "church planting specialist." He said he found this amusing as it all started with someone telling him that he insulted God. Whatever the cause, the whole congregation took a leap of faith, and their expectations were exceeded beyond their understanding, and the mountains moved once again. —*Jason Leo*

Jesus saves

I passed a billboard recently that displayed the words "Jesus saves." I didn't like it, and I didn't want to meet the person who had put up the billboard. A cartoon I had seen years earlier came to mind: A church and a bank were located across the street from each other. The church's sign said, "Jesus saves" while the bank's said, "You should, too."

Part of my negative reaction to the billboard, I later realized, arose from a dangerous spiritual pride on my part. As an educated (maybe overeducated) professional clergy type in The Episcopal Church, I don't use expressions like "Jesus saves." I believe he does save, but I don't talk that way. In my younger days, I looked down my long snooty nose at preachers who did talk that way, and maybe I'm not entirely past that even now.

There was another reason, though, that the "Jesus saves" billboard bothered me. It seemed to be trying to tell me what I needed without first getting to know me. But why should that have offended me? I have, after all, experienced in my own life the truth of the message the sign sought to convey—I know that Jesus saves, because Jesus has saved me, and I love telling people about it. The person who put up the billboard may have experienced something like what I have experienced. Perhaps we would become friends, even soulmates, if we met and shared our stories.

Sharing—that's the thing that was missing in the billboard. The communication was one-way. I was not asked who I was or what I needed or longed for. I felt lectured to, talked down to. So the message didn't come to me as "good news." —*Richard H. Schmidt*

Learning from creation

I love to watch God's creation at work. I love stopping whatever I'm doing to examine the world around me, taking note of the birds of the air, the fish of the sea, the creatures of the land.

Living in Sudan, with little electricity, no TV, limited access to the Internet, and an exceedingly small stash of books, I learned to appreciate creation in whole new ways.

I joined with friends to cheer as geckos stalked insects for their dinner, picking one gecko out of dozens as "mine," urging it on, directing it to the next tasty bug in its path. *C'mon, baby, get that one!*

I watched ants for hours, astonished at their ability to work together, dozens struggling to carry an insect carcass up the side of a building to their secret lair. *Don't give up! You're almost there!*

I giggled as the ewes deliberately turned in tight circles to keep the rutting rams away from them. *You tell him you mean it when you say no, honey!*

I adopted a pair of birds in the springtime, laid out bits of string and tiny sticks for their nest, kept watch anxiously as they brooded over their eggs, and celebrated when the babies were born. *The babies are here! Listen to them chirp!*

I squatted down and looked in wonder at new plants that had forced their way out of the parched earth, astonished that anything could grow there. *Where did these come from?*

I stopped in midsentence to stare in astonishment at wildly colorful birds swooping down over the schoolyard. *They are so beautiful!*

God's creation is endlessly fascinating, a feast for the eyes and the heart. *Thank you, Lord, for all that you have made, for all the blessings of this life.* —Lauren Stanley

Companions on the journey

In the early morning I stood at the entrance of the footbridge spanning a Spanish river on the Camino de Santiago de Compostela. Some of the younger pilgrims in the group had gladly started across, and the narrow bridge was bouncing and swaying. I froze. I don't like bridges. I am anxious even crossing them in cars, so a long suspension bridge constructed of wire and wood was more than I could manage.

Other companions noticed. Instead of teasing or chastising, the pilgrim who was a high school principal promised to go with me every step of the way. "Look around," he encouraged. "It's beautiful." Another young pilgrim stepped to my left side and linked arms with me. "I'll keep you safe." A voice from behind advised that I take a breath and step out in faith.

Surrounded by so great a cloud of witnesses, I stepped onto the footbridge and began to walk. Words of encouragement urged me to move into the beauty all around me: the mist on the water, the path curling and rising in the distant green. Before I realized, I was stopped in the middle of the bridge studying a glistening spider's web in the crisscross of wire. Now it was no longer fear but appreciation and wonder that gave me reason to pause. Once across, I hugged my companions and expressed my gratitude for their support. I heard, "You do the same for us, you know."

On my good days I am aware of the loving witness we share as Christians on the journey. In that pilgrimage moment my heart swelled with gratitude to our God. In loving wisdom, God sets the solitary in community, some families by blood and some families by the bonds of shared journeys in faith, and hope, and love.
—*Ruth Lawson Kirk*

Arcs

An arc is a curved line segment. If an arc is extended far enough it will eventually transcribe a circle that defines a center. The wider the arc, the longer it will need to extend to make a circle—and the more difficult it may be to visualize the circle that the arc will become. Its center point may also be difficult to imagine or locate. An arc moves from point to point without going through the space that is directly in between. So an arc is more indirect than a straight line in moving to a point, but it avoids some potential obstacles.

Martin Luther King Jr. once quoted the abolitionist Theodore Parker, who said, "The arc of the moral universe is long, but it bends toward justice." Sometimes we need to move from one point to another, but a linear progression is impossible. The next step cannot simply follow the previous one along a direct path. It would be tempting to push straight ahead, but that's not possible or helpful.

The real direction is more subtle, and changes along the way. It may be hard to see exactly where the path is leading because it involves a sequence of turns. The trajectory may be uncertain, with the final shape only visible to hindsight and reflection. But the arc's curve can also be a kind of quantum leap, moving over an intervening space or barrier to a new level, taking shape in ways that only become clear as the arc unfolds.

Even when the direction of things is unclear, we can follow the arc to its completion, and find its center. —*Rob Slocum*

Control

You shall not make for yourself an idol, whether in the form of anything
that is in heaven above, or that is on the earth beneath,
or that is in the water under the earth.

—Exodus 20:4

There was a time back in seminary when I doubted things I once had been certain about, and the path before me seemed impassable. I sought counsel from people I trusted and admired and I prayed faithfully, but I was still troubled.

The answer came from an unexpected source. All students were required to meet with the academic dean—whom I knew only in passing—prior to graduation. I ended up sharing with him my spiritual struggles.

"I feel like my life is out of control," I said.

After listening attentively, he swiveled in his chair and gazed out the window, where the trees were just beginning to bloom.

"You know," he said, "I think control is antithetical to the religious life."

In just ten words, he identified my struggle and showed me the way forward. I realized that I was placing too much trust in myself, in my beliefs and aspirations. I began to understand that idols aren't just gold statues; they can also be our own agendas, no matter how well-intentioned.

As I left his office, I felt my fists unclenching. I started to let go of my certainties, and began to wonder again who God wanted me to be. For the first time in a very long while, I was able to sit and pray and listen, without fear of what God might be saying. —*Robert Macauley*

God works in mysterious ways

Writer Reynolds Price, whose faith began during his North Carolina childhood, was diagnosed with advanced spinal cancer in 1984. Before radiation began, the Oxford-educated Price had a vision. As described in *Letters to a Godchild: Concerning Faith,* Price experienced himself reclining by the Sea of Galilee. A man approached, inviting him into waist-deep water where, from above, Price saw the horrific surgical scar running the length of his spine and tattooed lines to guide the coming radiation. The man beside him began pouring handsful of water over the scar. Recognizing Jesus, Price heard the words, "Your sins are forgiven."

"I didn't want that," recalled Price. "I asked, 'Am I healed?' Jesus stated, 'That, too.'" And the vision ended.

Afterward, Price wondered how seriously he should take that experience. He proceeded with radiation though the vision said he was healed because his trusted oncologist told him to. The radiation began and, as doctors had predicted, Price became a paraplegic.

After the vision, Price endured two frightful years of painful cancer treatment. No other consolatory visions came. Price said, "I never lost my faith, although I felt nearly tortured by what I thought was God. Speaking to the dark one night, I said aloud, 'How much more of this is there?' And although I don't think this could have been recorded by a microphone, I audibly heard a voice that said: 'More.'" Unbeknownst to Price, his prognosis was only eighteen months, but he ultimately lived another twenty-seven years.

Given his post-vision suffering and subsequent lifelong paraplegia, how did Price ultimately interpret his vision? "I realize mine was not a 'Lourdes-worthy' healing. I cannot explain it. I just know it happened. As the gospel song says, 'God works in mysterious ways his wonders to perform.'" —*John Van Nuys*

The comfortable words

It's almost time for school to begin again, and that always feels like the beginning of the new year to me. Our Knit Wits group will begin meeting again as will other groups that haven't met since spring. I almost want to say "Happy New Year! It's time to begin again!"

I'm remembering that often on the real New Year's Eve, we attended a service at a small chapel near us. The leader was Dr. Philip E. Hughes, who was an associate at that church. When he said in his slight South African/British accent, "Hear what comfortable words our Saviour Christ saith unto all who truly turn to him," I was more than ready to listen.

It was several years before I realized that he was reading from the 1928 *Book of Common Prayer*. We believe those words and they are a great comfort. No matter which Prayer Book you prefer, they are important words for our church and our people.

"Hear what comfortable words our Savior Jesus Christ says to all who turn to him." That's the way I introduce the comfortable words now when each month I visit the sick and shut-ins as a eucharistic visitor for our parish. Then I read to them the promises of God quoted in the current Prayer Book on page 332.

I'm pretty sure they like to hear those familiar words. After that, we exchange the Peace. Then we pray the Lord's Prayer together and share the bread and the wine. And each of us is comforted, knowing the Lord loves and cares for us in each new day, no matter what our circumstances may be. Thanks be to God! —*Lois Sibley*

Jesus shall reign

Some travel takes us to sunny beaches and lovely landscapes. Some teaches us about history or archaeology or world events. But then there's travel that shakes us to our bones and becomes a journey of the heart.

Such was the trip I took to Guatemala in 1992, with the Presiding Bishop's Fund for World Relief (now Episcopal Relief & Development), to see the work of this vital agency among the poor and disenfranchised. We observed Guatemala City's grinding poverty, where flimsy shacktowns flanked high-rise apartments. We saw children hawking handicrafts to earn a few coins, and little girls in the countryside bent double under loads of firewood. We visited tiny farm plots carved from mountainsides, with farmers scraping out crops of cabbages and corn.

We also talked with community workers, who daily risked being "disappeared" for nothing more than trying to bring water, electricity, and farm cooperatives to their villages.

On a bright Sunday morning, we attended the weekly English-language service at the Cathedral of St. James. There we sang "Jesus Shall Reign," which I have never heard the same way since:

> *Blessings abound where'er he reigns;*
> *The prisoners leap to loose their chains,*
> *The weary find eternal rest,*
> *And all who dwell in want are blest.*

In the providence of God's dream for us there is abundance for everyone, though our greed and indifference have turned this abundance into hoarding for a few and untold suffering for many.

I came home newly, acutely aware of God's calling: to share my abundance, to help his suffering children, and to dream his beautiful dream for this broken world. I'm still learning to respond. —*Betsy Rogers*

The death knell

When my husband and I were first married, we taught high school on an island in Micronesia. As we left school one afternoon, a funeral for a young child was about to begin at the cathedral next door. Walking into the dusty parking lot, we heard the death knell. *DONG*, an excruciating pause. *DONG*, the vibration took endless seconds to dull. We were frozen in our tracks, struck by the emotional power of a bell rung ever so slowly for this child unknown to us and for the deep sorrow of the mourners as they arrived in twos and threes. As late as the mid-1980s, telephones were rare. People still depended on church bells.

The evocative power of the death knell: twenty-five years later and I still recall how dirty my sandals were as I bowed my head to listen.

John Donne had it right. There is no need to send for whom the bell tolls. It tolls for each of us, every single time. "I am involved in mankind," he wrote, almost four hundred years ago. But isn't life much easier when we aren't involved, when we stay aloof? Christians are called to be involved, but the choice to actually do so remains ours.

Involvement is the act of choosing. I can do a hundred little things that will make a difference in my tiny sphere: a kind word, a note, a phone call, a batch of cookies, a held door, a well-timed wink, a squeeze to someone's arm, a witty email, a smile, a nod.

May we choose to be involved in the lives of people we encounter on the way. —*Heidi Shott*

The gift of friends

Now when Job's three friends heard of all these troubles that had come upon him...they met together to go and console and comfort him. They sat with him on the ground seven days and seven nights.

—JOB 2:11, 13

Jesus refers to this famous passage to assure us that God is with us forever and that our souls are nourished and safe in his hands.

Good friends are a gift from God. True holy friendship lasts, withstanding the trials of time and distance. Genuine friends celebrate and grieve with us. Lasting friends are loyal and responsive. They are the people who will drop anything to aid us.

My wife is undoubtedly my best friend, but I have others. Mark is such a friend. We've known each other for years and work out together at the gym each day. We know everything about one another. When his father passed away, I was there to comfort Mark. When I recently lost my job, many people prayed but Mark took the extra step and lined up interviews for me, allowed me to use space at his office, advised me on how to set up my own business, grieved with me. Our kids even turn to each of us as a second father. In any need we can call one another, day or night, and it would never be a bother.

Our relationships carry us through life and help buoy us in all situations. Let's make sure that these special friends don't go by the wayside because we choose to disconnect or are simply too complacent to pick up the phone. Make it your goal to reconnect today.

And remember Jesus is our most constant friend. —*Carl Kinkel*

What a friend we have in Jesus, all our sins and griefs to bear!
—JOSEPH SCRIVEN

Letting go

I remember the moment I first felt like a *former* parent. Our two youngest sons were departing for a three-week tour of Europe sponsored by their secondary school. We were glad for them, but felt bereaved without them. It wasn't merely the boys themselves we missed—it was also our sense of being in charge of them, our control over them.

God gives some people (like parents) limited control over some things (like children) for limited periods of time. Control feels good. Therefore we cling to it. But in time, control passes to someone else. Our children grow up and move away. We lose our jobs. Someone else becomes chairman, manager, chief-of-staff, principal, or rector. Our mental and physical faculties decline, and with them, our influence over others. Then we die. Each of us will experience these things; only the details will vary. Having fought all our lives for control, we must in the end relinquish all control.

Why does this depress me? Probably because I have not reached the point in my faith where I understand that my limitations do not separate me from others, but unite us all in a community of powerless people who share the experience of depending upon God.

We can trust God with our lives, our children's lives, our church, our work, our relationships, our death, and eternity. Or not. Trusting God, we embrace each new day as an opportunity—like the opportunity to rediscover each other that my wife and I received after our children grew up and left home. It's about trust. Even as we approach death, that final relinquishing of control, it remains a question of trust—either we trust God or we don't. I'm getting there. —*Richard H. Schmidt*

Fast forward

Once when I was serving in a large parish I went to the media center with another staff member. We watched a video on parish life, and put the video on "fast forward" mode to find a particular segment for an upcoming program. As I watched the television screen, images from parish life flickered by at two or three times normal speed. Meetings were held, hospitality was offered, pastoral conversations were shared, a Christmas pageant unfolded, communion was distributed at the altar rail—all at lightning speed.

I watched with fascination and horror. The "fast forward" mode created a distortion of the parish life video, but it showed the truth. Everything there was on "double time." Life and ministry were hectic, stressed, fast. "Fast forward" didn't work!

There are times when we need to rest. A rest in a musical composition doesn't mean the piece is over or lacking in energy. A field may lie fallow so it can again produce good crops. God commands the people of Israel to remember the sabbath day and keep it holy, doing no work on the sabbath (Exodus 20:8-10). The Prayer Book collect for Saturdays asks that God may help us to put away all earthly anxieties, and be "duly prepared" for the service of God's sanctuary, so our rest on earth can be a preparation for the eternal rest of God's people in heaven (*The Book of Common Prayer*, p. 99).

Jesus invites us to rest. We may recall Jesus' words of invitation: "Come to me, all you that are weary and are carrying heavy burdens, and I will give you rest" (Matthew 11:28). Jesus never asked his disciples to be hyperactive. He invites us to be centered, whole, and well in faith. —*Rob Slocum*

Lying awake

Many of us do not get enough rest. At morning gatherings usually at least one person is yawning, another reports not sleeping well lately, and someone else nods sympathetically while offering coffee. Many of us know the experience of lying awake.

Why do we lie awake at night? Why is it that only babies "sleep like a baby" and the rest of us only occasionally do so—and when it finally happens, we brag about it in the morning as if it were a conquest?

Practitioners of contemplative prayer say they are resting in the arms of God. For me, trying to be contemplative most often becomes a time when my mind goes off in a million directions and I end up composing a grocery list just to try to salvage something from the effort.

But even if I do not often experience it as such, contemplation is making room for a very deliberate kind of lying awake, a resting in expectation and assurance that the Holy One desires to gather us to the Holy Self in a place of safety and rest. Which is very different from the usual kind of lying awake, the mind-racing and heart-pounding variety, where everyday problems become mountains, obstacles become magnified, and peace is something that other people may have but not me.

And yet a glimpse of peace can be enough. A few moments of rest can provide a counter-experience to lying awake. I wonder—if I had more moments during the day of lying awake in peace in the arms of God, would I stop lying awake at night? —*Penny Nash*

Holy walking

It's a blessing to be able to walk to church. We live only two blocks away and Sunday mornings find us walking, looking up and all around. We enjoy the quiet, the beauty of the trees, the sounds of birds who seem to be joyfully going about their business.

The hardest part is crossing a busy street. Before the early service, there are few cars rushing down the street, but after that it is difficult to cross. I often pray my way across and when it proves to be an easy crossing, I say, "Thank you, Jesus," with much appreciation.

We walk on, with anticipation. What will the music be today? What scripture texts? What will we learn and understand about their meanings? And how can we best apply them to our own lives and situations? When we pause at the threshold, then step into the church, will we be ready and eager to join our friends in worship? For how many hundreds, thousands of years, have believers prayed their way along, walking up the hills to Jerusalem to worship God?

More than two hundred years ago, near a quiet village in eastern Massachusetts, Abigail Adams walked to church with her children. There were no cars. They passed a cow in the pasture, or they saw sheep in a neighbor's fields. Her husband John was off in Boston with his law practice, or attending sessions of Congress in Philadelphia, or maybe in France with Benjamin Franklin.

Talking with her children as they went along, Abigail called it "holy walking." I think of her explaining to them the blessings of freedom to attend the church of choice and to participate in holy walking, as we prepare to worship together the God who is Creator, Redeemer, Shepherd, and Friend. I tell my children of her example, and I hope and pray they will remember as they grow and do their own holy walking. —*Lois Sibley*

God's daily gift

Each one is a gift, no doubt,
mysteriously placed in your waking hand
or set upon your forehead
moments before you open your eyes.
—BILLY COLLINS, "DAYS"

At the end of each summer, my family makes its way to Maine's Acadia National Park for a few days of camping and hiking.

Waking up early in a tent somehow banishes the domestic and workaday worries that plague me the rest of the year. Somehow I'm able to appreciate more clearly the gifts of clean air and fresh water; of good food cooked over the campfire and the pleasure of reaching the top of a mountain with tired legs and a sweaty face. By mountain standards the peaks of Acadia are only biggish hills, but on clear days the views of the glacial lakes and the outline of the piney islands off the Atlantic coast take my breath away.

Each day—no matter where we awake—bestows its own gifts. Sometimes it's difficult to learn to let old gifts go and allow new gifts emerge. Each day God offers us some combination of the constant and the new: the constant of God's great love to reassure and empower, and the new to challenge us to grow in grace and in sharing that love with those we encounter on the way.

Each day as you awake, remember what you know to be true; remember you are well-loved. Remember it is worth the struggle to climb out of your cozy tent and into the new day to accept whatever is out there. —*Heidi Shott*

The feline ministry to the sick

There is a school of thought that holds that animals don't—or can't—really love the people with whom they're associated, that the (alleged) affection they display is based strictly on such pragmatic drives as gaining food and warmth.

Those of us who share our lives with pets know the scientific response to that theory: piffle.

In fact, science is catching up with what we've known all along; a rash of recent newspaper articles cites various studies that show that cats and dogs, at least, genuinely love the people with whom they share their lives. (I'm not so sure about ferrets, but then I've never cared for weasels.)

Finding the evidence is as easy as getting sick and taking to your bed. When you're genuinely unwell, if there's a cat in your home you're pretty sure to find yourself with a concerned and cuddly companion. They know.

My friend Margaret and I call this the "feline ministry to the sick," or FMS. As little as cats are known for pure altruism, this is an area in which they shine. I have sometimes had all three of the resident purrballs perched on and around me on my bed; at other times, they take it in shifts. But when I'm ailing, I'm seldom without furry companionship.

Some will hold that our pets are doing it only to encourage us to get functional again, so that we can attend to their food dishes. I don't think so. I believe that the unconditional, unjudgmental love and concern shown by cats in their FMS mode is a reflection of God's love, the divine love that runs through all creation and binds it together.

Deo gratias. —*Sarah Bryan Miller*

Moonlight

One of the most profound spiritual experiences of my childhood came one night when I was looking out over the ocean. There were no clouds, and the moon was bright and nearly full. It was rising slowly in the eastern sky, seeming to hover over the horizon. And there was a clear white path leading straight from the moon to me, the reflection of the moonlight on the calm sea.

I walked a few feet in one direction and then farther in the other, yet no matter where I went, the path of light pointed at me. It reminded me of the love of God, which comes directly to each of us, wherever we are. There is no escaping it, no matter how hard we might try.

I was also struck by the light of the moon, which wasn't its own. I knew even then that the moon only shone because of the sun's light reflecting off it. I could never have had that experience with the sun itself, which is so bright that you can't look straight at it. The sun also bathes the whole world not only in light but also in warmth, so the path sunlight takes straight to our heart isn't as obvious as the path taken by moonlight.

It seemed like wisdom was all around me that night: God's love reaching out to us as individuals, communicated to us not only directly but indirectly in ways that we're able to see, through the love of others, the beauty of the world, and the unexpected gifts that stay with us for the rest of our lives. —*Robert Macauley*

A new beginning

There are 1,050 videos that appear on YouTube when you search using the words "first day school bus." In most, a child appears at the edge of a front yard that bears the marks of late summer: green grass with yellow, parched spots. The boy or girl is dressed in shorts or a sleeveless top and, alternately, looks back at the camera and then down the street for the arrival of the big, loud, yellow, and inevitable school bus. On the child's back is an impossibly large backpack, and on the child's face is a miserable smile.

This for me is a little icon of what it feels like as an adult to stand looking into the fall with all its activities and obligations after summer vacation.

In the Book of Exodus, God tells Moses and Aaron that the year is to begin with the month in which Passover occurs, the event through which God delivered the Jewish people from their bondage in Egypt. With their liberation from slavery, then, God returned their time to them. From that time forth, they, not their oppressors, would decide how they would spend their time.

This way of seeing time is vital for us as we begin our cycle of activity anew each year. It means we will need to look at what we think are fixed obligations—things we "have" to do—and ask ourselves the hard questions of what in our freedom we want to choose to do. All this is in response to a God who gives us both freedom and dignity and asks us to choose a life worthy of both.

What do you want to do with your time in this coming year? What "oppressors" will you need to turn away from to have this time?
—*Melissa Skelton*

Get low

Go, and sit down at the lowest place.

—LUKE 14:10

In the aftermath of Hurricane Katrina, New Orleans police shot one man and severely beat his brother. The two were simply out searching for medical help. As the surviving brother was being interviewed, something incredible happened: The man suddenly burst into tears. Not tears of rage, but forgiveness.

"I forgive that police officer. I forgive him with all my heart. Because if I don't, God ain't going to forgive me when I do something wrong. I forgive him. I forgive him. And I'm trying to deal with this every day, but it's *hard*. It feels like something just is *gone* that I had in my heart—it's *gone*. I ain't never gonna get it back. I can't see him no more. We can't do the things we normally would do. I miss my *brother*. I *miss* him."

"Go," says Jesus, "sit down at the lowest place, so that when your host comes, he may say to you, 'Friend, move up higher'; then you will be honored in the presence of all who sit at the table with you."

The man who forgave his brother's killer knows what Jesus is talking about. He knows it because he is doing it. And so will we when we dare to go where Jesus goes and do what Jesus does. If we are humble, faithful, and loving enough to follow Jesus, then we truly will be beside our Host when he says, "You have a place at my table. Take and eat. This is my body and blood broken and shed for you. Do this in remembrance of me."

Your place at our Savior's table is secure—thanks to the costly grace of our humble, loving Lord who was willing to die for you. Follow him. Get low. *—John Van Nuys*

Grace is my river

Several years ago my husband and I were co-leaders with another couple at a retirement conference for bishops and spouses. One of our exercises was for each participant to draw his or her life as a river, with stops along the way for major events and crises. A clear voice in my head said, "Grace is my river." I wrote down my thoughts in a poem and after some additional work, this is what I came up with:

> *Grace is my river.*
> *It flows through my life, sometimes slowly,*
> > *sometimes overwhelming in its nourishing floods.*
> *It takes me around jagged rocks of death and disappointment,*
> > *missed opportunities and what ifs…*
> *Far more often my river holds waters of comfort for my soul.*
> *Its cleansing tides of love and faith move me through the shallows*
> > *of self-doubt and self-pity.*
> *Grace is my river.*
> *It flows through my life. When my frail boat of faith fails me,*
> > *I ask Grace to enfold me with its warm embrace.*
> *Oh Grace, carry me, carry me on*
> > *to the arms of Jesus at the throne of God.*

When I showed this to a relative who is a nonbeliever, he asked, "What is grace?" The best answer I could give him was something as wonderful as love and as undeserved as happiness, far more than we hope for or can work for, a pure gift from God. Kathleen Norris, in her wonderful book *Amazing Grace*, compares it to the delighted smile of a child who sees only friends as she looks around an airport. Webster's dictionary gives one meaning as "God's unmerited love for humans." Any of these definitions suits me. Please God, I need lots. —*Nancy R. Duvall*

Open my eyes, Lord

On a family vacation in St. Croix, I went snorkeling for the first time. As a neophyte, my first impulse when I jumped into the water was to remain upright, where I saw the same familiar world all around me—the surface of the water, islands near and far, the boat, my daughter, other people.

"Put your face in the water!" the native guide commanded, so I did, and what astonishment followed! Simply facing a new direction, reorienting and opening my eyes, I saw an entirely new world, a parallel but wholly different dimension. The water was crystalline, the sand dazzlingly white, and the fish so near I could have touched them. And what fish! Brilliantly colored in blues and greens and oranges and yellows and reds...striped, spotted, mottled...large and small...of varied shapes...swimming singly and in schools, including one huge mass of gorgeous blue tangs. All kinds of corals formed a spectacular reef, more of God's creatures in the most entrancing forms and textures.

The experience was amazing. What startled me most was the reality of this totally different world—to which I had been oblivious—right there, right beneath me, simply waiting for me to notice. Isn't that what the spiritual life is like? The reality of life in Christ exists right here, right now, waiting for us to open our eyes and be dazzled. The spiritual dimension of life is accessible moment by moment, if we'll simply loosen our white-knuckled grip on the familiar and step out in faith.

Open my eyes, Lord, says the familiar folk hymn. Such a simple prayer, with such life-changing implications. May I mean it when I pray it. —*Betsy Rogers*

Prayer takes many forms

Most of us will go through a period of time when it is difficult to pray. Maybe we don't sense God's presence with us, or events in our life may lead us to believe that God is far away. Sometimes there is just a sense of heaviness, such that it's difficult to come to God in prayer.

I went through a time like that once, and I felt really guilty about it. That was like adding insult to injury: I felt alone, and then I felt guilty for feeling that way.

I shared my struggles with a wise old priest. She asked me what I was doing with the time I usually spent in prayer. "I go on lots of walks," I said. I told her that I also spent time with friends, and listened to music, and read good books. And I was quiet a lot, just listening to my heart.

"And what exactly would you call that?" she asked, with a faint smile.

She helped me see that I had defined "prayer" very narrowly, and my experience was showing me that prayer can take many forms, as long as I remain open to God's voice. —*Robert Macauley*

What kindergarten teaches

Everything we really need to know, we learned in kindergarten. Robert Fulghum wrote that in his book, and he's right. Why?

Because everything we learned in kindergarten builds community.

Hold hands while crossing the street? That's building community. Share everything? That's building community. Be kind to little old ladies? That's so important to God in God's vision of community that God repeatedly tells us, especially in Deuteronomy, that we are to care for the widows among us.

When God created us, in that incredible act of love, God created us to live out that love in God's beloved community. And the best way to build community is to remember the lessons we learned in kindergarten. These are simple lessons, but what would the world look like if we actually followed them? We would live in a world where rejoicing would take place every single day, because we would live in a good world, in a world where we bless each other.

Fulghum mentions some other rules: Eat warm cookies. Drink cold milk. Then take a nap. Paul tells us, "Rejoice in the Lord always, again I say rejoice!" Be honest: If your life revolved around showering kindness on others, and having others shower kindness on you, wouldn't you rejoice? If you got to eat warm cookies and drink cold milk and then take a nap, wouldn't you rejoice always?

I like to tell people: The gospel isn't rocket science. So let's not complicate matters. God has told us, over and over, what we are to do. If the scriptures are too overwhelming, relax. All we have to do is remember what we learned as children.

—*Lauren Stanley*

School started this week

When I hear the motors, I know the yellow buses are starting to roll again and that I can expect them around 8:00 a.m. and 3:00 p.m. every day. Hearing and seeing those yellow buses each morning helps my day begin.

For a number of years after my children were grown, I felt a deep loss every September. No school clothes, no shoes, no list of pencils, pens, and other things to buy this year. I felt bereft, lonely, and sad. I had to give myself a talking-to: "Get over it. Find something else important to do. Life goes on, girl." It took a while, but finally, I was able to move on, find other things to do, and be happy in the moment with what God gave me to do next.

My years of PTA, band parents, and writing articles on school news for *The Towne Crier* are over, but I have good memories. One year I was in four PTAs at once. Our kids were in elementary school, middle school, junior high, and senior high—all the same year. It kept me busy going to meetings, but it helped me get to know other parents and teachers.

We don't live in that town anymore, but when I think of friends I knew there, I say a prayer for each one, asking God to bless them, wherever they are and whatever they are doing.

One of the biblical texts that helps me is in Paul's letter to the Philippians, where he cautions them to "rejoice...always...do not worry...but in everything by prayer and supplication with thanksgiving let your requests be made known to God" (4:4-9). Paul goes on to tell the Philippians to think about "whatever is true, honorable, just, pure, pleasing, and commendable." Good advice. Let's do it. —*Lois Sibley*

Rabid

One summer when I was working for the security police at Vanderbilt University, I heard a startling report from the radio dispatcher. There was a rabid dog in the university hospital! I went to the floor and ward in the hospital where the mad dog was said to be. I found him on the landing of a stairwell. The hound was sitting quietly and panting heavily in the warm (not air-conditioned) hospital stairwell. It was summer in Nashville. He was hot and drooling. He looked up at me sweetly through the window. I opened the door to the stairwell, and he followed me down some eight flights of stairs, with a little encouragement along the way.

The worried people in the hospital that day were judging only by appearances. They thought the dog was foaming at the mouth and began to panic. They jumped to a conclusion. I expect none of them had ever seen a rabid dog, but they were being vigilant.

Francis of Assisi had been disgusted by lepers. He hadn't wanted to touch them or see them. They smelled and looked horrible. But one day he encountered a leper on the road. Francis discovered that he could love a person with leprosy, despite all appearances. So he loved the lepers generously, as he loved many others.

Though it might be tempting to reach conclusions on the basis of appearances, prejudices, assumptions, and stereotypes can fool us. The latest gossip can bias us and keep us from knowing the person before us. The accuracy of an unfair judgment is not improved by many repetitions. The lepers that revolted the young Francis were not really horrible. Everyone seemed to agree that the hound was rabid, but he was merely hot and wet. —*Rob Slocum*

Different strokes for different folks

In my Father's house there are many dwelling places.
If it were not so, would I have told you
that I go to prepare a place for you?

—JOHN 14:2

Jesus said some things that were downright contradictory. One minute he's talking about the many mansions in heaven—some of which we haven't even heard of—and the next he's saying that "I am the way, and the truth, and the life. No one comes to the Father except through me" (John 14:6).

When faced with such disparate teachings, some people pick and choose. They selectively focus on what they think Jesus must have meant, because it's hard to face the possibility that God isn't exactly who we think. More than that, though, it's hard to fathom that the Son of God might not always have been consistent.

Jesus always spoke the truth, but he focused on what the people with him needed to hear. To the folks who thought they had it all together and didn't need God, Jesus said that everyone has sinned and needs God's help. To the downtrodden people the world had given up on, Jesus welcomed them as they were, reassuring them that his yoke was easy and his burden light.

Anne Lamott once wrote that "God loves us just the way we are, but loves us too much to let us stay that way." That's a pretty good description of the gospel of Jesus Christ, which explains why Jesus said different things to different people. His message is intensely personal and directed to each of us where we are. It may not be easy to hear, but it's what we need to hear. —*Robert Macauley*

It takes two

"For where two or three are gathered in my name, I am there among them."
—MATTHEW 18:20

They say that it takes two to tango. According to Jesus, it also takes two to summon the presence of God. It takes two to be a community, to be a church. It takes two to be Christians. It takes two to see the face of Christ.

That's a message we might not like to hear very much. Faith sure would be easier if we didn't have to deal with all these other people, with their different opinions and ways of worship. It's quieter, certainly, praying alone in our rooms than it is trying to worship in the cacophony of children and adults and music in a church service. It's more convenient to say prayers or read the Bible or reflect on theology on our own, without the added complication of the schedules and thoughts and desires of others.

But Jesus says our faith and life must be *grounded and rooted* in community. It's when two or three are gathered together that Christ comes among us in new and amazing ways. In the way that we disagree, but still find love. In the way that we forgive when we hurt one another. In the way that we challenge each other and learn from each other and grow together to be the people God created us to be.

Whatever your spiritual persuasion, it's important that you take the time to find a community of faith. Don't let past hurts keep you from a church. Don't let busy schedules get between you and weekly worship. You need other people: to comfort and challenge you, to support you and to keep you on track. It is there, in the midst of that difficult, messy, wonderful community of two or three or more, that you will find God. —*Melody Shobe*

Find the silence

Anthony Bloom, Metropolitan of the Russian Orthodox Church in Great Britain and Ireland, wrote of an old woman who complained to him that for fourteen years she had tried to pray, but God had never responded. Sit in silence, he advised her. Do not speak. Do not pray. Turn off the radio. Just listen.

Later, the woman returned and said that for the first time in her life, she had heard God speaking to her—because, she said, she had been quiet.

How often do we enter the silence so that we can hear God? How often do we even give God the chance to speak? Far too often, I think, we begin our prayer by telling God everything we want God to hear: our hopes, our desires, our needs. We talk and talk and talk. When we are done with our lists, our pleas, our demands, are we then quiet? Do we wait to hear God speak? "For God alone my soul in silence waits," wrote the psalmist (Psalm 62:1). Do we quiet our souls so that we can listen to God?

I know how hard this is to do. I will start out with the best of intentions: *Hello, God...*I quiet my mind, still my soul. And boom! *I forgot to...*a thought pops up. I push it away. Back to silence... Boom! *I need to...*another thought. Again, I push back. Back to silence... Boom! *My nose itches...am I getting a cold? Be quiet!* I tell myself.

Sometimes, we have so much noise in our heads, so much clutter in our souls, that we miss what God is saying to us. But just because we don't hear anything doesn't mean God isn't listening to us, that God isn't responding. Sometimes, we simply have to be quiet.
—*Lauren Stanley*

Lost in translation?

A tongue rested on each of them.

—ACTS 2:1-21

I recently visited Ground Zero. While New York hummed away in noisy activity, all of us circled around that great void were still and quiet. This place where the twin towers fell truly is hallowed ground.

The World Trade Center's collapse significantly damaged all the surrounding buildings—except for tiny St. Paul's Chapel. Although its graveyard and grounds were filled with rubble, the church, built in 1766, still stood. When the world as we knew it came crashing down, the church stood—physically and prophetically.

From September 11, 2001, until May of the following year, the tiny church not only stood—it served. Firefighters, police officers, construction workers, and countless others were provided meals, beds, counseling, and prayer. Medical personnel, therapists, pastors, and professionals and volunteers of all sorts transformed the Chapel into a place of rest and reconciliation. Over 14,000 persons of every faith from around the country and the world volunteered, cooked, sang, prayed, comforted, and labored to share their love, to try to say in one language that hatred was not going to be the only word—or the last word.

That's the opportunity you have today, to offer your life to speak another world into being, to say to a world consumed by greed, haunted by fear, and blinded by hate: "I'm not playing by your rules anymore. There is another way. Come, let's discover together a new city that can be built, lived, and shared today in lives that reflect the gracious love of God who loves us all."

Is your life being lost in translation? Find your voice. Speak the word of Love clearly and boldly. —*John Van Nuys*

Coming closer to the kingdom

Unless you change and become like children,
you will never enter the kingdom of heaven.

—MATTHEW 18:3

In 2011, on the tenth anniversary of the September 11 attacks, we tried to be intentional about remembering those who died. Our music and prayers were chosen with the hope of creating a solemn and dignified atmosphere.

When I walked into the sanctuary, there was a large oak tree in a huge pot in the middle of the center aisle. When I asked about the tree, I was told to bless it during the worship, as it would be dedicated to the victims of September 11. So I blessed the tree, and at the end of worship, during the final hymn, the ushers carried it out to the lawn in front of the church. Then they asked for volunteers to plant the tree.

Much to everyone's surprise, all of the children ran forward. They got right to work—shovels flying, dirt everywhere, laughter and shouting and joy. The adults in the crowd, myself included, wisely stood at a distance and watched. We all knew it was a special moment, a moment that transcended our planning and vision for the day.

We were, for a moment, moved to a new place, a little closer to the kingdom. And we were all made deeply aware that the good news of Jesus was unfolding before our very eyes—that God's determination to cause life is far greater than humanity's determination to cause death. God's determination to cause life surpasses all understanding, and fills us with the hope that our best days are always yet to come. The children showed us this in a way that we could have never planned, never imagined—and we were all surprised by joy. —*Jason Leo*

Looking for signs of life

Reading the daily news can be pretty depressing and confusing.

The world is a beautiful and broken place. The sun shines on the just and the unjust, and according to Matthew 5:45, this is God's own doing. Navigating this paradox is not for the faint of heart. It may be hard to understand what God was thinking, but God has given us this life to live fully in its joy and sorrow, its hard work and pleasure. Not in a "don't worry, be happy" kind of way, but in a "this is the day the Lord has made, I will rejoice and be glad in it" kind of way.

In the midst of it all—the good, the bad and the awful—we are called to be joyful in the Lord. We are called to remember that we belong to God—and what a truly wonderful thing that is. We are called to keep up with both the news and the Good News and to look for the signs of human beings fully alive, which is the Glory of God, according to Saint Irenaeus.

It is hard work to look for abundant life in the midst of so much meanness, pain, and tragedy. Still, I believe we are called to sift through the wreckage, looking for signs of life. And then to show those signs to the world, proclaiming the wonderful news that it is God's way to bring life out of death and joy out of sorrow.

It only works if we acknowledge—and mourn—the deaths and the sorrow, though. The world is both beautiful and broken, and to ignore either is a tragedy itself. —*Penny Nash*

The table

My wife Pam and I just gave away our dining room table. It had been my grandmother's. She lived across the street from me in the small Kentucky town where I grew up, and I recall many happy times with her around that table. I was delighted when my mother decided I should be the one to inherit Mimi's dining room table. For all but the first two of Pam's and my forty-four years of marriage, that table has been the site of tasty meals and happy times for our family. With all its leaves in place, it can seat sixteen people, and it has done it many times. The thing I liked best about Mimi's table was the scars it bore—from our children's carving their initials into it, left in place for twenty years but covered over with refinishing a few years back.

But now the table has gone to the home of our son Craig, in Chicago. Craig has married a lovely young woman who has a large extended family living nearby. The table will once again be the gathering place for children, grandchildren, aunts, uncles, and cousins. It will be—as it long has been—perfect for Thanksgiving. Pam and I now have a fine new table fresh from the furniture store. The only thing it lacks is a history; it has no stories to tell.

It's good to let things go and to know when to do it. An aunt of Pam's held onto her heirloom jewelry for years after she could no longer wear it, denying others the pleasure of wearing it. I wanted to hold onto that table, too, but it needed to go to Chicago. It goes with my prayers for those who will gather around it in years to come.
—*Richard H. Schmidt*

Relinquishing our demons

On a life-changing, knock-your-socks-off trip to the Holy Land, we stood on a hillside above the Sea of Galilee gazing across the water toward the land of the Gerasenes, where Jesus freed a tormented man from a legion of demons, sending them into a herd of swine which then plunged down the hillside into the water and drowned. When the story got around, the "whole town came out to meet Jesus, and they begged him to leave their neighborhood" (Mark 5:1-20).

Amazing! Here is a man with the astonishing power to free us from our demons, and we beg him to go away and leave us alone. Do we in fact like our demons, thank you very much? Are we unwilling to have Jesus cast them out? After all, there's a cost: I might lose a herd of swine, perhaps, or something else to which I cling.

It pays to ponder those things to which we cling, our latter-day demons. Perhaps it's intellectual certitude or narrow, rigid thinking. Perhaps it's wealth or power, food or drink, or any one of countless addictions. Perhaps it's nameless fear or unfocused anger. Perhaps it's our insistent urge to consume, that yawning "leanness in the soul" that in fact material things will never satisfy.

But the demoniac sits beside Jesus, clothed and in his right mind. And the good news is that this is where we too belong, sitting beside Jesus, free and whole. Our demons are powerless in the face of Jesus' authority. He can and will banish them, if we'll stop clinging to them. May we pray for the grace to relinquish our demons and let Jesus make us whole. —*Betsy Rogers*

When the morning stars sang together

Job was sitting there listening when the Lord said, "Who is this... and where were you when I laid the foundation of the earth...when the morning stars sang together and all the heavenly beings shouted for joy?" (Job 38:1-7).

Can you explain that, Job? What do you say?

Job wanted out of that argument, but the Lord said, "I will question you, and you will declare to me." Then the Lord spoke at length of his power until Job was humbled and satisfied.

Not that long ago, every morning when I came into my kitchen and looked out the window I saw the Morning Star in the southeast. The sky before sunrise was that beautiful cobalt blue. The star was very bright, and some mornings the moon was there with it. I don't know much about their orbits, so I was surprised but pleased to see them together.

Galileo observed the Morning Star in the seventeenth century, but God put it there in the sky many years before that. Later named after Venus, the Roman goddess of love and beauty, it is the second planet from the sun and the brightest object in the night sky, after the moon. Sometimes it can be seen during the day, if the sky is clear and the sun is low on the horizon. Venus is about the same size as the earth, but their orbits and rotation periods are different.

I am happy just to see the Morning Star, in the early morning and sometimes in the early evening, too. I thank God for it and for all of Creation. I hope Job looked for it, too, and that he learned to appreciate it. —*Lois Sibley*

Practice

My son played the cello for about six weeks when he was in the fourth grade. My daughter's violin career lasted awhile longer: eight months. My son took up the piano when he was fourteen, and that actually lasted for a couple of years. I miss the music. But what I don't miss is being the practice police—the constant nagging I had to do to get them to *practice*. I had to keep reminding them that it wasn't through the weekly lessons but the practice that they would learn.

I once led a retreat called "Practicing the presence of God." As part of our reflections, we explored a number of different spiritual writers, including Brother Lawrence, Meister Eckhart, Henri Nouwen, Pema Chodron, and Eckhart Tolle. What these folks have in common is their engagement in *practicing* presence. Although belief systems differ, the practice of presence is essentially the same: opening ourselves to an awareness of *what is* in the present moment. It is in this moment that we encounter God. At the burning bush, God said to Moses my name is *I AM*.

As I understand it, much of Zen and other eastern spiritual practice is sitting in simple awareness of the present moment. It often begins with an awareness of our breathing, inhaling and exhaling. It sounds easy, yet it can be so hard to sit in simple awareness, without our minds wandering off to the past or the future. But even in our limited capacity to do it "right," this simple practice makes us more aware, more mindful, in the rest of our lives. It changes us.

And so it is for so many things: we need to practice hospitality, practice justice, practice beauty. We learn not by thinking or theorizing, but by *doing* these things. And, as we practice, we encounter God along the way. —*Nancy Hopkins-Greene*

Pops

Thirty years ago, my mother remarried. It was a whirlwind romance and a tad surprising to the family, but she and her new husband were so happy that all we could do was smile in gratitude.

My mother was sixty-two when she married this man. My conundrum: What was I supposed to call him? I could have used his first name—after all, I was an adult by then. But that seemed distant, and as soon as I met him, I knew that I, too, could love him. Holding him at arm's length wouldn't do.

So I played with different nicknames. He couldn't be my "father"— my father had died right before I was born. He couldn't be "Dad"—that is what I called my stepfather, whom my mother divorced when I was ten. No way would I use "Daddy" or "Papa"—I was too grown up for that. Finally, I settled on "Pops." It somehow sounded right, and when I called him that for the first time, we both knew: this would be our intimate name, our way of entering into a new relationship and building upon it. The intimacy of that nickname both opened doors and drew us in closer. From the first time I called him that until the day he died, he was my "Pops."

When Jesus taught his disciples to pray, he taught them to call God *Abba*—"father," which can roughly translate as "Pops." *Abba* is an intimate form of address; using it brought the disciples closer to God in a whole new way.

What intimate names do we use for God? And does using them change our relationship, remove the formality, draw us into the loving arms of the one who has loved us from before time began?

Abba. Pops. —*Lauren Stanley*

Light show

There was a light sprinkle of rain and an offstage rumble of thunder as my friend Patty and I left the concert, a sprinkle that quickly turned into a heavy rain, with serious lightning flashing out to the west.

On the highway, the downpour was almost too much for the windshield wipers; I longed for the superior control of a stick shift as small waves blowing across the road made handling insecure. I put on the flashers, slowed to a safer pace, and found myself leading a small parade of the cautious, all with their own flashers working, in the far right lane.

Visibility was miserable. The only illumination came from the spectacular lightning flashes crackling all around, and a brief hail shower made things still more interesting. I focused on my driving and some heartfelt prayer until at last I made it home. From the porch, I could finally enjoy the light show, as thunder rattled the windows.

We have so many tools and can control so many things that were beyond our ancestors' knowing that sometimes we imagine we control it all; we expect the world to fall into line.

It won't, of course—not the winds and the rain, not the lightning, not the movement of the tectonic plates beneath our feet. Even now, with radar and satellites to show us the path of the storm as it hurls itself at us, with scientific names for different kinds of clouds and lightning, the best we can really do in its face is prepare, pray, and be mindful of the One who created all. —*Sarah Bryan Miller*

"We have bread of Jesus here"

Jesus called for them and said,
"Let the little children come to me, and do not stop them;
for it is to such as these that the kingdom of God belongs."

—LUKE 18:16

As a parish priest, I've studied a lot of theology, and week in and week out I strive to preach and teach the gospel. But for all my efforts, the best summary of the gospel I've ever heard came from my oldest daughter, who was three at the time.

Once a month our church held a free dinner for anyone who'd like to come, and it was usually a mix of families struggling to make ends meet, some migrant workers, and elderly folks on fixed incomes. It was a motley bunch, but the fellowship was rich.

My family was living in the rectory next to the church, so we'd go over to help prepare the meal. Typically I would greet people at the door and introduce them to our church. One very memorable time, though, I was in the kitchen when the door opened. My daughter, who was perhaps best known for being the first one at the communion rail on Sundays to make sure we didn't run out of "bread of Jesus," ran to answer it. I caught up with her a moment or so later, as she greeted a young couple with three small children.

My daughter didn't give the name of the church, or our denominational affiliation. She didn't talk about service times or our theological belief system. She simply said, "This is my daddy's church. We have bread of Jesus here."

I couldn't have said it better myself. In fact, I never have.
—*Robert Macauley*

Football players and little old ladies

Several years ago when we were going on a trip, our flight was changed and our seats were now in different parts of the plane. Sitting next to my assigned seat was a football player-sized young man. When I saw him I didn't think we would have anything in common, so I got out my book. I did look over and ask him if he was going home, and he said he was.

He asked me where I was going, and I told him that my husband, many rows in front of us, was a clergyman going to a church to give a storytelling workshop, and I was along for the ride.

That was all he needed. He was a seeking Christian, attending classes at the church where his fiancée was a member.

First, he wanted to know what I believed about the bread and wine at communion. He had so many questions that we never stopped talking the entire trip. He belonged to a 7:00 a.m. Monday morning group of men who encourage each other in their faith. His name was Jim, and I promised to pray for him. He said he would pray for me.

He was in the aisle seat, so when we got off the plane he went ahead of me. I saw him stop my husband, tell him we had had a wonderful conversation, and wish him well on his workshop at the church.

I never opened my book on that flight. God, bless Jim wherever he is today. Little old ladies and big, football player-sized men have a lot in common if they are both seeking to be good Christians.
—*Nancy R. Duvall*

Turning around

I was an undergraduate intern in the psychology department of a Veterans Administration hospital in Nashville. One day the clinical director went to give some important tests to a patient, taking along a graduate student and me. We were serious about the significant task ahead, and moved quickly through the hospital. We passed a patient who was sitting on the floor near an elevator. He turned his head slowly, painfully, side to side. His eyes were half-closed and he seemed to wince. All three of us passed by him on our way to the appointment. But the clinical director, Dr. Joe Mancusi, then turned around to offer help, and we followed him back.

I would never have stopped for the patient. We had important work, and I would have kept going. I was busy and had to be someplace. I was in a hurry. At least someone turned around. Someone saw the person who was right before our eyes, and I followed. That was my conversion.

Jesus was ready to interrupt what he was doing for an unexpected ministry opportunity when he entered Jericho. He noticed Zacchaeus, a rich tax collector who had climbed a sycamore tree to see Jesus. So Jesus called him to "hurry and come down" so they could meet at Zacchaeus' home. That visit was the occasion of his conversion. He promised to give half his possessions to the poor and pay back four times what he had taken by fraud from anyone (Luke 19:1-10). This was a surprising encounter with a wonderful outcome.

Unimagined possibilities and new directions can appear for us. But we may need to suspend our plans and agendas. Our real mission may be something unexpected that's right in front of us.
—*Rob Slocum*

Transformed by teachers

God has appointed in the church first apostles, second prophets, third teachers.
—1 CORINTHIANS 12:28

My thirteen-year-old son recently began a new school. It was a time of transition for him, stepping into a completely new community and also moving from a public school to a parochial school. "Dad," he moaned, "religion class twice a week. I don't know anything about religion." I reminded him that he probably had learned more in Sunday School than he was aware of, and I sent him on his way.

The first few days were a little rough. The frustration on his face was obvious, and I waited for some hopeful sign. I figured one small victory would do the trick. A few days into the first week, he came home with a smile. He'd had a great day—in religion class. The teacher had asked the class who had written the four gospels. My son shared with me that a lot of the other students had some good guesses, like Moses, Jesus, King James, and some guy whose initials were R.S.V. And then he told me that he raised his hand and said "Matthew, Mark, Luke, and John." He observed that the teacher looked kind of relieved.

In my denomination, we have bishops, and those bishops get a lot of attention, and that's probably a good thing because they have a lot of responsibility. We also have Sunday School teachers, and they don't get as much attention as bishops do, but I was thinking at that moment that maybe they should. They share their faith in Jesus in wonderful and creative ways. They have the habit of transforming people's lives.

From that day on, my son started to embrace his new school, and his life was in no small way transformed. The grace of that came from Sunday School teachers, and the power of the Holy Spirit working through them. —*Jason Leo*

The fate of the auk

Three hundred years ago, the great auk flourished on the coasts of the North Atlantic. A powerful diver and swimmer, the great auk also had the misfortune of being totally useful to human beings. Its eggs and flesh were tasty; its feathers made for soft bedding; its carcass was rich with oil. As a result, the great auk was hunted into extinction. The last one was seen in Waterford Harbor in Ireland in 1834.

If anyone spoke up against the extermination of the great auk, I expect the counterargument would have been as it is today—given a choice between jobs and birds, jobs come first. It's a classic conflict. Most people eschew the extremes: "Never kill a bird for any purpose" and "Create jobs at any cost" are positions rarely defended. But how do we strike the right balance between birds and jobs?

In the creation stories in Genesis, God instructs human beings to "till and keep" his world and gives us "dominion" over it to care for it. We ourselves are part of the world we are to care for, and providing gainful employment is part of caring for human beings. The tragedy of long-term unemployment isn't only bodily hunger (which is often relieved by social agencies and family), but the spiritual devastation resulting from feeling unneeded and unwanted.

But to serve, nurture, and protect the world also requires that we not meet our own needs in a way that exterminates other creatures or abuses the earth itself. Never again will the great auk glorify its Maker. When God looked at the world he had made with all its creatures, he "saw that it was good." The task of keeping it good, God has delegated to us. —*Richard H. Schmidt*

Inscribed on God's palms

See, I have inscribed you on the palms on my hands.

—ISAIAH 49:16

In this moving passage from Isaiah, God tells Israel that her exile in Babylon is over, the desolation of the land is coming to an end, the multitudes will return to rebuild the ruined Jerusalem, and the people of God, inscribed upon his palms, will take up his high commission to be a light to the nations.

Like the Israelites, we too are inscribed on the palms of God's hands. The One who calls us by name, who knew us in the womb, who counts the hairs on our heads has written our names on his hands. We too are commissioned to do his work in the world, to be a light to the nations, to care for the dispossessed, to tend the sick, feed the hungry, clothe the naked, and provide shelter for the homeless.

Imagine! These all-powerful hands, which spread the stars across the heavens, shaped the planets, and set in motion this amazing cosmos with all its physics and chemistry and biology—these very hands bear our names. In the infinite vastness of all his universes, God knows each one of us and holds our names upon his palms.

In my humanness I find this hard to believe. Who am I, that my name should be written on God's hands? But when I ask in prayer if it can be true, I find that it is. There it is, *Betsy*, on his palm... and, when I raise my eyes just a little, I find in his wrist the mark of the nails. —*Betsy Rogers*

A true shepherd

There are a lot of sheep images in the Bible, ranging from "The Lord is my shepherd" (Psalm 23) to the Parable of the Lost Sheep (Luke 15:3-7). If you really think about it, though, being compared to a sheep isn't exactly a compliment. They're not very smart, they can barely see, and they're so focused on following their leader that if one sheep jumps over an imaginary obstacle, all the sheep following will jump in the same spot, even though nothing's there.

The power of these images isn't in the sheep, it's in the shepherd who loves his flock so much that he is defined in relation to them (after all, you can't be a shepherd without sheep). And Jesus goes even further in this parable, by telling his listeners that the shepherd will leave the herd—even risk his own life—to find just one lost sheep.

That's not very smart, either. The more sensible approach would be to let one sheep go, because if the shepherd is killed, who's going to protect the rest of the flock? But God, as the true shepherd, isn't sensible. He's not driven by conventional wisdom, but rather by an unbridled love for his sheep.

So while being compared to a sheep may not be a compliment, having a shepherd who loves us infinitely is the greatest gift anyone could ever receive. —*Robert Macauley*

Does God ever stop nagging?

Many years ago, when our twin sons were toddlers, we spent one long afternoon at a car dealership. Watching me entertain them, an older woman sitting nearby suddenly proclaimed, "Fifteen is God's way of showing parents that they won't mind their boys leaving home someday."

It was hard to imagine then that our sons would someday no longer depend on us for everything. Fifteen has come and gone and, happily, they've remained engaging and kind through their high school years. Still, they've become much less needful of us. Gradually I've learned to give up control over things that don't matter so the boys could make mistakes and learn from them.

Perhaps this business of growing independence plays out in our own walk with God.

Throughout my own youth and college years, I felt the presence of God hover over me like a benevolent seabird: nudging, nagging, keeping me safely near shore.

In the years since it's not that I've lost the ability to sense the presence of God but perhaps God—having accompanied me to a certain juncture—is trusting me to get it right with less supervision. Does that freedom allow us to flourish as Christ's disciples in ways we might not if we were more closely shepherded and nudged along the way?

We live on a millpond, and to get to the open lake we must motor our boat under a low bridge. I can't help but remind our boys to duck. Recently, as we approached the bridge, my mouth opened just as one son dutifully bent over, well beyond need of admonishment.

But still: "Jay!" I barked to our friend behind him, who at age sixty-two should know the drill, "Duck!" —*Heidi Shott*

The Petoskey stone

It's small and round, highly polished and shiny. When I hold it in my hand, it feels cold. I try to warm it in my hands, and it doesn't really warm up. But it comforts me. I like to hold it and think about our amazing God who made Petoskey stones and all things.

Petoskey stones are composed of fragments of rock and coral reef, or fossilized coral, that was deposited about 350 million years ago. They were formed as a result of glaciation. Sheets of ice plucked stones from the bedrock, grinding off the rough edges and depositing them in the water and sand of the beaches of the Great Lakes.

Petoskey is the English translation of the name of an Ottawa Indian chief, Pet-O-Sega, which means "rising sun," "rays of dawn," or "sunbeams of promise." It is said that when he was born, rays of the sun fell upon his face and so he was named.

In its natural state, and if dry, the Petoskey stone looks like ordinary limestone, but when wet or polished the stone is a mix of gray and brown with a distinctive mottled pattern showing a six-sided coral fossil, making these stones distinctive and collectible. Sometimes jewelry and other decorative objects are made of Petoskey stones. It is the state stone of Michigan.

There are many references in scripture to stones. Joshua set up a "large stone" as a witness because "it has heard all the words of the LORD" (Joshua 24:26-27). Peter refers to Jesus as "a stone, the cornerstone, chosen and precious" (1 Peter 2:6). So I sit quietly and hold my stone and think about the Lord God, who made all of us and Petoskey stones.
—*Lois Sibley*

Trouble in Technoworld

There's nothing like losing something to make you realize just how much you depend upon it.

Today I had planned a rich, full, work-related schedule, chock-a-block with phone interviews, electronic story filings, and the usual social media and email. It didn't quite work out that way.

First, my landline went out, with a dial tone that turned into a fast busy signal that turned into a strangled stutter and then into a fuzzy undead quiet. At the same time, my company's email server quit. I called my editor using my mobile phone, and met my most pressing deadline by sending the copy in creative ways: at least one of them made it through.

This might make a good subject for a meditation, I thought—and then, of course, I couldn't log into my website. Had it been hijacked? Was the host server down? Was this Purgatory Day in Technoworld?

Eventually, phone service was restored, email returned, and, finally, the website appeared when summoned. It's all incredibly minor stuff when you think of what others have suffered in the recent past—floods, earthquakes, tornadoes, tsunamis—or consider the day-to-day realities of life in places like the Arab world, Rwanda and Sudan, Myanmar, and North Korea.

I wasn't too badly inconvenienced, after all; a lot of people would be thrilled to have nothing worse on their plates. Days like this should serve as a gentle reminder to consider how very blessed we are—a reminder to take nothing for granted, a reminder to offer our praise and thanks for all God's gifts, every morning and every night. —*Sarah Bryan Miller*

Soul searching

Indeed, all who want to live a godly life in Christ Jesus will be persecuted.
—2 TIMOTHY 3:12

I was impatient, shoes in hand, being patted down by security. I'd done everything to board my flight quickly and painlessly, to no avail.

Another passenger was being searched—by three guards. Unlike me, he had not done everything to avoid scrutiny. For there stood a tall, quiet, bearded man in a long brown robe and a white head wrap. As his every article was meticulously searched and as he was being escorted to the metal detector for a second time, he was impassive—not impatient. I was frustrated. He looked peaceful.

As security searched my body, I searched my soul: What accounted for our differences in attitude? While my search was an unexpected imposition, his was an anticipated trial. With that foreknowledge, he patiently endured. If my faith asked me to dress in a way that would cause at best inconvenience or at worst prejudice, would I keep that part of my faith? Probably not. I hate inconvenience, let alone hardship.

I've read that spiritual maturity is a willingness to be inconvenienced for the gospel. Fredrick Buechner writes: "To sacrifice is to give up *something* important for *someone* more important." How willing am I to be inconvenienced for my Lord? My "sacrifices" are small and seldom. I rarely want to ruffle feathers, much less stand up and be counted. But what does God want?

God wants us to incarnate humility, generosity, and compassion in a world filled with pride, haunted by scarcity, and lost for lack of love. Forsaking self, ignore the stigma, incur the cost, and incarnate the blessing. If we do, God will ensure that we arrive safely at our ultimate destination. —*John Van Nuys*

What the tea tells us

Tickets to the Japanese tea ceremony are hard to come by. The first day, we left home early but arrived too late. "Let's go first thing in the morning," my friend Linda said. What if we got all the way there, and still missed out? Better not to bother. But Linda, sensibly, said, "Let's just leave a little earlier."

And so we did, and got our tickets for the first seating: O me of little faith.

The purpose of *chado*, the ritual of tea, is contemplation. The preparation, serving, and consumption of tea are, one might say, only the outward and visible signs of an inward and spiritual search for enlightenment.

There was some jostling for place as the group approached the tea house. One by one, we removed our shoes and crawled through the tiny door that demonstrates the equality of all in the teahouse, taking our places on the straw mats that cover the floor.

"The four basic principles of tea," our teacher said, indicating a scroll hanging in a niche that also held a vase of artfully arranged flowers. "*Wa*, harmony; *kei*, respect; *sei*, purity; *jaku*, tranquility."

As she demonstrated and explained each step, the principles began to sink in. The group, sharing a new experience, became more cohesive and friendlier. Our bowing became easier with practice and bowls of thick green tea.

We left through the little door, bowed, chatted, and took pictures, unwilling to go. For a little while, we'd had a glimpse into the deep heart of another culture, a glimpse into a kind of sabbath that we should give ourselves regularly, but rarely do. Such sabbath time is a treasure; sometimes it is contained in a bowl of thick green tea. —*Sarah Bryan Miller*

The bad wolf

One night when my daughter Claire was about four, she had a really scary nightmare. She dreamed a giant wolf was tearing through the wall and coming to get her! She screamed bloody murder. I was amazed that a child so small could make a sound so chilling and piercing. She was terrified when I reached her, and not about to be persuaded otherwise. It was impossible to reason with her to prove there was no wolf in the room, or in the closet, or under the bed.

Have you ever been afraid? Did you fear a noise in the night, or a sudden threat, or a wrenching loss? Did you fear your own weakness, or even your own strength? Did you fear pain, or failure, or humiliation? Fear can seem to take over everything, and it can spread like a stain. It can lead to cloudy judgment and bad decisions. The fear made it hard for Claire to sleep in the following days. The wolf was still with her.

It took a few days, but we finally chased the bad wolf out of her room. I held her hand, and she tightly held mine, and we went looking for the wolf several times a day. We'd knock on pieces of furniture to scare him out. We'd check the closet and under the bed. We'd tell him to *go away!* These were our wolf hunts. Finally she laughed and the wolf was gone.

One of the most frequently repeated commands in the scripture is to "fear not." Fear no evil, not even in the valley of the shadow of death (Psalm 23). As we let go of fear and anxious self-concern, we can trust and share the faith we're called to live. —*Rob Slocum*

Open to grace

One moment you're waiting for the sky to fall;
the next you're dazzled by the beauty of it all.

—Bruce Cockburn, "Lovers in a Dangerous Time"

On a recent morning, after lying awake for thirty minutes, I turned to discover it was 4:30 a.m. I'd been thinking about fifty-three different things I had to do. Rather than do any of them, I put on a sweatshirt over my pajamas and set off for a walk around my neighborhood. As I ventured into the early morning, gulls and osprey were fishing for breakfast, noisily swooping low across the water of the lake.

"Pretty nice," I sniffed, too deeply engaged in thinking about the logistics and politics of thing-to-do #14 to be moved by any early morning beauty. But as I rounded a corner and a vast field of lupine unfolded with the head of the river in the distance, God got me at last.

Earth is like heaven when you can recognize God's grace in the midst of the most stressful week.

My pace slowed. By the time I got back to my own yard, my sneakers were wet with dew, and spider webs in the tall grass shown in sparkles as the sun began to rise. As I approached the house, not one of my fifty-three things-to-do seemed quite so important. My reclaimed calm wasn't about the work I do for the church. It was about God's loving voice saying, "Here it is. Here it's always been. Here it will be. All of it, for free."

Inside I turned on my computer and did twelve or fifteen things before it was time to make lunches and whisper "Good morning" in everyone's ear.

May God's kingdom come that way more often.

—*Heidi Shott*

Saint Francis Day

Today is animal blessing day! It's the feast of Francis of Assisi; in his honor, the church offers to bless your critters. I tell people: Bring your dogs and cats, your birds and fish, your spiders and snakes (shudder!). Let's gather and bless, bless, bless!

When the time arrives, I put on my vestments and go out to greet all of God's creatures visiting this day. I try to be filled with joy, but I temper it with reality: *Not all these critters like each other.*

I pull apart two dogs that are fighting, hunching to keep blood off my vestments. I pick up a mouse; it promptly pees in my hand. The next animal is a cat: *What do I do about the mouse pee? Will the cat attack?* (Surreptitious wipe on my vestment.)

I approach the llama cautiously; a friend was bitten once and still bears the scars. I ask the tarantula's owner to leave the beast in its cage: *My blessing will go through the glass.*

I step over the cow "pie," and stroke Bessie's sides, receiving her gentle moo in return. I dip my hand into the waters of the fish tank, and let the fish investigate and nibble. I stroke the *back* of the parrot, not the head—I've been nipped by parrots before.

I pray for them individually, and then for them all:

> *Heavenly Father, you created the birds of the air and the fish of the sea and the animals of the land. Send your blessings upon these creatures gathered here, and all others in your beloved creation, and make us good and loving stewards of them. Help us to protect, feed, and care for them as you protect, feed, and care for us. In Jesus' name we pray. Amen.*

—Lauren Stanley

I love you—but change

Behold, I make all things new.
—REVELATION 21:5

In my church people generally don't like new things. Every once in a while we try something new—a new hymn, a new worship schedule, a new kind of coffee, a new Sunday school curriculum, a new preacher. Every so often we try something new and people usually struggle with it. The responses are pretty predictable: that's the way we have always done it; if it was good enough for so and so. At some level it is probably not surprising that people refer to us as God's "frozen chosen."

But the truth is that we are really a whole lot more flexible than we first think. God is transforming the church, and indeed the world, all the time, and there is overwhelming proof of this all around us. Consider just one example. My mother was born into a church were she was not permitted to be an acolyte. My daughter was born into the same church where women are now consecrated bishops.

We greatly underestimate our flexibility and our openness to what is new and unfamiliar. Jesus did not say, "I have come that you might have traditional values and rigid customs." Jesus did say, "I have come that you might have new life, and life abundant" (John 10:10). And that new life is happening all around us and within us.

I know that God loves us just as we are, and way too much to let us stay that way. I am increasingly aware that God also loves the church just as it is, and way too much to let it stay that way.

And so our journey continues, and all things will be made new.
—*Jason Leo*

Changed by a miracle

There was a wedding in Cana of Galilee.

—JOHN 2:1

At Cana, Jesus turned water into wine. It wasn't a one-time-only occurrence. Turning water into wine, turning the ordinary into the holy, is what God does all the time.

At my son's third-grade awards ceremony I recognized a boy who had bullied my son earlier that year. My parental instincts kicked in. I silently seethed anger at that boy. I thought about the school paddlings I'd received and how much I would enjoy giving a paddling to him.

But something odd happened. As children were called up to the podium to receive award after award, I realized that this boy was all alone. Everyone from his class got something for doing something right—everyone except him.

I thought about a kid I went to school with who was just like that boy. I thought of how his life had turned out—not well. I thought about my classmate's home life, which I discovered years later was a living hell. I focused again on the nine-year-old boy before me. What would his future hold? What kind of home life did he likely have? Suddenly I felt my anger ebbing away, replaced by sorrow and compassion.

Awakening to that change within me yet not accomplished by me, I thought: *God is in the house.* Just as God was at an out-of-the-way wedding in a tiny Palestinian town, God was present in a little school amidst Hoosier cornfields, doing something way more important than changing water into wine. God was working on my heart, changing it—yet again—away from my darkness toward God's saving light. —*John Van Nuys*

Forgiveness means letting go

Many of us pray every day: forgive us our trespasses as we forgive those who trespass against us. But we're not always sure we want to forgive. What does it mean to forgive? It might help to first say what forgiveness is not.

Forgiveness is not saying that the wrong someone did to you was okay. It is not letting the other person "off the hook." It's not pretending you were not hurt. It's not an invitation for the other person to continue to do you wrong. Those things are not forgiveness, which is making a decision to let our anger and resentment go.

We don't, most of us, do forgiveness well. We think we need to hold on to our anger, to hold that grudge, in order to hold the perpetrators' feet to the fire. We want to keep punishing them for what they said or did to us. And we want them to keep feeling our anger.

And maybe they do keep feeling it. But more importantly, we keep feeling it. We keep letting anger, resentment, and hurt take up precious room in our own lives and poisoning our hearts. Saint Augustine says, "Resentment is like drinking poison and hoping the other person dies."

Forgiveness doesn't mean "no consequences." Tell people they hurt you—and then let it go. Tell people they need to make restitution for the things they took from you—and then let it go. Let them suffer the consequences of their actions—and then stop dwelling on it yourself.

Sounds simple, but we all know it's not. And so we continue to daily pray: forgive us, Lord, as we forgive others. —*Penny Nash*

Legato: lessons for living

Those of us who sing in choirs, including amateurs like me, know the term *legato*, referring to a smooth, flowing articulation that joins words together in a continuous sound. Singers, often even good ones, easily fall into legato's opposite, *staccato*, hammering hard on every beat and punching out words like a nail gun—appropriate for, say, a military tune, but unsuited to mystical melodies or heartfelt hymns of love.

Legato in Italian means "bound" or "binding," referring to the tie or slur mark connecting notes so they make a smooth, unbroken sound. Accomplishing this kind of articulation means stressing the vowel sounds and connecting them with minimal interruption by hard consonants. So there is a sense in which one sings "from the inside," the voice dwelling at the center of the words.

Legato articulation often implies peaceful, gentle, serene, undisturbed. But it also implies an inner strength, a quiet persuasive force that lifts and carries those who sing it and those who hear it.

Sometimes I feel like I live my life in staccato. Pounding rhythms, hard edges, disconnected sounds, and abrupt separations abound. This is the sound track of a high-stress life and its insistent demands, so many of which are of my own making.

And then, miraculously, God touches me. It might be in prayer or worship. It might be as I work in our food pantry or talk with my husband or sit with a friend or sail on Lake Michigan. It might be in a Rachmaninoff concerto or the smile of a child.

At those times my life shifts into legato. The Spirit's tether binds me together with all around me; I'm drawn to the Center and filled with God's strength and peace...and inexpressible gratitude.
—*Betsy Rogers*

Newborn

When my daughter Rebecca was born, I cut the umbilical cord and immediately held her in my arms. "I love you, Rebecca," I said. "I love you." This was before she learned to say a word, or played drums in the high school marching band, or was elected to Phi Beta Kappa. This was before she chipped a baby tooth running away from the big girls at church, or went to prom with her first boyfriend, or learned to speak Spanish. She just was. And I was there with her, and I loved her.

Unconditional love can seem so impossible. There must be a catch—as if we had to prove something, earn a prize, or close a deal. But God's love is just there for us. God *really* loves us. Before anything we do, or say, or plan. And even after some of the things we've done, and said, and planned. God loves us, unconditionally, tenderly, like a newborn in a parent's arms.

Jesus says we must receive the kingdom of heaven like a little child (Mark 10:15). Our openness is essential for the life of faith. The little baby in my arms was totally available to receive what she needed to receive. She had no hidden motives or calculated agendas. She was just there to love and be loved. And as she loved, she grew.

We are the limiting factor in the divine-human relationship. Our human limitations cause all kinds of obstacles in relationships, and we may even hurt the people we love the most. But there's no limit to God's love or God's invitation for us to draw nearer and be healed. The first steps of faith may seem like a precarious movement into the unknown, but we're in good hands. —*Rob Slocum*

Stars, sand, and understanding

Years ago I was privileged to spend five weeks in Jerusalem at St. George's Anglican College. A week of the course was spent in the Negev Desert. Days were extremely hot and dry, so we were required to carry a liter of water to drink each day. The body overheats quickly without humidity in the air. That can be dangerous.

Nights were another matter. It was bitterly cold, with a constant wind. We slept in sleeping bags on the ground, with blankets inside those, and luggage at our heads to deflect the wind. I would not want to do this now, but thirty years ago it was a challenge happily endured.

I had always thought that the sky was black with a sprinkling of stars. Wrong! Out in the desert, with no ground lights, the sky is white with stars and planets everywhere. Shooting stars are common and when we were there the moon was full. No lights were needed to see what was around us. The infinity of space in the crowded sky was striking and humbling.

With this experience, particularly that of the hot, dry days, we began to understand why Moses' flock grumbled and argued as they traveled in the desert. When the Bible talks about the tree in the desert, it means literally *the* tree. There is very little shade—anywhere.

Life is primitive in the desert. Bathrooms are nonexistent. We were well fed; the children of Israel were not.

Oh God, who made stars too numerous to count, sand beyond comprehension, and heat and cold in terrible extremes, take pity on us, your most rebellious creation, and help us also to be the most loving as we care for your earth and each other. —*Nancy R. Duvall*

The miracle of God's love

*"A certain creditor had two debtors; one owed five hundred denarii,
and the other fifty. When they could not pay, he canceled the debts
for both of them. Now which of them will love him more?" Simon
answered, "I suppose the one for whom he canceled the greater debt."
And Jesus said to him, "You have judged rightly."*

—LUKE 7:41-43

Sometimes we feel overcome by our sinfulness. Maybe we've done something really bad, or something that just *seems* really bad. Either way, it's hard to feel forgiven, to believe that God could still love us.

That's human reasoning, though, not divine reasoning. Jesus said that the more someone sins, the more that person needs to be forgiven. Then he went on to say that the more someone is forgiven, the more that person must be loved. The miracle is that the love of God is infinite. We're never going to "use up" God's love; we're never going to run out of divine forgiveness. There is nothing that God won't forgive us for, if we ask.

So while sin is never part of God's will, it is always an occasion for divine love and mercy. For if we haven't sinned very much—or, at least, don't recognize how much we've sinned—God's love might seem nice. But if we truly acknowledge the darkness that resides in our hearts, we can recognize God's love for the miracle that it is. And in the midst of our remorse, there is also reassurance, as God's love shines forth even more brightly in the darkness. —*Robert Macauley*

Coping

While driving through Missouri one day, I saw a personalized license plate that intrigued me. The plate consisted of six letters: COPING. What did that driver intend to say? It depends on the punctuation, but there was no punctuation. Here are the possibilities that came to my mind:

COPING? Perhaps the driver meant to ask me a question as I pulled up behind him. "Yes," I would have answered, "I'm coping okay just now. But then, of course, the kids aren't screaming in the back seat, and I'm not late in getting to the hospital, although I will be if you don't move soon. Anyway, thanks for asking. I didn't know you cared."

COPING! An exclamation of triumph! Perhaps the driver had been through two nervous breakdowns, was just out of detox, was three times divorced, had lost his job, and suffered from a brain tumor, paranoia, and ennui—and yet here he was able to drive to the store for a gallon of milk! Congratulations to you, sir. Well done!

COPING... An ellipsis would suggest a tentative statement, perhaps to be replaced next week with something like I QUIT. Sometimes I feel like that. I've managed to get through another day and will probably keep on top of things at least through lunchtime tomorrow. Beyond that, I'm not sure.

The secret to coping, I think, is to recognize that no one can cope. Life is too perplexing, demanding, and unpredictable. Perhaps God made life that way on purpose, to drive us into his arms. God can cope, and if we turn to him, we don't have to worry about it. When we try to get through our lives alone, we end up thrashing around, getting nowhere, and then wondering where things went wrong.
—*Richard H. Schmidt*

Sing a new song

How could we sing the LORD'S song in a foreign land?
—PSALM 137:4

The psalmist weeps over the bitterness of captivity in Babylon while longing for Jerusalem and the comforts of home. A song from the musical *Godspell* echoes this psalm: "On the willows, there we hung up our lives. For our captors there require of us songs and our tormentors mirth...But how can we sing? Sing the Lord's song in a foreign land?"

Sometimes we find ourselves in such sorrowful situations. The anxiety of changing schools or moving away to college, a job transfer and relocation, selling our home, changing churches, or going to prison. Life is hard and it might not get easier.

Years ago our rector (and close friend) lost his mentor to an automobile accident. A week later he and his family joined us on Cape Cod. He and I took a sunset stroll on the quiet beach. My friend was low, very low. As we approached a jetty I suggested he go out and have a one-on-one with God. From a distance I could see him flailing his arms and letting it all out. He took it to God and together they handled it.

We all have times when our lives are turned upside down. During times of transition and challenge God wants to help us refresh ourselves and move forward with a renewed spirit. We must reconstruct our lives or we will wallow in self-pity and bitterness.

There is a season for change. When we are there, we turn to God and allow him to transform the situation. We may need to alter our lives or create an action plan and implement it. In any event, we can't leave our lives on the willow branches.

If we pray for guidance, in time we will receive a new song to sing. —*Carl Kinkel*

An extraordinary life

This is the extraordinary life of Samuel Isaac Joseph Schereschewsky, whom we remember today: he was born a Lithuanian Jew in 1831; he trained for the rabbinate, converted to Christianity, emigrated to the United States, and was ordained an Episcopal deacon in 1859 in New York. Responding to a call for missionaries, he sailed for Shanghai that year and mastered Mandarin Chinese en route. Once in China and priested, he translated the Bible and the Prayer Book into Mandarin. He continued his scholarship after his 1877 consecration as Bishop of Shanghai and ultimately translated the gospels into Mongolian and the entire Bible into Wenli, 2,000 pages of which he typed with a single finger after Parkinson's disease paralyzed him.

Who could have imagined, when little Samuel was born, what curious twists his life would take, or what astonishing things he would accomplish for God?

Schereschewsky had an exceptional gift for languages and a calling to take the gospel to those who hadn't heard it. Most of us don't have his facility with languages, but we do have our own gifts and the same calling to share the good news of Christ.

The obstacles Schereschewsky faced were daunting: mysterious tongues, millions upon millions of unreached souls, and, toward the end, a debilitating disease that sought to trap him in his own body. But he would not be trapped, and he persevered to the end.

We face our own obstacles. They might pale by comparison to Scherschewsky's, or perhaps they seem just as insurmountable. But God shows us in this wonderful example of service and devotion that we can indeed do all things through Christ who strengthens us.

What astonishing things does God have planned for us today? —*Betsy Rogers*

Planning your funeral

Because I was living in a war-torn nation, where death stalked the land and its people on a constant basis, I decided to plan my own funeral. I chose the prayers, hymns (lots of them!) and readings.

My family and friends found this exercise macabre. "We don't want to talk about it," they said. "Why are you doing this?"

"Because," I said, "in Sudan, it's too easy to die. From disease. Accidents. Attacks. Bad water. Bad food. Need I go on?"

One of the hymns: "I come with joy to meet my Lord," an old African American spiritual, set to the tune Southern Harmony.

On the day that I die, this is how I want to meet my Lord: in complete joy, seeing God face to face, meeting my heavenly Father, knowing God's complete love in ways I can only imagine in this life.

"Aren't you afraid?" people asked me as we consulted about my funeral.

I grinned and looked at them.

"The worst thing that will happen to me is that I will wake up and have breakfast with Jesus. Since that's what we pray every time we pray the Nicene Creed, I'm thinking this is a good thing."

I really do believe that these lives we live on this fragile earth, our island home, are but a short part of our lives in God, that we have to achieve the Omega of this life in order to enter the Alpha of our next life.

So yes, I planned my funeral. I had a blast doing so. I sang all the hymns, prayed all the prayers, read all the readings. I pray that when my time comes, I truly do come with joy to meet my Lord.

—*Lauren Stanley*

"Why me?"

Most of us have a highly developed sense of the fair and unfair, at least as the terms apply to our own special selves. For evidence, watch any small child when goodies are being divvied up: no scientific scale exists that can measure cookies with the exactitude of a suspicious six-year-old.

This same sense usually comes into play when something bad happens to us: "Why me?" Why should I be sick? Why should I be burdened with a parent with Alzheimer's? Why should my child have emotional or physical problems?

It's a perfectly natural question, particularly when we've done our best to live good and healthy lives. It's the wrong question, though, if we haven't also asked it when we feel blessed: Why should I have the talents that I do? Why should I have such a loving family? Why should I have been hired over another, equally qualified?

Since I tend not to ask "Why me?" about good things, it seems to me hypocritical to ask it when the news is negative. No life is without sorrow; no life is without pain. Jesus never said it would be easy; he only said we'd have comfort and assistance when things got hard.

Better than complaining, it seems to me, is to say, "Thy will be done. Lord, I can bear this burden only with your aid." Ask for God's help, and it will surely be granted. —*Sarah Bryan Miller*

Tyler's gift

*Each of you must give as you have made up your mind, not reluctantly or
under compulsion, for God loves a cheerful giver.*

—2 CORINTHIANS 9:7

After worship, an usher handed me a pledge card. Placing it in the
stewardship mailbox, I noticed the handwriting—and got a lump in
my throat. The pledge card was from a child. The scrawled name read
"Tyler." Eight-year-old Tyler loves baseball and sings in our youth choir.
Then the lump in my throat got bigger and tears welled up. Tyler had
pledged to give God through the church $1.00 per week.

I asked Tyler's folks if they knew about this. His mom Jennifer
said, "Oh, yes. Tyler asked us specifically for *his* pledge card."

Giving him the card, Tyler's parents explained his gift was included
in the pledge they had already made. Tyler replied, "I know that you
give for us, but I want to give God something from me. I don't give
anything now, but if I do next year, just think of all the good things
God will do through my gift! That's why I want to pledge." His parents
smiled as Tyler placed his card in the plate.

Jennifer said, "After church, Tyler kept talking and talking about
his pledge, asking us which chores he could do to earn his $1.00 each
week to give God." Hearing this completely humbled me—and inspired
me to be a more generous giver.

Later that week, I saw Tyler's grandmother and asked her if she had
heard about Tyler's gift. Grandma Nanette nodded and said, "Tyler still
hasn't stopped talking about his pledge. He now wants to do even
more chores so that he can give God $2.00 each week."

May we all share Tyler's spirit. God loves a cheerful giver.
—*John Van Nuys*

Change of seasons

The change of seasons speaks to my spirit. Winter reminds me of all that is dormant yet possible in my life and the world. Spring proclaims the possibility of new life in places that feel dead. Summer breeds color, creativity, and warmth. And then there is fall...

By October I've finally gotten around to putting away my hummingbird feeder, its customers long gone. I've cleared away most of the vegetable plants. What is left—my fall crop of spinach, lettuce, and beans—grows very slowly. I clear away the spent raspberry canes and perennials and start raking leaves.

I love many things about fall: the cool air, the beauty of leaves changing color. But this season feeds my spirit in other ways too. As I watch the trees shed their leaves, I join creation in this annual ritual of emptying and clearing. I love the fruitfulness—the "bounty"—of my summer garden, but by October I'm ready to let go of it, to let it fall away. As I watch the trees shedding leaves, I ask myself what needs to be shed in my life.

De-cluttering can be a spiritual practice: de-cluttering our desks or email inboxes perhaps, but also our wardrobes, budgets, and calendars—and maybe even some of our ideas. Letting go of these things, I am reminded that God gives me what I truly need.

And so, I watch the trees shed their leaves and ask God what needs to be shed in my life. I can think of a few things today: my anxiety about the future, the need to control, the bag of clothes in the basement. Like trees releasing their leaves, I gently let them go.

—*Nancy Hopkins-Greene*

Now!

Have you ever been at your wits' end and not known what to do? Has it been so deep a problem that it made you sick, angry, full of despair? Did you feel you had no one to turn to, no one who would understand?

Welcome to the human race. No matter what you think when you look at people from the outside, they all have or will have a time they feel just that way. I have felt that way. It is a terrible way to feel. The only thing I have known to do is to turn to someone I know loves me (and who is not the problem) and ask for help.

While we were in seminary I felt that way. We had no money, a new baby, it was the first time I had ever been away from home, and I was very young. The people I met seemed to have it all together. I felt inferior, unappreciated, worthless.

I called the priest with whom my husband worked on Sundays. His church was on the other side of Washington, D.C., and I lived in Alexandria, miles away. He came immediately, but it took him over thirty minutes to get there. By the time he arrived, just knowing he had dropped everything to come to my aid was enough to make me see that I was not worthless—someone really cared.

Now I forget what I was upset about. But I will never forget that he came immediately. He was like a lifeline. When you know someone is hurting, don't make an appointment for three days from now to talk to them, don't let your precious time or schedule get in the way of that precious person's need. Go—now! —*Nancy R. Duvall*

Strangers and angels

Do not neglect to show hospitality to strangers,
for by doing that some have entertained angels unaware.

—HEBREWS 13:21

My wife and I recently welcomed our third child. It was a long and challenging pregnancy for her, ending in both joy and relief. Her doctor was a real blessing throughout the whole experience, and I have to say our insurance company was nothing but helpful from start to finish.

The baby's two-month checkup was great, but a few days later a letter came from the insurance company denying the claim. I called, and after a whole lot of button-pushing I found myself speaking with a real live person. When I explained the situation, the woman responded that the insurance company had no record that the baby existed.

My frustration level and temper immediately began to rise. In the letter to the Hebrews, the writer reminds us to show hospitality to strangers—and this, to me, falls under the category of "hard sayings." I took a deep breath and asked the woman if she might scroll up on the computer and view our prior claims. She allowed that she could. A period of silence and then: "Oh my goodness, you did have a baby, didn't you!"

She was very apologetic, and shared that she too was pregnant. We had a long conversation about the joy of having children. She asked about our baby's name. Yes, it was taken from scripture. Yes, we were members of a church, and yes, we were planning a baptism. She even said she would offer prayers for us. I felt I had made a new friend.

She had been an angel to me, and had reminded me that probably before long, that same opportunity would be in front of me. Do not neglect to show hospitality, for it is a door into the kingdom. —*Jason Leo*

Stillness in prayer

Be still and know that I am God.

—PSALM 46:11

Sometimes I think we make the Christian life harder than it really is. Sure, there is a lot of self-sacrifice; Jesus, after all, commanded us to take up our crosses and follow him. But at the same time he assured us that his burden is easy and his yoke is light. Nowhere is that more clear than in prayer.

There are lots of ways to pray. One popular method is abbreviated ACTS: adoration, confession, thanksgiving, supplication. That way we cover all the bases—we declare our love for God, we say we're sorry for what we've done wrong, we give thanks for the gifts of this life, and then we share our concerns. That's a wonderful way to pray.

Sometimes, though, words get in the way. We might get so caught up in checking things off the list that we lose sight of the fact that we are blessed simply to be in God's presence. "Be still and know that I am God," the psalmist writes. God wants us to let the words go, no matter how honest and beautiful they are. God wants us simply to slow down—to stop, even—and rest in his presence.

That's harder than it sounds. Words sometimes are the easy way out because at least then we have a formula to follow. To stop requires us to enter God's presence without bringing anything along. Just us and God, trusting in his promises, completely undeserved and unadorned.
—*Robert Macauley*

God's hand at work

As we look at the beauty of nature around us, we see the change of seasons at work. We savor brightly colored leaves as a feast for our eyes. Soon these orange, yellow, and red leaves will have fallen to the ground, as the trees make ready for winter. Some of us enjoy the promise of cooler weather, while others mourn the departure of summer with its warmth.

It's not hard to see the hand of God at work in all this. The sheer beauty of our natural environment is often breathtaking, and creation itself seems to sing out in praise of God. As the psalmist wrote, "The heavens declare the glory of God" (Psalm 19:1).

When we see the colorful leaves of autumn, gentle flakes of winter's snow, radiant green shoots of springtime, or the wildflowers of summer, most of us enjoy the rhythm of the changes. We know that the changes are anticipated, expected, because there is constancy in the overall shape of seasons. We trust that cooler weather will lead to warmer weather, which will bring us back to cooler weather again.

I wonder if it is possible to see the changes and chances of our whole world this way? What if we treasured the constancy of God amidst life's great changes? It's easier to enjoy the cycles of nature, because we perceive nature to be a gift from God. Our anxiety with "worldly" things often stems from our sense that these things belong to us. If we can learn to understand that everything in our world is a gift from God, we might learn to be less anxious and more grateful.
—*Scott Gunn*

Love song

There is salvation in no one else, for there is no other name under heaven given among mortals by which we must be saved.

—ACTS 4:12

Some Christians love this verse; others hate it. Those who love it point to its affirmation that Christ is the only way to God (salvation) and is Lord of all; those who hate it feel it demeans other faiths, suggesting they are nothing but dead ends.

It helps to know what kind of literature we're reading. We don't read a sonnet the same way we read a baseball box score, or a legal document as we read a recipe. The Bible contains a wide variety of literature, including hymns, court records, short stories, historical narratives, legends, sermons, letters, accounts of dreams and visions, poetry, and one play. What sort of literature does this verse seem to be?

It sounds to me like a love song. Lovers addressing their beloved say things like "You're the only one" and "Your name is the only name under heaven." Such statements pertain only to the beloved—they are not meant to negate other people's beauty or worth. Love songs have a context, and their meaning derives from that context. I look at this verse not as a statement about other religions, but as an expression of Peter's love for Christ, a love he is eager for others to share.

This statement works for me as well, as an expression of my own love for Christ. Are other faiths wrong? Like Christianity, they probably contain elements of truth, and like Christians, their proponents have often done unfaithful, even awful things. People are like that, of whatever faith. But for me—and I hope for everyone—no one compares to Jesus Christ.

—*Richard H. Schmidt*

Gathered fragments

After the miraculous feeding of the five thousand, Jesus tells his followers to gather up the fragments left over from the five barley loaves and two fish, "so that nothing may be lost" (John 6:12). James DeKoven (1831-1879), a controversial Episcopal priest, preached one of his last sermons on this passage, reflecting that only in God are the broken fragments of our lives to be gathered up and made whole.

DeKoven could well have felt that his own life was fragmented. He was elected Bishop of Illinois, but concerns about his theology prevented him from receiving the necessary consents for his election. Many people opposed him. And yet he pointed to an integration and wholeness of life that was beyond the limits of his own story.

Gather up the fragments! The miracle is visible in every piece that remains when the five thousand have eaten. Gather the fragments. That is a prayer for the broken pieces in our lives, and the love of God that is present. Gather up the hurts, the disappointments, and the missed opportunities. Gather up the things that could have been, and the relationships that were lost. Gather up the things that were never tried, or misused. Gather up all the shards and broken pieces. Gather everyone left standing when the music stopped. Gather them all into a greater whole, with divine hands more capable than our own.

Gather the fragments. —*Rob Slocum*

I will walk among you

I will walk among you and will be your God,
and you shall be my people.

—LEVITICUS 26:12

What a great promise the Lord told Moses to tell to his people. Of course, it was given first of all to the Jews, but the Bible later makes clear that God includes people from all the nations among his people.

In Isaiah 49:6 we read that the Lord is going to adopt people from all the nations. They may be Gentiles, but God will adopt them into his own people, equal with them, to be counted with them—a special people, saved by the Lord.

As Saint Paul reminds us, "Isaiah says, 'The root of Jesse shall come, the one who rises to rule the Gentiles; in him the Gentiles shall hope'" (Romans 15:12). Paul is telling us Gentiles that when Jesus comes again, we who believe in him shall be included in God's people.

When Jesus walked on the earth, he healed some who were Gentiles. He talked with the Samaritan woman who asked about the Messiah (John 4). And he told her, "I who speak to you, am he." She in turn went to other Samaritans and asked them, "Can he be the Messiah?" And they believed and were counted as part of God's people.

There are many examples, but we each must decide: Is the Holy Spirit calling me? Will I believe in Jesus? Will I obey him? Will I be a part of God's people? Will I walk with God? —*Lois Sibley*

Heaven on earth

After the funeral of the mother of a childhood friend, I went to the dinner for family and friends. Sitting around the table we told stories about Doris, who loved to entertain. She could barely finish a meal without planning for the next one, whether for a party or family dinner. She made her house a gathering place for friends, music, and parties. It was clear why the family chose for her burial service the passage: "I was hungry and you gave me food...Just as you did it to one of the least of these who are members of my family, you did it for me" (Matthew 25:35, 40).

The kitchen and table were not her only worlds. After the life squad saved a daughter's life, Doris led the charge to get a new ambulance. She organized the first community sports teams for girls at a time when there were no such sports.

After Doris lost her husband, she was an inspiration in how she remained committed to life, to family and friends. As Psalm 90 says, "Teach us to count our days that we may gain a wise heart." It was a wise heart that Doris opened to all sorts of people.

It was during her final illness, when her body was giving out, that her family and friends witnessed Doris's shining spirit most profoundly. Her disease was not a lesson in dying but a lesson in living each day to the fullest, with love, humor, courage, and grace. She hoped her family would not cry, because she had faith that the next life would be the best and be everlasting.

Throughout her life, Doris showed her family and friends what it means to live in heaven on earth. —*Noël Julnes-Dehner*

Come

Come to me, all you that are weary.
—MATTHEW 11:28

We've all probably read those comfortable words a hundred times. They are a favorite for those falling on hard times and seeking God's comfort. God's promise is there: the promise of love, of open arms, of a companion in carrying our burden. But all too often, we overlook the very first word of that verse: Come. Before God issues the promise of easy burdens and light yokes, God issues a call—God asks us to "Come and get it."

God has come, is coming, and will come again: we proclaim it every Sunday, and it is true. God offers us rest, refreshment, comfort, and solace. That is the good news that we know and believe. But that is only part of the story. God also calls us to come. God asks us to make an effort, to step out, maybe to leave home—definitely at least to leave the comfort of our armchairs.

Maybe you are being called to come into something, or to come out of something. Maybe you're being called to come home, or to come away from home. Maybe you are being called to come to church, or maybe to come before God in personal prayer. I don't know where God is calling you to come, only that God is calling, and that when you come, you will find God's promise of rest.

The next time you hear that comfortable, wonderful verse, I invite you to listen to that first word, "Come," and consider accepting God's wonderful invitation. —*Melody Shobe*

May the circle be unbroken

*Be kind to one another, tender-hearted, forgiving one another,
as God in Christ has forgiven you.*

—EPHESIANS 4:32

My home church recently voted to leave the Presbyterian Church (USA). I grew up in that little country church—as did six generations of my family. The exit was over sexuality and ordination, the ongoing fight rending many denominations. As an ordained pastor serving another congregation, I was asked on my last visit home if I would be leading my congregation to leave as well. When I said no, responses ranged from bashful silence to visible disappointment.

John Calvin said, "It is vain to seek a church free of every spot." If any of us ever find the perfect church, our presence there will render it imperfect—for all of us have sinned and fallen short of the glory of God.

It's easy to take sides and make judgments about issues. It's more difficult when those issues involve people. Especially people you have known and loved your whole life, with whom your family has been friends for generations.

I grieve my home church's departure. I wish they would stay. Regardless of who we are, individuals and groups need a loyal opposition, clear-eyed critics who can spur us to greater fidelity. Conservatives need liberals; liberals need conservatives; we all need each other.

Pray for and love those with whom you disagree. Uphold your convictions with humility. Avoid "us/them" language, remembering that on the other side of the issue are persons who love the church just as much as you. As Paul counsels in Ephesians 4:30, do not "grieve the Holy Spirit"—whose deepest hope for us all is mutual, Christ-like love. —*John Van Nuys*

OCTOBER 29

Unexpected pleasures

One of the unexpected pleasures (and I am pretty sure there aren't many) of not doing the yard work is the abundance of rose hips in the fall garden. Had I been more diligent about deadheading the roses, these beauties would not now be appearing and growing ever larger all around the yard.

Sometimes we learn from experience that not getting around to something can yield unexpected pleasures. It turns out that not everything has to be done on time or even done at all. (My family holds this to be particularly true for raking leaves. Maybe they will all just blow away...)

Not getting around to cleaning out a closet or drawer preserves that odd little thing we might have thrown away that now is just perfect for another use. Not weeding allows a lovely volunteer flower to appear in the garden. Not pressing for resolution of a knotty problem at church or home or work allows a solution to emerge organically, gracefully relieving us of the burden of being really too pushy.

I am glad as winter approaches that I didn't get around to trimming off all the spent blossoms from the heavy late summer bloom. Now all winter I (and the birds) will enjoy these unusual beauties decorating the bare branches, until they are eaten by the local wildlife or simply wither away in their own time.

There is wisdom in taking the wait-and-see approach sometimes. I'm pretty sure God knows this. Look at how some of us turn out to be late bloomers ourselves, if we are given the time, bearing unusual fruit that nourishes the world around us in surprising ways. —*Penny Nash*

Conversion

Centuries ago a treadmill was constructed at the top of Canterbury Cathedral's central Bell Harry Tower as a way to hoist construction materials to the tower's roof. At the yank of a rope that hung to the floor in the crossing, a workman would start walking the treadmill, turning it and lifting the load to the top. The treadmill continued in use until recent times.

One day, a schoolboy from King's School in the cathedral precincts was passing through the nave and on a whim grabbed the rope with both hands and pulled. Before he had a chance to let go, he began to rise through the air. A workman was pulling him skyward. The stunned and frightened child hung on for dear life, all the way through the dizzying heights to the top. The surprised workman lifted him out, unharmed, on the Bell Harry roof, 250 feet above the cathedral floor.

What a wonderful image of conversion! Perhaps some people experience conversion in a predictable way; in my experience, it comes at the most unexpected moments and in the most unlikely forms. Skimming along, oblivious to God, I'll take an unsuspecting yank on a metaphorical rope and suddenly I'm spinning upward to a new level of faith and vision and understanding. Often, too, it is the hard work of another person that God uses to convert me. My faith is God's gift to me through many who, by their love and prayers, have walked the treadmill to lift me from truth to truth.

For all this I give thanks—for all the "ropes," the opportunities to learn and grow; for the faithful workmen and women in my life; and for the new vision God offers us day by day through a lifelong process of conversion. —*Betsy Rogers*

Hallowed but frightening

Today is the day when we dress up and try to shock and humor people into giving us treats. It was named for All Hallows' Eve, the night before All Saints' Day, which we celebrate tomorrow.

But before jumping ahead, I recommend praying that old Cornish prayer about "ghoulies and ghosties and long-legged beasties, and things that go bump in the night," that then asks, "Good Lord, deliver us."

I know all about things that go bump in the night. Living in a mud hut in Sudan, with creatures inhabiting the straw roof, there were all kinds of bumps and long-legged beasties to accompany my sleep. At first, those noises kept me awake. *What was that? What was THAT?* After a while, I adjusted and began to sleep through the commotion. *Just another bug,* I would think. *Maybe it's a gecko. (Please don't be a spider!)*

Until one night, I heard a mad scrambling above my head, and felt dust and dirt falling onto my mosquito net, and then... *suddenly!...*a great...big...*thunk!...*and the net swayed dangerously, the air filled with shrieks, and I shot up in bed, convinced we were under attack. My heart raced, and my skin prickled. I was *scared!*

I grabbed my flashlight and frantically shone the light. The net was dancing maniacally, but I couldn't see a thing. And I grew even *more* scared. Then I heard another *thunk!* I shone my flashlight around the room, and there they were, the culprits who had scared me so much, two large geckos, one atop the other...um...*What are they doing? Oh! They're...um...making babies!*

Good Lord, I breathed, lying back down, *deliver me.*
—Lauren Stanley

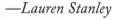

Aiming for sainthood

And there's not any reason, no, not the least, why I shouldn't be one, too.
—THE HYMNAL 1982, #293

People who didn't grow up in the Anglican tradition often roll their eyes at the children's hymn "I Sing a Song of the Saints of God." It's so quaint; it's so British; it's so…cheery. I loved it as a child; I love it now. Part of the reason is that it's so quaint and British and cheery, and that I grew up with it; part of the reason is that its message is an important one. The saints of God are among us now; they're not just sanctified ancients with halos attached. They truly are "just folk like me." We do meet them in our daily lives—and we really can aspire to be saints, too.

Saints, of course, are human, and that means that they are imperfect. Like us, they dwell in the context of their times, and with the fashions and prejudices of those times. Like us, they are susceptible to the vicissitudes of day-to-day existence; some of the finest saints I have had the privilege to know could be cranky before they'd had their morning coffee, or prone to a little pottymouth when provoked.

The saints of God live their faith the best they can, bringing God's light into a murky world, witnessing God's love to those they meet. And I mean, God helping, to be one too. —*Sarah Bryan Miller*

> *I sing a song of the saints of God,*
> *patient and brave and true,*
> *who toiled and fought and lived and died*
> *for the Lord they loved and knew.*
> *And one was a doctor, and one was a queen,*
> *and one was a shepherdess on the green;*
> *they were all of them saints of God and I mean,*
> *God helping, to be one too.* —Lesbia Scott (1898-1986)

Roscoe

The path of the righteous is like the light of dawn,
which shines brighter and brighter until full day.

—PROVERBS 4:18

As a Hoosier farm boy who knew every four-letter word from helping Dad as he cursed and castrated uncooperative pigs and wormed unwilling sheep, I was astounded by our neighbor Roscoe Poe who trucked our livestock to market. Herding unwilling, fattened animals into the sorting pen or loading chute, Roscoe never said one cussword.

To me, as a young boy, his example really stood out. Years after he died, I found the language to describe the gift Roscoe had given me. Working in ankle-deep manure with headstrong animals, Roscoe, through his living example, was teaching me all about holiness.

In our country church, Roscoe served as head usher, which he did for forty years. Every Sunday Roscoe would come forward with the offering as we all stood, singing *The Doxology*. Even though Roscoe was all dressed up in his Sunday-best coat and tie, it was the bib-overalls-wearing Roscoe who was preaching to me.

As Christ bids me to be *in* the world, but not *of* the world—to be a man without being profane or ungodly—Roscoe is with me. I understand the charge Christ gives me through the example Roscoe gave me. Roscoe is one of my heroes of the faith. His continuing presence is part of that great cloud of witnesses that continues to lead me as I endeavor each day to be a new creation in Jesus Christ.

Give thanks for the saints who continue to bless you. And remember: somewhere, someone is looking up to you. Be worthy of God by being worthy of them. Like Roscoe, let your light shine. —*John Van Nuys*

"What do you need?"

When our city opened a winter shelter for people who are homeless, churches and other groups volunteered to supply meals, bedding, and clothes. In charge of the new facility was a city administrator who attends our church.

I asked her what was needed at the center that I might supply. She said, "Books." Many clients were the working poor who could not get two months rent together to rent an apartment. They would love to have a book to read.

I was surprised. To my chagrin, I realized that I had stereotyped homeless people in my mind as people who would not or could not read. I was ashamed and quickly changed my attitude.

Books and reading have meant pleasure for me since my mother held me in her lap and read to me. Many a night I have read into early morning hours.

I told my daughter, also a reader, about the need for books at the shelter. She brought bags of paperbacks. I pulled books from our shelves. A neighbor brought over more bags of books. We have continued to take books to the shelter each year. We learned of a women's prison that needed books. Our project enlarged. Now a school near the church needs library books.

At Christmas my book club decided to bring books for the shelter or prison. They brought five large boxes full. Now we do this several times a year. I hope we can also keep the school supplied with books.

Of course I am not really talking about books, but about caring for those around us, about sharing what we have that others don't. There are many simple things we can do to help others if we ask what they need. It is a blessing to them and to us. God's blessings abound. —*Nancy R. Duvall*

Two copper coins

The widow put two small copper coins into the temple treasury. Her gift seemed petty in comparison to the large sums donated by the rich people, but Jesus praised her gift. She gave more, Jesus said, because she gave everything, all she had to live on, while the others gave from their abundance (Mark 12:41-44).

The value of a gift is seen in the heart of the giver, not the gift itself. The widow dropped a meager two copper coins into the temple treasury, and it probably didn't look like much. But, it was an incredibly generous offering from her. The rich will return to their remaining riches, but this widow sacrificed everything.

Despite the widow's extreme generosity, we don't know her name. "Sine Nomine," which means "without name," is the name of Ralph Vaughan Williams's famous tune for the hymn *For All the Saints* (*The Hymnal 1982*, #287). Both the tune's name and the words fit very well with the reading from Ecclesiasticus (44:1-10, 13-14) for All Saints' Day, which sings the praises of famous ancestors and then recalls: "but of others there is no memory; they have perished as though they had never existed." They died "without name." And yet they gave what they had. They were also faithful and godly, and their righteous deeds are not forgotten.

The widow's name is lost to us, but we remember her generosity. We also may never be mentioned by name in histories or memorials, but we can give what we have. We can take our place in the communion that shares Christ's name in faith. —*Rob Slocum*

Election Day

It's not pretty.

We are now approaching the conclusion of a particularly vicious election cycle. I, for one, can hardly wait for Wednesday's dawn, no matter who wins.

The electioneering letters and postcards outnumber the bills and catalogs in the daily mail. Today I received six oversized postcards and a pair of dueling letters in one race alone, all containing mirror accusations of utter slime-coated, puppy-eating, baby-hating wickedness from and toward a pair of candidates that I'd earlier considered about equally qualified and equally benign.

The telephone keeps ringing with eager, anxious pollsters: my unlisted number and lifetime membership in the Do Not Call club avail nothing against them. They have no interest in nuance: "Do you consider yourself a conservative or a liberal?" I'm a raging social liberal and a bedrock fiscal conservative. "You must not find many people to vote for," replied one young man, clearly frustrated by my answers.

I don't find many people for whom I enjoy voting, it's true. Part of being a grownup, however, is acknowledging that human beings are imperfect, that the electoral process is beyond imperfect, and that we must all weigh our choices and go with the individuals and philosophies we think will do the most for our communities and all God's children.

Not voting is not an option, it seems to me, if we want to continue to live in a representative democracy: elections like this one are the price we pay for having some say in how our country is run, and we can't complain about crooks in high places if we do nothing to stop their ascent.

All the same, I'll be grateful when Wednesday morning finally comes around. —*Sarah Bryan Miller*

Love your enemies

Love your enemies, do good to those who hate you,
bless those who curse you, pray for those who abuse you.

—LUKE 6:27-28

Some people are really hard to like. Maybe they stand for something we detest, or they've treated us in a cruel and callous fashion.

Jesus didn't command us to like our enemies, though; he commanded us to *love* them. That's not easy either, but it's possible, because while liking someone is an emotion that we have little control over, loving someone is an action we can choose to do. Loving people is being kind to them, looking out for them, considering their needs above our own. We can do all those things, regardless of how we feel about a person.

One way we can love others is to pray for them. We can pray that they find peace and meaning and that God heals whatever drives them to mistreat us. In the process, God may change our hearts, too, for in praying for people we begin to see them through God's eyes, with God's infinite mercy. And maybe, in the end, we might start liking them a little, too.

That happened to me a few years ago, when some people I'd considered friends treated me badly. I was hurt and angry, so I decided to focus my prayer on them. Every day I asked God to show kindness to them and bend their hearts to his will. Pretty soon it became a routine: start praying for them, and then ask God for what I needed. Along the way my heart was touched, and one day their slights no longer seemed so great, and I was ready to move on, wishing them well. —*Robert Macauley*

The day I lost my wedding ring

One day, after twenty-four years of marriage, I lost my wedding ring. I had removed it at an athletic field, so I returned to the field and searched every square inch of the playing field, the dugout, and the stands. I searched my car and all the clothes I had worn. I posted notes at the field with my phone number. As days passed and no one called, my hopes of finding my wedding ring waned.

What I experienced felt like grief. I recalled the day twenty-four years earlier when my wife Pam and I had selected our rings at a jewelry store in downtown Louisville. I recalled the moment she had slipped the ring onto my finger as we exchanged our vows. I remembered the ring's inscription, with both of our initials and the date of our wedding. I felt almost as if I had lost Pam herself.

But of course I had not lost Pam. I still had what really mattered. The ring was important only because it symbolized Pam's and my commitment to each other, a commitment that continues with or without a ring on my finger. I thought of the Holy Eucharist. It is so important to me that I sometimes go far out of my way to receive it on Sunday. But what if I were denied the eucharist? I would grieve, but Christ would still love me and I would still love him. That commitment is symbolized by the sacrament but it does not depend on it.

Two weeks later I found the ring, hidden next to a caster on our bed frame. Of course I was delighted with the discovery, but I was also delighted to have been reminded how steadfast and indestructible is the love of Christ for me. —*Richard H. Schmidt*

Words

The battle lines were drawn. The combatants came armed with their verbal ammunition. Sharp disagreements were slicing through those gathered in the church hall. You could feel the tension in the room. Hard to believe that only a few minutes before, the same people were kneeling together at the communion rail, receiving the sacrament of Christ's body and blood.

Even good-hearted church members can succumb to the temptation to see one another as enemies when resources seem scarce and choices have to be made. Territories are fiercely defended even if it means ruin and destruction for someone else's favorite ministry.

The pastor stepped to the podium and cleared her throat. "Before we begin this meeting, I want to say a few words." She went on to remind them where they had just been and then said something I'll never forget. She said, "You are about to use your mouths to speak words to one another, the same mouth that just received the real presence of Jesus. Remember Jesus in your mouth and make sure that the words you speak, you can speak through him." Then she led the room in prayer.

Somehow during the prayer, the lines drawn across the room shifted to form a circle, and the words that were weapons were disarmed. Instead the truth was spoken in love, and a compromise was reached that allowed the church to move forward together.

When fear clouds the way forward and anger electrifies the environment, discernment and wisdom disappear. This is true in one heart or in an assembly of good-hearted people. In that moment I remember how close Jesus is to us. "The word is near you, on your lips and in your heart" (Romans 10:8). In remembering this again, I know his saving grace. —*Ruth Lawson Kirk*

The tipping point

A beam balance provides very accurate measurements of weight by using a pivoted beam with weighing pans suspended from each of the beam's arms. The unknown weight is accurately measured when the beam doesn't tip on its fulcrum, indicating balance with the known weight in the second pan.

The tipping of the balance is the moment of decision for us in our lives. It's the turning point, the outcome of the crisis that hangs in the balance, the decision that could go either way. As my physician often asks when presented with a new condition to treat, "Is it getting better or getting worse?" Which way is the balance tipping? Should the trend be encouraged to continue, or is an intervention required?

We may consider a crisis to be by definition a bad thing—a hostage crisis, a monetary crisis, or a health crisis. But crisis itself, like any turning point, is just a moment of discernment and decision. It's not bad or good in itself. It's the place where the path divides and we must choose one direction from multiple options. Our own future may seem to tip before us to disclose a new world. As this happens, we may seem to tip between times of consolation and desolation, as Ignatius of Loyola describes them. We may tip between joyful hope and bleak despair.

The wandering knights of the Arthurian legends would sometimes come to a fork in the road. Each path would lead to its own particular adventures and dangers. Which way to take? Sometimes there was a cross planted at the fork in the road, a reminder of Christ present at the tipping point between possible directions and available in all our choices. —*Rob Slocum*

God has put his hands on us

"I am a selfish and sinful man, but God put his hands on me, that is all," says Theophilus Msimangu, a young priest in Alan Paton's powerful 1948 novel *Cry, the Beloved Country.*

In truth, this entire novel is about people on whom God puts his hands. Set in pre-apartheid South Africa, *Cry, the Beloved Country* is a profoundly moving story of sin, forgiveness, and redemption. The son of the black priest Stephen Kumalo shoots and kills the son of a wealthy white landowner. The two fathers come to know each other, move through their anguish toward each other, and together experience unimaginable grace. Reconciliation breaks like a shaft of light through the lowering clouds and hints at new understanding between black and white in the little village of Ndotsheni.

God puts his hands on each of them. Numerous other characters, white and black, also feel God's powerful touch as they give and receive mercy and truth and goodness.

God puts his hands on you and me, too, molding from our shapeless clay useful vessels for his purposes in a hurting world. Our stories might be less dramatic, but in every life there are opportunities to serve, to help, to heal, to reconcile, to bless and be blessed.

We respond to his touch when we reach out with love, listen with compassion, act with kindness, share with generosity, speak up with conviction for those unable to be heard—when we glimpse with sudden clarity the astonishing possibilities with which God has infused his world.

We are selfish and sinful people, but God has put his hands on us.

—*Betsy Rogers*

Veterans Day

"You will hear of wars and rumors of wars," said Jesus to the disciples privately (Matthew 24:6). And there have been so many wars since. Even in our young country, our history includes many wars. There are countless memorials and cemetery flags to remind us of it.

Some who are alive now remember vividly World War II and the Vietnam War. We have posters about the war effort and guns from World War II, as well as sabers, swords, and guns from the Civil War—popular items brought to TV's *Antiques Roadshow* for information and assessment. It's unbelievable how much value those tools of war have.

Every Veterans Day we memorialize those who served our country, especially those who gave their lives in that service. I remember the flags that hung in people's windows during World War II—a blue star meant a family member was deployed and a gold star indicated that a family member had died serving our country. There were so many Gold Star mothers. On November 11, now we have parades and special services at memorials in honor of those who served and died.

Jesus said not to be alarmed when we hear of wars and rumors of wars because "this must take place, but the end is not yet" (Matthew 24:6). He cautioned that it was just the beginning, in fact. There have been thousands of years of war and hostility. It is still happening and will continue until that day when Jesus comes again. We long for that day even as we trust him to know when is the right day to come.
—*Lois Sibley*

> *What a day of rejoicing that will be!*
> *When we all see Jesus, we'll sing and shout the victory.*
> —"When We All Get to Heaven," ELIZA E. HEWITT

Living code

The naval officer and computer pioneer Grace Hopper helped build one of the very first computers to help America win World War II. In the 1950s, Hopper discovered that most errors resulted not from computer error but programming error. So she designed a better way to program computers—not with mathematical code, but with everyday English words and commands. She ended up writing one of the very first computer languages. She called it COBOL: "Common Business–Oriented Language."

In essence, what Grace Hopper did for computers is what we are to do for God. We, in our actions, words, habits, and life, are to develop a code—a living language—to make accessible this deep mystery called God. We are to decipher the deep mysteries and truths of the Christian faith—creation, fall, sin, and salvation—into everyday language, actions, and interactions people can understand, experience, and discover.

How on earth can we do that? Paul gives us this solid strand of starter code: "Be at peace among yourselves. And we urge you, beloved, to admonish the idlers, encourage the faint hearted, help the weak, be patient with all of them. See that none of you repays evil for evil, but always seek to do good to one another and to all. Rejoice always, pray without ceasing, give thanks in all circumstances; for this is the will of God in Christ Jesus for you. Do not quench the Spirit. Do not despise the words of prophets, but test everything; hold fast to what is good; abstain from every form of evil" (1 Thessalonians 5:13b-22).

By grace, that is the eternal truth we are to express in the everyday language of our lives through our faith, hope, and love. As we live that way for God, God will live that way in us.
—*John Van Nuys*

Christians behaving badly

"O, God! You're so strict!"

—FATHER FYODOR, IN *THE TWELVE CHAIRS*, MEL BROOKS

Human beings behave badly, on a distressingly regular basis. Christians are human beings. Ergo, Christians behave badly, on a distressingly regular basis, even though—hello!—we're supposed to hold ourselves to a higher, more heavenly standard.

When we fail, the rest of the world is watching, with barely restrained glee.

There are evangelists who preach to the poor, collecting their dimes and dollars, who live in multimillion-dollar compounds filled with luxurious furnishings and fleets of luxury cars, enormous boats, and private jets. ("I don't make any more than I'm worth," one told a reporter here a few years ago. "We're definitely within IRS guidelines.") There is the regular—by now predictable but always freshly horrifying—spectacle of sexual predators in positions of sanctified trust, and those who protect them instead of the victims.

This all started early in the Christian era, and it has never let up over two millennia. Today, however, the whole world is watching and the whole world is judging.

Christians, of whatever stripe, should be open and honest in their dealings. Christians, of all people, should lack any sense of entitlement and not pretend that the end justifies the means. Christians, of every creed and covenant, should walk humbly with our God and do our stumbling human best to keep Jesus's commandments to us, his people. As often and inevitably as we fail, we owe that effort to our Lord. —*Sarah Bryan Miller*

Becoming

"Do not be conformed to this world, but be transformed," says Saint Paul (Romans 12:1). Be changed into what God has called you to be.

Yes, we know that, but change can be painful. There is loss in transformation. Even when what we leave behind is negative (extra pounds, bad habits, dysfunction), it was comfortable, known, dealable-with. We love our routines, even when they become deep ruts. Remember the Israelites who wanted to go back to Egypt after they had escaped Pharaoh? They may have been slaves in Egypt, but the food (cucumbers! melons! garlic and leeks!) was a lot better than what they were getting in the wilderness.

We wonder, who are we without our old habits and pounds and dysfunctions? Are we really any better? Says who? Do we even want to know?

Whether we welcome it or not, we are always in the process of transformation. We are losing our rough edges as we move through life; we are losing our narrow view as we are exposed to more and more (even things we don't want to be exposed to). We are preparing to take on new life—becoming partners, parents and grandparents; becoming generous; becoming wise; becoming trusting; becoming peaceful; becoming hopeful; becoming.

Making way for that new life means shedding part of the old. Shedding mistrust, anxiety, ignorance, tight-fistedness, and hard-heartedness, shedding the prickles that keep others at arm's length.

We are always in the process of transformation, in the process of becoming. And like the ugly duckling in the fairy tale, we may not even realize that what we are becoming is beautiful.

—*Penny Nash*

Photographic memories

It was time for us to take a photo for the Christmas card we would send to our friends and family members. So hard to do. Especially with five active, lively children jumping around.

We had the children sit and stand around the piano, each one smiling as I made faces at them. Dad took a picture. Later in the week, after a snowfall, we tried for an outside photo. On Sunday afternoon, we made the children put on their warm coats, scarves, hats, and mittens. They were not pleased to have to go out into the cold again. This time I asked them to make some snowballs and pretend to throw them at me as Dad took another photo. That one might be good, too.

That was before digital, so we had to take the film in to the local film developer, wait for its return, and then choose the photo and the card and place our order. It took time, and we waited patiently. Finally, we had the right photo with the right card, and we sent them out.

I'm remembering all of this now because recently a friend in Canada sent me that very Christmas card. She had received it in the late '60s. Cleaning out some papers, she found it and thought I would like to have it. I am thrilled to have it, and it is now on my fridge with other priceless family photos.

Memories are good. Photos that help us remember are great. And it is such a privilege to sit down quietly and remember our past and our God who has walked through each day with us. May we always be faithful as we trust him to make a way for us. —*Lois Sibley*

Bread

Bread is a very powerful symbol in the Bible. Jesus said, "I am the bread of life" (John 6:48). He shared bread and wine with the disciples on the night before he died. One of his most famous miracles was about the loaves and fishes.

It shouldn't be surprising, then, that baking bread can be a very spiritual experience. Yeast is a living organism that allows the bread to rise. The act of kneading allows the baker to feel the dough forming and changing under his hands. And some of the most wonderful breads are made with "natural yeast," not the kind we buy in the store but the kind that is all around us in the air we breathe. It just takes a little more patience, since natural yeast takes longer to work.

That might be the most profound spiritual lesson of all, especially in the hustle and bustle of modern life: you can't rush bread. It needs time to rise and proof and bake.

There are times when we need to work the dough and times when we need to leave it alone. It's a wonderful reminder that we are not in control and that we can't achieve our goals through sheer force of will. Sometimes we just need to watch and wait. And in those times of waiting, we have the chance to quiet our souls and recognize the miracles that surround us. —*Robert Macauley*

Keep watch, dear Lord...

Keep watch, dear Lord, with those who work, or watch, or weep this night, and give your angels charge over those who sleep. Tend the sick, Lord Christ; give rest to the weary, bless the dying, soothe the suffering, pity the afflicted, shield the joyous; and all for your love's sake. Amen.
—THE BOOK OF COMMON PRAYER, P. 134

I was in Virginia the night of the earthquake in Haiti. This was my prayer. Over and over again, I prayed it as I anxiously watched the television and monitored the Internet and checked my phone continuously. *Keep watch with those who watch this night...*

I had been a missionary in Haiti for six months. These people who were dying? They were *my* people. My friends. My adopted family. My colleagues. My acquaintances on the street.

As the days went by and the magnitude of destruction became better known, I wept saying this prayer. So many dead. So many more injured. Who knew who was still alive? How many were trapped under the rubble? *Keep watch with those who weep this night...*

Fourteen of my parishioners were killed. We couldn't stop to mourn, because we were working frantically to help those who yet lived. *Bless the dying, soothe the suffering, pity the afflicted...*

Then the good news began to trickle out: This friend was alive! That friend was injured but would survive!

I had never really understood the next line in the prayer—*shield the joyous*—not in my heart, at any rate, until that moment when, upon my return to Haiti, I found my friends on the streets. Standing across from a refugee camp with 6,000 homeless people living in it, we erupted in joy: "You're alive! I've found you!" *And all for your love's sake. Amen.* —Lauren Stanley

No power—but plenty of light

You, O LORD, are my lamp; my God, you make my darkness bright.
—PSALM 18:29

A few weeks ago, there was a big storm on a Saturday night that knocked out the power in the whole neighborhood. The Sunday morning experience at our church changed big time. No lights, no organ, no coffee. The junior warden announced that we probably shouldn't flush the toilets because the septic system was electric. This was not well-received, and I could feel a growing sense of doom. Someone said "Are we going to have church?" Before I could respond, someone else said "We are church; we're going to worship."

It was very dark in the sanctuary, really hard to see. It is an old Victorian building, so even with all the lights on, it is a relatively dark space. Before long, candles appeared, the piano rang out some newly chosen hymn that everyone knew, I called out into the void "Blessed be God, Father, Son, and Holy Spirit," and a loud voice from a crowd that I could barely make out called back "and blessed be his kingdom, now and forever..." At announcements the senior warden reminded people to get current with their pledges so we could get the electricity back on, and at communion, people helped one another make their way to the communion rail. At the dismissal, I think we were all a little sad it was over.

It was a Sunday that we would remember for some time. A Sunday when there was darkness, but when there was also energy, and power. And there was light. And we were church. —*Jason Leo*

Forgiveness

"I keep having these revenge fantasies," the parishioner said. She had been horribly treated at her work and eventually lost her job. It was office politics at its worst, and she had come out on the losing end.

"I want to go to my old boss's house and throw stones through his windows or slash his tires. And the guy who spread all the rumors about me—I just imagine running into him on the street with all his cronies around and giving him a full dressing down!"

"Have you done any of these things?" She assured me she had not. All she did was think about them and keep revisiting them in her mind.

"What do I do with all these revenge fantasies?" she asked.

"Enjoy them," I said. "Don't act on them," I added. "But don't try to suppress them, either. The more you try and hold them back, the more they will want to come out. It's all part of the forgiveness process. You'll eventually get bored with these fantasies."

Forgiveness is a process. It doesn't happen overnight. And eventually we realize that we forgive others, not for their sake, but for our own.

The parishioner came back to me after the revenge fantasies faded away. She told me she forgave the people who treated her so badly.

"I didn't do it for them," she said. "I did it for me. I got tired of them spending so much time in my head. I wanted to get on with my life. They weren't worth all the energy and anxiety I was giving them."

We gain strength from forgiving others, regardless of what that forgiveness does for them. —*Stephen Smith*

The ringing bell

The Rule of Saint Benedict states that the monks will immediately set aside what they're doing when the signal (such as a ringing bell) is given for the community's daily prayers. They respond "with all speed" so nothing is "preferred to the Work of God" (Chapter 43). The moment the bell rings is the time for response without hesitation or delay.

God is available to us in the everyday moments of life, and we share God's presence by responding with our attentive hearts and minds. Without delay. If this is the time to know and be known by God, there's nothing more important to do. Shonna Storz, a yoga teacher of mine, once said, "There's no better place for you at this moment than to be here." Our meeting God will be in a present moment, and not in a time or place when we are absent.

Procrastination can be very harmful. We can buffer ourselves from God, and the moment of God's encounter can be missed. There will be other times to encounter God in the future, but each present moment is precious and not to be wasted. Our commitment is to be here, really here, to find and be found by God.

Our encounters with God may not be punctuated by any sound, but we can be attentive to God's presence. We can be alert for the unexpected opportunities and coincidences of life. We can listen to others with our hearts as well as our ears, and make ourselves available without delay or distractions. We can be present where we are. We can listen for God. We can know God in all the moments of our lives, clearly, like a ringing bell. —*Rob Slocum*

A lot to be thankful for

Now thank we all our God,
with hearts, and hands, and voices.
—*THE HYMNAL 1982*, #396, 397

I am especially thankful for the voices, when there are many of them crowded into a small space. I'm glad when they all come, with lots of loud talking and laughing, even if it is confusing, crowded, and tiring.

There used to be quite a few of us—our children, their spouses, grandchildren, and friends. Grandma Johnson's big table with all the leaves was never big enough, so we set up a card table in the living room just a few feet away, so nobody would miss any of the jokes, teasing, and laughter.

We had a lot to be thankful for as we remembered all the things that had happened in the past year. Even the young ones could say "Thank you, God," when it was their turn to pray.

This year there may be just two of us, because jobs have called and families have gone to other parts of the country. Now we are thankful for email and "family news" that we often share through our computers. I have even learned to share photos electronically.

One of our traditions after Thanksgiving dinner is to draw names out of a hat to choose the family member for whom we will buy a Christmas gift. Someone picks for those who are not present, and someone else writes it all down. This year we will have to send the list around via email.

A day of thanks, yes, for all God's blessings—and a day to be together and find joy in each other's company, or to remember each other with joy if we are apart. —*Lois Sibley*

Blessed and thankful

In you all the families of the earth shall be blessed.
—GENESIS 12:3

Thanksgiving is a secular holiday designed around a most sacred practice: the act of giving thanks. It's a beautiful thing really, that people of faith and differing faiths and no particular faith at all can gather around a table, joined in the holy practice of gratitude. Across the country, people will take turns naming aloud things for which they are grateful. It's something to be treasured, something to be commended, something worth doing.

And yet, I wonder, in all these moments of listing the blessings in our lives for which we give thanks, if there isn't a crucial element missing. As people of faith we are called, not only to bless God, but also to be a conduit of God's blessing to others, so that through us the whole world might be blessed. It's a high calling, but a sacred one that we ought not to neglect. It calls for us not only to receive all the blessings that God gives us in this life, but also to be nourished by those blessings so that we might pass them on to others.

This year on Thanksgiving, as you make the mental list of all the blessings of your life, consider also how you might be a blessing to others. Maybe you could serve others at a soup kitchen before you chow down at home. Perhaps you could invite someone lonely to join you at your family table. Whatever you choose, make Thanksgiving about more than just your blessings—make it about being a blessing to others as well. *—Melody Shobe*

Thanksgiving has no boundaries

Thanksgiving in a foreign land. It's just not the same as being at home.

In Kenya one year, we ordered a turkey from the market. When we arrived to pick it up, we were shocked: It was alive! It escaped from the seller, so we chased it through the market, tackling it just before it scooted into the street. No one told us we would have to kill it ourselves, gut it, pluck it. But we did. We used dental floss to sew up the skin, eyebrow tweezers to remove the feather shafts. It took hours and hours to cook in a balky oven. That was one good turkey.

Years later, in Sudan, one of my colleagues told my cook that this was a special day for me. She arose before dawn, went to the market, picked out a goat, had it slaughtered, and brought me fresh liver for breakfast. "It's your day of giving thanks," she said. "I brought you something special." That was one good goat liver.

Fast forward more years, this time to Haiti. We want turkey, we told a Haitian friend who sometimes cooked for us. And yams. And potatoes. And green vegetables. And cranberries. Is that possible? "Of course," she said. "I would love to cook all of that for you."

The tough old bird that might have been a turkey was in a stew, with the potatoes and yams thrown in. Instead of vegetables, we had avocados. And *piklis*, Haitian coleslaw so spicy it can bring tears to your eyes. Instead of cranberries, we had mangoes. It wasn't quite the traditional American Thanksgiving. But it was one good stew.

Thanksgiving meals made in love are the best Thanksgivings of all. —*Lauren Stanley*

Ray's woodpile

As Saul was going along and approaching Damascus,
suddenly a light from heaven flashed around him.

—ACTS 9:3

Dad always said, "If it ain't growing, it's going." Barns were painted; tools were put away. If something didn't work, it was gone.

Ray was a woodworker, making grandfather clocks and restoring antiques. His workshop included a tangled woodpile that didn't look very productive to my ten-year-old eyes.

When an antique chair leg splintered, we went to Ray—who went to that pile. Emerging with a dusty piece, he said: "See the up-and-down saw marks on this barn beam? It was hand cut. Poplar. I'll turn a new leg from this that'll match exactly."

Sure enough, the repaired chair looked perfect. I confessed to Ray how I'd thought that old pile was good for nothing but a match. Smiling, Ray said, "Just because something is broken doesn't mean it should be thrown away. That pile has pieces of wood you can't find anymore: elm, chestnut, sassafras. I may not have a use for all of them today, but I will have a use for each of them someday."

It seems like the way Ray thought about wood is the way God thinks about people. We are quick to condemn, but God is sure to save. God didn't throw Saul the persecutor into the fire of condemnation. God threw Saul into the fire of transformation. The fire of the Holy Spirit blinded Saul so he could see the light and become the wholly/holy new person Paul.

If there are pieces of your life that don't fit, if your life seems broken beyond repair, trust God to find a way to make the pieces work—beautifully. —*John Van Nuys*

Brush with royalty

I once had a brush with royalty. When I was in high school, my family took a trip to London and we hit all the usual hotspots: the Tower of London, Big Ben, St. Paul's Cathedral. Toward the end of the day, we ended up in the famous Tate Gallery. At some point I wandered off by myself, and when I turned around I came face-to-face with…the Queen Mum.

I'm not much of a royal-watcher, but even I couldn't miss this one. There she was, in all her glory, wearing a bright purple dress with matching shoes and handbag. She was short but dignified and quite, well, old. While she was at least ninety-something at that point, she still made a striking impression. And there she was, close enough that I could have reached out and touched her were it not for the large bodyguard with his hand inside his sport jacket, ready to blow anyone away who even looked at her funny.

While keeping tabs on the British monarchy may be good fun, there is, of course, only one King. And when we reflect upon Christ the King, our earthly notions of kingship must be suspended. Jesus isn't about the trappings of earthly monarchs—he was born in a stable, not a palace; he had a group of nomadic followers, not a royal court; he had "nowhere to lay his head," not a royal bed chamber. It's a different kind of kingship and a different kind of kingdom. And yet, as the Son of God, Jesus is the only king in the history of kingship who could authentically lay claim to Divine Right. —*Tim Schenck*

Word games

Some friends and I have taken to playing a Scrabble-like game on our mobile phones. It's an enjoyable diversion, and I think it's helped to push back the chemo-induced fog in my brain.

To do well, of course, requires a good vocabulary, but that isn't enough by itself. You need skill as well, the knowledge of how best to place the tiles. Nabbing a triple-word score is great, but if you play an X or a Z on a triple-letter spot, you may do almost as well. If you can't get the triple score, you may at least be able to block your opponent from using it.

I arrived with the vocabulary and I'm developing the skills. The sad truth, though, is that you're only as good as the letters the game turns up for you. If you get only single-point Ts and Rs, instead of big-point Js and Qs, you're unlikely to rack up the spectacular scores. If the game gives you only consonants or only vowels for several turns, you're unlikely to get very far. The luck of the draw is as important as ability.

Fortunately, it's only a game.

Life is a little like that. You arrive with talents, you develop skills—but the circumstances around you play a big part in what you do with them.

But God does not flip the tiles randomly or maliciously. God loves us and will guide us if we pay attention. The importance of the luck of the draw recedes when we have faith. —*Sarah Bryan Miller*

Selfless giving

It is more blessed to give than to receive.

—Acts 20:35

I didn't understand what generosity was until I went to Africa. I grew up in an affluent community in the United States, and my family supported many charities, but we did so from a position of power and comfort. We could *afford* to give money away, because there was always enough left over.

My wife and I spent some time as missionaries in Uganda, and the people there taught me about true generosity. When we were invited over to someone's house for dinner, they would serve us meat, even though the family would never indulge in such extravagance for themselves. One meal could cost a week's or a month's wages, and it would go on for hours.

We also learned to be careful about complimenting people on their home or their belongings. That's a rather standard politeness in America, but in Africa if you admire something that someone else owns, more often than not they'll try to give it to you. Even if it means a lot to them. Even if it's the most valuable thing they own.

That sort of selfless giving is almost unheard of in wealthier parts of the world, and it convinced me that only the poor know how to be truly generous. It also made me wonder about what the world would be like if the rich were equally so.

If the rich gave away as much of their belongings as the people in Uganda did, we would all be richer for it. —*Robert Macauley*

Making love real

We wandered into an antique shop just to have a look around.

On the wall was a framed piece of needlework that had a message I pray to accomplish every day. Embroidered on a white cloth were the words: "Making Love Real."

We took it down and looked at the back. There was a note that said it had been given to a lady who taught an adult Sunday School class for over thirty years. I don't know how it arrived at an antique shop, unless the teacher had died without heirs. I might have taken it to the grave with me! What higher honor could anyone receive than to be told he or she made love real?

We bought it, of course, but before I could find a place to hang it, we got a phone call. A dear friend, now in her eighties, wanted to give me a birthday party—for ten or a hundred, it was up to me. We chose the smaller number, feeling grateful for her love and hoping the affair would not be too much for her.

I then stopped trying to find a place to put our new purchase. I knew exactly where it should go. When the day came, we carried it with us and presented it to our lovely friend. She has had a lifetime of making love real for many people.

She put the needlework over the doorway from her living room to the dining room, where many delicious meals have been shared. As we held hands and a blessing was said, I felt humbled to be chosen by her as a friend. That is why I often say I have world-class friends. She is one. —*Nancy R. Duvall*

Prepare—and wonder

We are about to embark on the "most wonderful time of the year." You'll hear that 1963 Christmas classic piped into the stores, its lyrics waxing nostalgic about kids jingle belling and everyone telling you "be of good cheer." When your ear catches the tune you may be stomping impatiently through a store attempting to satisfy the desires and expectations of your loved ones.

There is another way to prepare for wonder at Christmas. The point is not to add to the list of things to do, but to develop an attitude or an approach to the mystery of Christ's coming.

Advent marks both the birth of a humble Savior, whom God sent into the world to redeem it from the darkness of sin and death *and* the second coming, when the majestic splendor of Christ will come again to "judge the world with righteousness and the peoples with his truth" (Psalm 96:13). In the first coming, we welcome Emmanuel, born to be God with us. Wonder what it means to shape your life as a cradle to contain him. For that second coming, we prepare to meet the one who looks for truth deep within us, for actions and gestures that demonstrate a life in right relationship with God and neighbor. Wonder for a moment today what truth Jesus reads in you when the Author of Salvation opens your life story. —*Ruth Lawson Kirk*

> *Once he came in blessing, all our ills redressing;*
> *came in likeness lowly, Son of God most holy;*
> *bore the cross to save us, hope and freedom gave us.*
> *Still he comes within us, still his voice would win us*
> *from the sins that hurt us, would to Truth convert us:*
> *not in torment hold us, but in love enfold us.*
>
> —*The Hymnal 1982, #53*

Improbable disciples

The Bible is full of stories of faith and trust and revelation found in unlikely people. The Samaritan woman at the well recognized Jesus as a prophet. The prostitute in Nain washed Jesus' feet with her tears. Jairus, a part of the religious establishment, knew Jesus could save his dying daughter. Of the ten lepers healed of their deadly disease, the lone Samaritan was the one who returned to worship at Jesus' feet. Zacchaeus, a hated tax collector, repented and made amends. The Roman centurion in Capernaum amazed Jesus with his faith.

Thank heavens that improbability doesn't disqualify us as Jesus' followers! Not so many of us, I suspect, would stack up as "likely" disciples, caught up as we are in our secular lives, captivated by the consumer culture's glam and glitz, sunk in the seemingly limitless self-absorption of our age. We are improbable followers indeed of the One who gave up everything—his family home, his dependable trade, his very life—for others, for human-kind's salvation.

Yet God calls us out of our small lives. Improbable though it seems, he reaches out an all-powerful hand and touches us, awakening our minds and hearts and spirits, giving us dreams to dream and visions that burn through the scales on our eyes. And with Zacchaeus we can hear him say, "Today salvation has come to this house" (Luke 19:9). —*Betsy Rogers*

Christmas is not *your birthday*

John said to the crowds that came out to be baptized by him, "You brood of vipers! Who warned you to flee from the wrath to come? Bear fruits worthy of repentance"… The crowds asked him, "What then should we do?" In reply he said to them, "Whoever has two coats must share with anyone who has none; and whoever has food must do likewise."

—LUKE 3:7-8, 10-11

There are twenty-four shopping days until Christmas. Retailers are anxious; consumers are stretched; and the already frenzied Christmas season continues to accelerate. But it can be different.

The Reverend Mike Slaughter of Ginghamsburg United Methodist Church near Dayton, Ohio, preaches a John the Baptist-like message about Christmas that is hard to hear, but good to follow. Slaughter preaches that Christmas is *not* your birthday—it's Jesus' birthday. So, instead of buying yourself a bunch of presents, why not focus your giving on Jesus by giving to him?

Slaughter challenges his parishioners: "If you buy your kid a bike, then you also buy a bike for a needy child. If you give your daughter a Barbie, you give a Barbie to a little girl who otherwise wouldn't get anything. Whatever you spend on your family this Christmas, you give the same amount to others." Use your moral imagination: toys or Heifer Project animals or mosquito nets—the possibilities are many and the blessings are rich.

It took our family a couple of years to grow into this 1:1 ratio of family spending to neighbor giving, but it has made our Christmases much more meaningful.

Try Slaughter's challenge. As you do, you may find this Christmas to be the best one yet. —*John Van Nuys*

Preparing for an out-of-town guest

My parents used to drive for the Thanksgiving holiday from Kentucky to wherever my family and I were living. Prior to their arrival we cleaned the house and made certain fresh sheets were on the guest room bed; we gave our three young sons baths shortly before their grandparents were expected; my wife Pam cooked a lot of food. Such preparations were made because we wanted our guests to be comfortable in our home.

Thanksgiving is over now and the guests have come and gone. It is time to prepare for another guest. We know how to prepare for a visit from relatives—but how do we prepare for a visit from the Son of God? What things will make Jesus feel at home with us? Perhaps we should abandon the thought of a big turkey dinner and serve simple sandwiches, giving the difference in the cost of the meal to charity. Or perhaps we should invite a few homeless folk to dine with us so Jesus can see our concern for the poor. What will make Jesus feel comfortable in our presence?

The greater problem may be how to make ourselves feel comfortable in Jesus' presence. We will be comfortable with Jesus if we have prepared properly for his coming—if we have swept our house clean of all things petty and mean, if we have frequently entertained the poor, the helpless, and the needy at our table, and if, in our efforts to fill our home with "the finer things of life," we have known that the finest things are those that can be neither touched nor seen? Into such a home Jesus could come. Both he and his hosts would be comfortable.

Are we ready to receive him? —*Richard H. Schmidt*

Picture perfect

When I was a child, my family received a Christmas card from friends who lived on a farm with their five children. On the outside was a photograph with everyone dressed in their Sunday best, sitting nicely and smiling for the camera. Even the family chicken was peacefully sitting front and center on the lap of one of the kids. But when you opened up the card there was another shot of the family. This one showed everyone laughing and whooping it up, with chicken feathers flying every which way.

We often strive for perfection, yet reality always lurks beneath the surface. Even when the kids are whining that there's nothing "good" to eat, despite the fact there's more food on the table than any pilgrim saw in a lifetime; even though the cranberry sauce just got dumped on my lap; even though Norman Rockwell himself would be horrified, God's presence abides in the midst of our holiday chaos.

A good metaphor for faith may be the way I wrap Christmas presents. Unlike my wife, who wraps gifts beautifully as if she works in a Hallmark store, I'm the worst wrapper this side of the North Pole. It's embarrassing: tape and paper everywhere, ends and corners sticking out, and a ribbon two sizes too big.

Our faith is a gift. But it isn't a perfectly wrapped gift with exact folds and a precisely tied bow. It's more like the way I wrap. Fortunately faith isn't about being neat and tidy, and the good news is that God remains in the middle of it all. —*Tim Schenck*

Seeking God

Seek the LORD while he may be found.

—ISAIAH 55:6

The life of faith is sometimes like a game of holy hide-and-seek. God isn't obvious or always visible; many times we wonder if God is around at all. It would be much easier, we often believe, if God would just make himself clearly, definitively known: skywriting a message with the stars, or issuing a booming proclamation in a clap of thunder. But for better or worse, that's not how it works. We, instead, are called to seek God, even as we are sought out by God, to engage in a lifelong game of holy hide-and-seek.

Too often in our lives we are willing to hide, but not to seek. We tuck ourselves into corners, in out of the way places, and wait for God to find us. Again and again, we find the most difficult of hiding spots, believing that God, who really cares, will search for us once again. But we're unwilling to take our turn at being "it," to spend the time and effort and energy it takes to seek God. We only want to play a one-sided game.

A one-sided game is no fun at all. Instead we have to be willing to engage in the back and forth of seeking and being sought. We have to be willing to pursue God, even as God pursues us. Seek out God—go back to church, even if we've been burned; go on a mission trip or pilgrimage, even if it's outside our comfort zone; read the Bible, even if it seems intimidating. The amazing thing about this amazing game of hide-and-seek is that God's not that hard to find at all. God's standing out there in the open, all around, just waiting for us to take our turn at seeking. —*Melody Shobe*

Change

It's a cliché that nothing is certain in this life but death and taxes. I would add a third certainty to that list: change.

Some change will be for the better. Some will not. Some of it will be natural and organic in the way in which it unfolds. Some will come as a surprise, even as a shock.

My great-aunt Eleanor was ninety-six when she died in 1990. Her generation saw change unrivaled in human history, from horse-drawn conveyances and rutted roads to automobiles zooming along on superhighways to men walking on the moon.

Lately, I think that our own generation may rival hers in terms of sweeping change. Changes come so fast that it's hard to keep up with them, especially in terms of the instantaneous and widespread dispersal of information. Many people spend a large portion of the day glued to various glowing screens that Aunt Eleanor could not have imagined.

Most change is on a smaller scale, more incremental, but still of enormous import in our own lives. The seasons bring new rhythms. A child goes away to school or launches herself into the adult world. A job is lost or gained. Families are built or broken. We move up to a larger house or scale down to something more manageable.

Change is inevitable in this world. A shark must keep swimming or die. We must react to new challenges. But for all the changes that we have experienced and will continue to experience, God never alters. Our perceptions and understandings change, but God remains unchanged and unchanging, the same today and tomorrow.

It's important to be open to changes and challenges, to listen to the Spirit and follow where God leads. To ignore them means stagnation; to rise to them will fulfill us as God's people.

—*Sarah Bryan Miller*

"I've been good!"

My husband, a bishop, was asked to tell the story of Saint Nicholas to the children at our church. He decided to go in full attire—purple cassock, red chimere, gold pectoral cross, and red miter.

The room was packed with young children and their parents. Little ones gathered around him on the floor as he told the story of the good bishop who dropped gold coins down chimneys at houses where young girls lived who could not marry without dowries.

One-three-year old kept putting up his hand and his mother kept pulling it down, until the story was done. Up shot the hand again, and my husband asked, "Do you have a question?"

Standing on tiptoe and leaning forward as far as he could, the little boy said firmly, "I've been *good!*" Laughter broke out, and he said loudly, "And my name is John." With that established, he sat down at peace, sure that he had gotten the word to the right person.

Unfortunately, he had not gotten the word to the right person. The person to whom he reported was not the person who would give him gifts for Christmas.

Do we do the same thing? Do we ask the wrong things to get us through the day? Are we relying on alcohol, drugs, food, cigarettes, lying, pornography, or other things as crutches?

It won't work for long. God gives us the freedom to make our own decisions and often we make the wrong ones. God does not take away the consequences of our actions. God loves us through trials and tribulations, but we must want to change bad habits and addictions.

We must give up our pride that we can do it ourselves and ask God to help us. —*Nancy R. Duvall*

Imagine

A voice cries out: "In the wilderness prepare the way of the LORD, make straight in the desert a highway for our God. Every valley shall be lifted up, and every mountain and hill be made low."

—ISAIAH 40:3-4

In *The Good Book*, Peter Gomes writes of the Bible as "a book of imagination." We can get caught up in believing that scripture is about things that happened long ago, or we may look to it as a book of rules and regulations. But the Bible is a book of imagination, opening up new possibilities of a God whose word keeps coming to us.

Nowhere is this more true than in the writings of the prophets. Every Sunday during Advent, we hear from them. As we await the coming of Christ, we join these prophets in imagining a new world.

Jane Addams, the founder of the Settlement House movement in the United States in the late nineteenth and early twentieth centuries, said of the world where she worked in inner city Chicago, "much of the insensibility and hardness of the world is due to the lack of imagination."

This is still true today. We so often get stuck in reality, in our limited visions of what is possible. Or we get stuck in the daily grind. We spend our energy gathering data and delaying action. Good organization and planning has its place, but sometimes our vision is too small.

Advent calls us to imagine a new world, where mountains are leveled and valleys are exalted. Can we imagine it? The lion lying down with the lamb? A world without war? A world where all are fed and have their basic needs met? Can we imagine our own lives content, stress-free, and trusting God? This is what the prophets did and still do: they call us to look honestly at the present and imagine a new future. —*Nancy Hopkins-Greene*

Simplicity night

When I tell my kids that over a billion people in the world survive on less than a dollar a day, they have a hard time believing me. They look around at all that we have—two cars, a nice house, plenty of food in the pantry—and it seems as if I'm telling tales.

So we started having "simplicity night" once a week. On that night, we have a basic dinner (usually just soup and bread), with water to drink. We read about how other people struggle to survive, and we take the money we would have spent on dinner and put it in "the Africa jar," which we then contribute at the end of the year to an international charity.

I think that this weekly observance impacts how we live our lives—and how we view the world—far beyond that one evening. I, at least, am more acutely aware of the blessings of this life, which I don't take for granted. And it's great to take the time we would have spent making dinner and spend it together as a family, knowing that someone else far away is being blessed as a result. —*Robert Macauley*

Finding the way home

In this you will rejoice, even if now for a little while
you have had to suffer various trials.
—1 PETER 1:6

Our neighbors have a dog named Fred. He came from the pound and was very nice, but not too smart. He always looked dirty, like he could have used a good bath. But Fred always wagged his tail at people and was about the friendliest dog anyone could remember.

One summer our neighbors went away for a long vacation. On the last day of their vacation, Fred saw a squirrel and was gone in flash. Our neighbors searched high and low for many hours but could not find Fred. He wore no dog tag, not even a collar.

The family was crushed. The drive home was misery. When they told us the news, we were all sad and tried to console them.

On Christmas morning, almost five months after Fred disappeared—I'm not making this up, couldn't if I tried—there was scratching at their front door. When they opened the door, Fred came charging in. We figured Fred had traveled over seven hundred miles and through or around at least two major cities. Fred was obviously a little worse for the wear, but he was home.

A long time ago a follower of Jesus named Augustine cried out to God and said "Oh God you have made us toward yourself, and our hearts are restless until they rest with you." The same pull that brought Fred home is in each and every one of us, calling us back to God our Creator, calling us to be in relationship with God. All of us. You and me. When we answer that call, and journey toward God and God's kingdom, we find our way home. —*Jason Leo*

Still so misunderstood

"I want to create the perfect Christmas this year," I once heard a woman say. I figured right then that trouble lay ahead. For that particular woman, I knew this would include buying, addressing, and mailing over a hundred elegant greeting cards; erecting a large tree in the parlor with designer-coordinated ornaments; buying, wrapping, and mailing dozens of packages; changing the color scheme of her house to red, green, and gold; entertaining friends and their children; cooking (or hiring out to a caterer) gobs of food; and doing more work at church than she would normally have agreed to do—all the while emitting an unnatural cheery glow. Observing Advent as a time of quiet reflection on the coming of the Savior? Certainly not on her list.

I'm not sure there is any such thing as a "perfect" Christmas, but if there is, I don't think it includes a distracted, strung-out woman at the center of it—the Blessed Virgin, possibly, but she was anything but distracted and strung out.

What or who would be at the center of a perfect Christmas? What is the purpose of Christmas, the "reason for the season?" When you have answered that question, make a quick list of the things you're planning to do to prepare for the holiday and then ask yourself which of them further that purpose and which of them hinder it. Next lop off the list everything that detracts from the purpose of Christmas, and do the remaining things with a more focused intention.

Perhaps the perfect Christmas isn't a matter of how much you do and how well it comes off. Maybe it's about sitting quietly and thanking God for his love, and then doing a few small things to let others know that God loves them, too. —*Richard H. Schmidt*

Goat under the mountain

My thoughts are not your thoughts,
nor are your ways my ways, says the LORD.

—ISAIAH 55:8

My nine-year-old surprised me on the way home from worship one Advent Sunday. Sam said, "It all makes sense now. That last hymn. Now I get it—'Go Tell It on the Mountain!' Ever since I was little I thought that song went 'Goat under the mountain.' I never understood why we sang about some goat being under a mountain! Now I know what that song is really saying."

We had a good laugh, but later I thought that Sam isn't the only one among us who has had a misunderstanding during Advent or about Christmas. Most of us don't get it either.

Christmas, as it is presently culturally observed, is a season of enforced good cheer in which we ratchet up our crazy-busy activity another notch. We consume more commercially and calorically, leaving our pants tighter and our wallets lighter. We can whiz through Christmas without really getting what Christmas is all about.

Christmas at its core is about the Incarnation of God's redeeming love into broken humanity estranged from our Creator. Advent is the time to prepare for the gift of the Incarnation by making our lives more open to and reflective of the One who comes to save: Emmanuel—God with us. If we can fix our gaze on the light of that shining truth, our darkness shall be overcome.

One thing kids do get right about Christmas is that Christmas is not about giving, but all about receiving. It is about receiving all the love our gracious God comes to give. That is the saving truth. Go tell it on the mountain. —*John Van Nuys*

Watching and waiting

Our son Nick, aged eleven, contracted an illness with the improbable name of Henoch-Schoenlein Purpura. HSP is not typically life-threatening, though it can be in some cases. It mostly strikes young boys, manifests itself in a succession of symptoms, and usually runs its course in a couple of weeks.

Nick's case was different. The illness did not run its course but kept cycling through the same succession of symptoms again and again. He would come to the cycle's end, we would hope he'd get well, and then it would all begin again. His pediatrician, a wise and experienced doctor, had never seen HSP continue as Nick's did. Still, there was no medical cure, nothing she could prescribe that would bring it to an end. Nick suffered with severe abdominal pain, immobilizing swelling in his joints, kidney inflammation, and other miseries.

One December evening, as I walked the dog and said my prayers, I kept returning to the pediatrician's words: "We just have to wait. He will get well."

Watching and waiting, hoping and praying. These are the disciplines of Advent. In the darkest days of the year, we watch and wait and hope. There's no hurrying Christmas, as there was no hurrying Nick's healing. We can only wait. But we wait in confidence and certainty, knowing not just that we will again celebrate God's Incarnation, but that Christ will be born anew in our hearts and that he will come again at the last day, to restore all creation to God.

Advent came alive for me that night. I came to trust that Nick would get well, and he did. And I learned in an unforgettable way to keep Advent, to watch and wait, to hope and pray.

—*Betsy Rogers*

In the wilderness

In the wilderness prepare the way of the LORD,
make straight in the desert a highway for our God.

—ISAIAH 40:3

In Sudan, I lived on the edge of the desert, in the sub-Saharan Sahel, the semi-arid flatlands of grass and acacia thorn trees—a true wilderness where you can see for miles and miles, with few landmarks to guide you.

One night, returning to Khartoum, eight of us—laity, priests, and bishops—wandered in the desert for hours in our trucks. I knew we were heading in the right general direction, west, because I was keeping tabs on the setting moon. Suddenly, our trucks slammed to a halt.

"Laurens," said my new friend Joseph. "Can you read a compass?"

"Yes."

"Can you tell me which direction we are heading?"

"Joseph, I don't need a compass. We're heading west. See? The moon is setting there."

"But, Laurens, are you sure? Please look."

"Yes, I'm sure. Look," I said, taking him by his shoulders and turning him south. "See that constellation? That's the Southern Cross." I turned him around. "Look? See that? It's the North Star."

We were lost, he said. We could not find the path. We were wandering the wilderness, where no highway had yet been made, for God or for us.

"Follow the moon, Joseph," I assured him. "God put it there to guide us." We got back in the trucks and followed the moon. Eventually, we found the White Nile River. Hours later, Khartoum. God prepared a way for us, in the middle of the wilderness that is South Sudan. —*Lauren Stanley*

So beloved

Advent is a good time to remember our baptism.

There was a baptism at my church recently in which four babies and one adult were received into Christ's flock. The adult was to be a godfather, so he went first. Then came the twins. Both studied the minister's face in complete contentment. Next were the other two babies. None cried as water was poured over their heads. All four babies were dressed in beautiful gowns made especially for the occasion. All five were marked with a cross using holy oil on their foreheads, making them Christ's own forever.

After we had received the newly baptized into the household of God, the fathers carried their babies down the center aisle as we sang "Jesus Loves Me."

As the procession passed my row, one of the fathers caught my eye. All were proud parents, but this man was aglow, joy beaming out from his face, radiating light as he passed. He was totally in love with his son. It was beautiful to watch.

That is when it hit me that God feels the same way about all of God's children, no matter their age, dress, condition, address—even in a stable, wrapped in a swaddling cloth, with a mattress of straw and a feeding trough of rock for a bed. Our Savior, born so humbly, but so beloved.

That is why Advent is a good time to contemplate what being a baptized person means to each one of us. We remember God has proved to us, all over again, that we are God's, and God's love is forever.

—*Nancy R. Duvall*

Saul in the basket

Saul of Tarsus was a major threat to the early Christian church, but Christ encountered him on the way to Damascus and asked him, "Saul, Saul, why do you persecute me?" Saul was blinded by the brightness of the light that shone about him. He obeyed the Lord's direction to go to Damascus, where he took the next steps of faith (Acts 9:1-19).

The Jews in Damascus plotted to kill Saul, but his disciples helped him escape. At night they lowered him in a basket through an opening in the city wall. He fled to Jerusalem, where he tried to join the Christians. But they were afraid of him, and didn't believe he was a disciple. Finally Barnabas convinced the apostles of Saul's conversion (Acts 9:23-27).

It must have been difficult for Saul. He was respected, forceful, articulate, and accustomed to speaking for himself. His escape from Damascus required him to sneak out of the city in a basket, literally depending on others to hold him up as he fled. And he couldn't bring about his own acceptance into the community of disciples in Jerusalem. He had to keep his mouth shut while Barnabas told his story and persuaded the apostles to believe him. He would certainly have been glad to speak for himself, but anything he said in that context would have seemed suspicious and self-serving.

Our greatest personal strengths can sometimes become our most significant weaknesses. And we may be amazed by the possibilities available to us when we seem most helpless and vulnerable. We may find unexpected strength beyond ourselves as we let go of pretense and control. Like Saul, we may find healing, new direction, and acceptance in the hands of others. We can begin with trust. —*Rob Slocum*

The wind

A few years ago I went on a leadership training expedition in the Sea of Cortez. On our off-days I would often get away by myself for a little while to write in my journal. One afternoon I found myself on a rocky beach, and I'll always remember how the wind took me by surprise. The gusts came unexpectedly, because there was no grass or trees to bend or move, no visual clues. I had no warning when the wind would come.

In the Bible the same word means both *spirit* and *wind*. The Holy Spirit is often likened to wind or breath (literally giving "inspiration"). That day on the rocky beach helped me understand how the Spirit works. Most of the time the Spirit works through things we can feel and touch and anticipate: the people in our lives, the world around us. At those times we can see the Spirit moving.

At other times, though, the Spirit takes us by surprise. There is no warning, and we're not even sure from what direction it's coming. It may be silent and invisible and impossible to grasp, but it is also undeniable. We know when it has touched our lives, for we are awakened and amazed. And we will never be the same. —*Robert Macauley*

It's almost time

This week we begin to hear the beating of angels' wings. That means it's almost time, time for Mary and Joseph to arrive in Bethlehem and find no room in the inn, time for Jesus to be born. A stable will do for the birth of the King. Time for the shepherds, the angels, the wise men from the east—all coming to worship the baby in the manger, just as the prophets had foretold and as God promised.

Excitement is building. Everyone is practicing for the pageant. The altar guild is busy planning decorations for the church, getting out the special candlesticks, cleaning and polishing. "Greening of the church Sunday" is nearly here. Cookies will be made and packed and taken to the homebound. There will be an Open House at the rectory or parish hall for all the congregation, and a special luncheon for the church staff and volunteers. The choir is having extra practices. The office staff is swamped with extra leaflets to prepare for extra services.

But that's okay. They are all enjoying themselves, loving what they do in serving God here with one another. They will be tired but satisfied as they enjoy the twelve days of Christmas and then begin another year together. The biblical stories of the coming of the Messiah will be read again, to reveal, enthrall, teach, and maybe even surprise with a new word or thought all who come to worship.

And the story is not over. Jesus will come again, as he said in John 14:3: "I will come again and will take you to myself, so that where I am, there you may be also." That's the promise we hold dear as we await that day, trusting God for the best time, the best situation, and the beginning of life eternal with Christ who loves us and gave himself for us. —*Lois Sibley*

Preparing the way in the...snow

One Friday after a messy snowfall in Seattle, I took the day off and began preparing my little house for Christmas. I could not get my car out of my parking spot, so I walked to a nearby tree lot, bought a Christmas tree, asked the tree man to tie some rope to the end of it, and then dragged it the eight blocks to my house.

"Keep on the ice and snow the whole way!" the tree man shouted after me, as my tree and I made our way out of the parking lot.

It turns out to be hard work to drag a six-foot tree for eight or so blocks, even if you do stay on the ice and snow. But as is often the case, hard work has its rewards—rewards like cars yielding you the right of way, just so that the people can watch you and laugh, or like dogs barking at you because they've never seen a person walk a tree before.

Preparing the house is important during Advent. And so, to be honest, I found myself a little upset by the mess and the disruption that the snowfall had brought to my preparations. I had planned to do so much, but now would have so little ability to get things done.

But the One who comes at Christmas—the One born to a peasant teenaged girl at a time when no inn could receive him, the One born to a people who would not be ready for him—is a God who comes with blessing, ready or not.

In what ways are you ready and not ready for the coming of Christmas? What blessings might you receive, ready or not?
—*Melissa Skelton*

Bring light to the world

The light shines in the darkness.

—JOHN 1:1-18

"The light in the darkness—come see the light! It's Jesus Christ our Lord," is the first stanza of "The Light," the first song that our small parish church has sung for the past twenty years at our annual Christmas Living Nativity outdoor pageant.

It is a sight to behold as our teens act out the birth of Christ with a full entourage of animals—horses, cows, sheep, a donkey, and other barnyard animals that we scrape up from our rural New England community. We hold this magnificent event on the front lawn, often in the snow, for the community. Publicity, flyers, sponsorship, and plenty of work are all part of the Advent preparation. The eager crowds come and families, small children, grandparents, and the curious all watch. For some, it is the only truthful reality of Christmas that they will experience in this harsh and often dark world.

As we look toward Christmas this year, how are we each preparing our hearts for the birth of Jesus? We live in a fallen world of sin, and we all must shoulder and carry this difficult burden. For some it is overwhelming. But we are not alone—our God saves if we but take a small step into his light.

How does God call you to action, and what will you do for your Advent? Pray that today God will open the eyes of your heart to fully experience his brilliance. Help one another.

As we give our struggles and difficulties to the Lord in prayer, we open our spirit and reflect the radiance of God in our lives. Because of Jesus, light has come into the world and is forever with us. —*Carl Kinkel*

Wise guys

There's a great scene in the 1982 Barry Levinson film *Diner* in which Kevin Bacon's character gets drunk and punches out the Three Wise Men. In his underwear. It all takes place at a life-sized nativity scene outside a church in a respectable Baltimore neighborhood. A church, I might add, where I sang in the boys' choir as a child.

Now, I'm not encouraging you to go out and do likewise. But there is something about this scene that warms the heart. And I'm not just referring to the Christmas spirits involved. It's because if nothing else, Kevin Bacon's character, Fenwick, is *engaged* with the nativity scene. He is literally in the midst of it; especially when he lies down in the manger.

And while our engagement is hopefully a bit more metaphorical, it's so often something we fail to do. Because we usually set up our little crèches and simply admire them from afar. And they may well be beautifully crafted, hand-painted works of art. But when we put them on the mantle and tell our kids to look but not touch, we miss the power of the Christmas story. Because the reality is that Christ entered *our* world, not Fantasy Island. He entered a place with real people and real passions; not a world where the Three Wise Men kneel in handcrafted glory.

The power of the Incarnation is only unleashed in our lives when we engage it. Not by punching out the Magi, but by incorporating the message of salvation into our lives. By meeting Jesus as he comes to us: first as a little child, but ultimately as the risen Christ. —*Tim Schenck*

Solstice

I sat down to write this as the hour of the solstice approached; it will be winter before I finish.

In the northern hemisphere, this is the shortest day; in some places closer to the pole, the sun barely makes an appearance before rolling back over the horizon. In the American Midwest, where I live, the weather at this time is often gray and cloudy, making the light even more abbreviated than the patterns of the Earth's rotation alone would dictate.

In the church, this is when we count the hours until the Nativity and try to get everything needful accomplished. In this past year, the usual Energizer Bunny approach didn't cut it for me. I was on the sidelines as my body was poisoned to cure the cancer that threatened it.

Part of me observed, almost clinically, the physical changes, the fatigue and string of minor ailments that accompany the chemotherapy; part of me chafed and attempted to carry on as usual. Working was like trying to swim through molasses, but I was compelled to try. My job was to wait and prepare.

A little while ago the Earth began its journey toward summer; the lightening will begin tomorrow morning, although few of us will notice an extra minute or two of sun. There are still many weeks of darkness before the change becomes apparent.

So, too, with my illness: the tumor began to shrink and I began to heal, although with months to go—and a lot more to endure—before it was over. The changes were gradual, but they did come.

Meanwhile, now the greatest change of all is coming, the birth of Jesus, that Son of Righteousness that lightens all: I will watch, and wait, and rejoice. —*Sarah Bryan Miller*

Waiting and rejoicing

O come, Desire of nations, bind in one the hearts of all mankind;
bid thou our sad divisions cease, and be thyself our King of Peace.
Rejoice! Rejoice! Emmanuel shall come to thee, O Israel.

—THE HYMNAL 1982, #56, ST. 7

This is the verse set aside specifically for this day, December 22. It's actually the seventh verse of the hymn that so many of us sing in Advent, a hymn that is both beautiful and haunting and speaks to so many of our souls.

Calling upon the "Desire of *nations*," which means *all* of the people? Asking that Desire to "bind in one the hearts of *all* mankind?" Oh, my, what a peace that would be, to have all our hearts bound together in peace, to have all of our sad—and sad they truly are—divisions cease.

Many of us, I suspect, think this is a Christmas hymn, but it is not. It is a hymn of waiting, of waiting for the Incarnation that once was and is about to be and will be again and forever. It is our plea for God to be with us. God already *is* with us, but we don't always see him, hear him, feel him, know him. There are days, we all believe, when God is more absent than present, and we feel more abandoned than loved.

Come, Desire of nations—so that we may be one.

Come, Emmanuel—so that we may know you in our lives.

Be thyself our King of Peace—because we live in a war-torn world of our own making, and we have no idea how to end the wars, how to get out of the mess that we have made of your creation.

Rejoice! Rejoice! Emmanuel! —Lauren Stanley

Love never fails

Love is patient; love is kind;…it does not insist on its own way…
Loves bears all things, believes all things, hopes all things, endures all things.
Love never fails.

—1 CORINTHIANS 13:4-5, 7-8

Less than six months after my ordination, my rector asked me to help with the annual Christmas pageant. Simple enough, I thought.

After many meetings and rehearsals, the big day arrived. About five minutes before the curtain went up, a mother came running into the parish hall and announced that she wanted her two children to be in the pageant. They had not attended a single rehearsal, and I gently indicated that it wouldn't be possible as we were about to begin. She insisted. I excused myself and headed for the sanctuary.

The play went off without a hitch. But as the whole cast gathered at the manger and the congregation stood to sing "Hark! the herald angels sing," I noticed two small children processing down the center aisle. As they came closer, it was obvious that they were Roman Soldiers.

The determined mother had found costumes in the box marked "Easter Play." I looked at the rector; his expression was not encouraging. When the two soldiers arrived at the manger, they knelt with solemn respect and dignity, gazing at the baby Jesus with wonder and awe. I looked around the room. People were moved. Afterward, it was all anyone talked about. The best Christmas play anyone could remember.

The story of our faith includes many critical moments: an escape from Egypt, a new beginning after a flood, and a young mother who offered her son unconditional love. One year at a Christmas play, I encountered a mother's unconditional love for her sons. And that love was a blessing to us all. —*Jason Leo*

Let me hold you, little Jesus

Little Jesus, I heard you crying as I passed by the stable, so I came in. Now I hear the chilly rain falling against the stable roof. The swaddling rags are keeping you dry and warm, but they are coarse against your soft skin. Your parents are frightened and tired, so let me hold you, little Jesus.

I have held many babies, but never one like you. I want to hold you now because in a time to come, you will hold me. Years from now, I will stumble and fall by the side of a road far from this stable. Darkness and cold surround us here tonight. A different sort of darkness and cold will close in around me as I lie on that roadside. Then, in the coldest, darkest moment of my night, you will come to me. But you will no longer be a helpless infant then. When you come to me in that night, you will come as King of kings.

You will call my name. You will tell me you have searched for me for many years and in many places and that when you finally found me, your heart leapt within you. Then you will pick me up. Your arms will be strong by then, not the tiny infant arms I see in the manger tonight. You will cradle me in your arms and it will be well with me.

But this is the night, the one night since before days and nights began, when the creature holds its Creator. This is the night of grace when the Lord of heaven and earth stoops down, reverses roles, and invites the finite to minister to the infinite.

And so, my helpless, needy, little Jesus, on this one night, let me hold you. —*Richard H. Schmidt*

Hearing the gospel

Several years ago I was serving a church as the music director. One year, when we didn't have a Christmas Day service, I decided to worship—to do something that people who work for the church don't get to do often enough. I found a local Episcopal church and joined a small group, all seated in the choir stalls near the altar.

Fortunately for me, the organist was there, and he played as if the church were full. We all sang with gusto. The readers proclaimed the word with care. And then it was time for the sermon.

The preacher said he had been working with a tutoring program, teaching inner-city kids to read and write. He told us he would be reading a letter from one of the elementary school-aged kids as his sermon that Christmas Day. I must confess my first cynical thought was that this was an easy way out of writing a Christmas sermon.

And then I realized I was hearing the gospel. The gospel for our time. This young boy said that he didn't really need any more toys or clothes for Christmas. All he really wanted was for no more bullets to fly through his neighborhood. He wanted his friends to live long enough to become grown-ups. He hoped everyone in his neighborhood would have enough to eat.

What is Christmas about, if not this? God sent Jesus into the world so that we might have salvation and peace, not so that our malls could fill. It seems so obvious, but that young child's simple letter captured the Good News and the hope of Christmas so perfectly that I remember it all these years later. May I never forget. —*Scott Gunn*

Love, incarnate

At Christmas we kneel before the manger to worship the presence of God in the form of a helpless child, God and humanity now inseparable in Christ Jesus. It is a reminder to us that God embraces human flesh. Our bodies are worthy of God's graceful redeeming; our human nature is profoundly empowered and sanctified.

Because of the Incarnation we will not denigrate human flesh, but value and protect our bodies as temples of God's indwelling. The Incarnation leads us to honor flesh and blood.

Because of the Incarnation we understand that we take on Christ's nature in our flesh, giving him our hands to serve, our hearts to love, our mouths to proclaim Christ's word today. The Incarnation leads all Christians to minister as Christ's body today.

Because of the Incarnation we will seek and serve Christ in all human beings, respecting their dignity and worth. The Incarnation leads us to justice and true welfare for all flesh.

In John's first epistle, he writes, "Beloved, let us love one another, because love is from God; everyone who loves is born of God and knows God. Whoever does not love does not know God, for God is love. God's love was revealed among us in this way: God sent his only Son into the world so that we might live through him. Beloved, since God loved us so much, we also ought to love one another" (1 John 4:7-9, 11).

Let the rest of this Christmas be a time to honor God, who became flesh and blood that we might truly know the glorious power and increasing joy of God's holy love. Enter into every opportunity for worship that your heart needs to remember the Word made flesh, full of grace and truth, in Christ Jesus and in us all.

—*Ruth Lawson Kirk*

Keep the peace

They shall beat their swords into plowshares,
and their spears into pruning hooks;
nation shall not lift up sword against nation,
neither shall they learn war any more.

—ISAIAH 2:4

How on earth could that ever happen?

On Christmas Eve 1914 during World War I, without permission, frontline troops called an informal truce. British and French soldiers climbed out of their trenches; German troops laid down their arms; and they did it for an odd, wonderful reason: they wanted to sing. Missing home and fallen comrades, they wanted to sing—if only for one night—about a Child who was born to put an end to their hell. Refusing the world's ways of death, an estimated 100,000 enemies became brothers to sing Christmas carols. They shared cigarettes and biscuits. Impromptu soccer matches broke out in the middle of No Man's Land. Atop that blood-soaked soil came an inbreaking of Christ's peaceable kingdom.

Inevitably, orders came to stop. They still do. The world is moving on from Christmas. But thankfully we don't have to. We can gladly defy the principalities and powers that are presently ordering us back to business as usual.

Don't let Christmas go. Don't end the Christmas peace. Extend it. Surrender your grudge. Lay down anger to take up compassion. Pound your wounded pride into the shape of forgiveness. Unclench your fists. Embrace peace. Let the Prince of Peace continue to be born again in you today. —*John Van Nuys*

Hands

Into your hands, O Lord, I commend my spirit.
—*THE BOOK OF COMMON PRAYER*, P. 132 (COMPLINE)

Our hands distinguish us from other created animals. We don't have paws or claws. We have opposable thumbs, making it possible for human beings to write letters, paint landscapes, or perform brain surgery. A violin comes to life in the hands of an accomplished performer. In many ways, our hands represent our ability, our creativity, and our humanity. We may shake hands when we greet another person, thereby presenting ourselves for relationship. A person who can do many tasks of building and repairing is called "handy." We offer our help when we "lend a hand." We may "give a hand" by applauding at a concert or speech. We may "hold hands" with a loved one.

Hands also provide important ways to represent God's loving presence and our response. At Compline, we commend our spirit into God's hands, and bless the Lord as we lift up our hands in the holy place (Psalm 134:2). Michelangelo's fresco for the Sistine Chapel depicts the hand of God nearly touching Adam's hand at the Creation. The essential divine and the essential human draw near each other, and new life is shared through their hands.

God's life works in our hands. A powerful experience for priests and eucharistic ministers is to see parishioners' hands—the worn, the rough, and the delicate—opened to receive the bread of communion.

May we open ourselves as we open our hands in love. —*Rob Slocum*

Be opened

Then looking up to heaven, he sighed and said to him,
"Ephphatha," that is, "Be opened."

—MARK 7:34

In the region of the Decapolis, south of the Sea of Galilee, Jesus and his disciples encountered a man who was deaf and had an impediment in his speech, whose friends begged Jesus simply to lay his hand on the man. He did, and immediately the man's ears were opened and his tongue released. I wonder what he heard first. Birds singing? The breeze blowing in the olive trees? The amazed and happy exclamations of his friends? Perhaps it was the rush of angels' wings, as heaven and earth intermingled in this moment.

When Jesus turns to me and says "Ephphatha," what in me needs to be opened? Perhaps it's my eyes, to see and truly apprehend the loveliness of all the human family and the whole creation. Perhaps it's my mind, to grasp new truth outside the narrow strictures of my own thinking. Perhaps, like the Galilean who was deaf, it's my ears, to listen with compassion to those who would share themselves with me. Perhaps it's my heart, so often cold and hard, to give and receive love beyond measure.

It is a holy moment when Jesus commands us to "be opened." We're human, and as fallible creatures all too often we just snap closed again. We must return to Jesus over and over again to experience this miracle of grace and healing. But in these holy moments, we see with new eyes and hear with new ears as the angels sing out their joy, because heaven and earth are dancing together. —*Betsy Rogers*

How long are you staying?

Roger Rosenblatt's memoir *Making Toast* is about his journey through the hell of losing a child. His daughter Amy, a gifted physician, suddenly died of an asymptomatic heart condition, leaving a stunned husband and three small children.

Just settling into their anticipated golden years, the newly-retired Rosenblatt and his wife Ginny were thunderstruck by the worst news that can befall any parent. They rushed to their daughter's home to help their surgeon son-in-law and their grandchildren: six-year-old Jessica, four-year-old Sammy, and one-year-old James. Taking up residence in the guest room, the Rosenblatts were quickly immersed in full-time parenting: changing diapers, 2:00 a.m. feedings, reading stories, and trying somehow to help three little souls whose mother was never coming home.

The morning after the funeral, Sammy turned to his Grandpa Roger at breakfast and said, "Boppo, how long are you staying?"

Without hesitating, Grandpa Roger replied, "Forever."

That is the Christmas answer God gives us in the Incarnation. In an eye-for-an-eye world of dashed hopes and innocent suffering we often cry, "God, where are you?" In Bethlehem, God says, "Right here. I am with you. I'm one of you. We are kin."

"When are you leaving?" We ask. "Never."

If you are like me, then some far-off god floating high above it all on a cloud won't do. But if you want a God who has felt pain, suffered rejection, been hungry, tested, tormented, bedeviled, crucified, and vindicated, then truly what a friend we have in Jesus.

The date of Christmas passes, but the truth of Christmas continues. "How long, O God, are you staying?"

"Forever. I will never leave you." —*John Van Nuys*

A new tradition for New Year's Eve

Tonight my wife Pam and I shall stay home. When we were younger, we often attended parties on this night, where we ate heavy hors d'oeuvres, drank more than we should, and tried to enjoy ourselves by engaging in convivial chatter. It was hard work. Finally, at midnight, we watched on television as the shiny ball descended into Times Square, then sang "Auld Lang Syne" and hugged and congratulated one another. As soon as possible after that, we said our goodbyes and went home.

New Year's Eve parties have always seemed strained and artificial to me. What are we congratulating ourselves for at 12:01 a.m.? Have we accomplished something noteworthy? Do we think the world will be different tomorrow morning? The only things about tomorrow that will be different are the calendar on the wall and the prevalance of dull headaches.

Oh, some things do change. People die; people are born. New books are written, new music composed, new buildings erected. Travel becomes faster and information more readily accessible. But the one sure thing is that today will become yesterday, tomorrow. The Teacher was right: "Vanity of vanities, all is vanity" (Ecclesiastes 1:2).

But some things do matter. Every year gives birth to blessings, little acts of thoughtfulness, devotion, courage, and self-sacrifice. Smiles unexpected and unasked for. Silent, hard-won victories over evil. Slights forgiven, adversities transcended, broken hearts mended. Such blessings change and enrich lives, and one generation passes them along to the next. On this final day of the year, rather than engage in meaningless chatter, why not leave some small blessing for those who will follow after you? If enough of us do that, next year really will be different and a year from now on New Year's Eve, we can celebrate something real. —*Richard H. Schmidt*

Contributors

NANCY DUVALL is a poet and journalist who has just had one of her poems set to music. She and her husband of fifty-five years live in Columbia, South Carolina, near their three children and six grandchildren.

SCOTT GUNN is Executive Director of Forward Movement. Before accepting this call, he served as a parish priest in Rhode Island. Prior to ordination, he worked in technology positions, working at the *Atlantic Monthly*, the MIT Media Lab, and Education Development Center. You can read his blog at www.sevenwholedays.org (http://www.sevenwholedays.org).

NANCY HOPKINS-GREENE, an Episcopal priest who works part time at The Church of the Redeemer in Cincinnati, Ohio, is a parent, clergy wife, slow runner, composter, and gardener. She is also an assistant editor at Forward Movement.

NOËL JULNES-DEHNER, an Episcopal priest and assistant editor at Forward Movement, is a poet and documentary filmmaker. Her current film project is *The Right Track*, about formerly incarcerated women and men re-entering society. She is also a founder of inner city reading camps in Cincinnati, Ohio.

CARL KINKEL is Director of Marketing for the Christian Association of Youth Mentoring. He is the youth choir director and director of musical arts at the Church of the Nativity in Northborough, Massachusetts. A former sales and marketing executive for three Fortune 500 companies, he resides in Northborough with his wife and has three daughters.

JASON LEO is rector of Calvary Episcopal Church, Cincinnati, Ohio. He was formerly director of youth ministries for the Diocese of Southern Ohio and has contributed to *Forward Day by Day*. He is author of Forward Movement's Advent booklet *We Shall All Be Changed*.

ROBERT MACAULEY is a pediatrician, bioethicist, and priest who lives in Shelburne, Vermont, with his wife and four children.

SARAH BRYAN MILLER is a frequent contributor to *Forward Day by Day* and other Forward Movement publications. She is the classical music critic for the *St. Louis Post-Dispatch* in St. Louis, Missouri.

PENNY NASH is Associate Rector for Youth, Children, and Families at Bruton Parish Church in Williamsburg, Virginia. Prior to her call in Williamsburg, she served parishes in the Diocese of Atlanta. She blogs regularly at *One Cannot Have Too Large a Party* (http://penelopepiscopal.blogspot.com/).

BETSY ROGERS is an editor, communications specialist, Christian educator, and member of the Forward Movement Board of Directors. She and her husband are the parents of three grown children and divide their time between Belleville, Illinois, and Sister Bay, Wisconsin.

TIM SCHENCK is rector of St. John's Episcopal Church in Hingham, Massachusetts. He is battle-hardened, not only as a parent of two sons but as a former Army paratrooper. Tim writes a syndicated newspaper column and blogs regularly at *Clergy Family Confidential* (http://frtim.wordpress.com/).

RICHARD H. SCHMIDT was a parish priest for thirty years. He is author of five books on Christian spirituality and was Editor & Director of Forward Movement from 2005 to 2011. In his retirement he resides with his wife of forty-five years in Fairhope, Alabama.

MELODY SHOBE is Associate Rector at Emmanuel Episcopal Church in Cumberland, Rhode Island. She lives in Rhode Island with her husband, Casey, who's also a priest, and their daughter Isabelle. Melody has written for several publications, including the *Episcopal Cafe* blog.

HEIDI SHOTT is Canon for Communications and Social Justice for the Diocese of Maine. Praised widely for her writing about faith in daily life, Heidi writes for a variety of publications and blogs. She lives in coastal Maine with her husband and two sons.

LOIS SIBLEY has written book reviews for *Episcopal Life, The Episcopal Journal,* and other publications. She worships at St. Peter's Episcopal Church in Glenside, Pennsylvania. She and her husband are the parents of five, grandparents of nine, and great-grandparents of one—so far.

MELISSA SKELTON is rector of St. Paul's Episcopal Church in Seattle, Washington, and canon for congregational development in the Diocese of Olympia. She has contributed to Forward Movement's devotional booklets for the bereaved and those experiencing a divorce.

ROB SLOCUM is an Episcopal priest who has served in the dioceses of Louisiana, Milwaukee, and Lexington. He is author of *The Theology of William Porcher DuBose: Life, Movement and Being* and *Light in a Burning-Glass: A Systematic Presentation of Austin Farrer's Theology,* and editor of *A Heart for the Future: Writings on the Christian Hope.* He lives in Danville, Kentucky, with his wife, Victoria, and their many greyhounds and cats.

STEPHEN SMITH, rector of St. Patrick's Episcopal Church in Dublin, Ohio, is the author of *Saving Salvation: The Amazing Evolution of Grace* (Morehouse 2005) and of numerous articles. He plays a blistering lead guitar in the band Rev'd Up, an ecclesiastical Eddie Van Halen!

LAUREN STANLEY is a priest in the Diocese of Virginia who has served as a missionary in Sudan and Haiti. She was a journalist for over twenty years prior to her ordination in 1998.

JOHN VAN NUYS has contributed to *Forward Day by Day* and to Forward Movement's booklet on divorce. He is pastor of Wabash Avenue Presbyterian Church in Crawfordsville, Indiana.

Author Index

Notes and Reflections

Notes and Reflections

Notes and Reflections

Notes and Reflections

Notes and Reflections

Notes and Reflections

Were you inspired by
Walking With God Day by Day?
Consider these Forward Movement resources.

Forward Day by Day

If the meditations in this daybook have touched your heart, stirred your soul, or just made your day a little brighter, we invite you to subscribe to *Forward Day by Day*, which has guided the daily prayer of millions of readers around the world since 1935. Issued quarterly, *Forward Day by Day* brings you an assortment of authors,

both clergy and lay—bishops, priests, missionaries, schoolteachers, biologists, medical professionals, and more—who share their reflections and abiding faith in God as they write on a scripture passage for the day, taken from the Episcopal Church's lectionary. *Forward Day by Day* is available in regular or large print, email, Spanish, and Braille, and as a single subscription or a bulk standing order.

Advent & Lenten Meditation Booklets

Each Advent and Lent, Forward Movement publishes a booklet of meditations to support your daily prayer and help you keep the season. Beautifully written and sized to carry with you, these booklets are among our most popular publications.

Wisdom Found: Stories of Women Transfigured by Faith

Edited by Lindsay Hardin Freeman

Forty spirited women tell of everyday challenges, life's most profound joys, and its deepest sorrows—echoes of your own experiences, told sometimes in shouts, often in whispers, but always in voices luminous with faith and rich in wisdom. Find comfort and strength as they share stories of finding a balance; work and play; motherhood; at the altar; illness, pain, and healing; grief and sorrow; and lessons of the heart. A full-color, hardcover, gift book to be cherished and shared.

For more information about these resources, visit our website at

www.forwardmovement.org
or call us at **1-800-543-1813**